T0125151

Love Three

Love Three   A Study of a Poem by George Herbert

Aaron Kunin   Wave Books, Seattle and New York

Published by Wave Books

www.wavepoetry.com

Copyright © 2019 by Aaron Kunin

All rights reserved

Wave Books titles are distributed to the trade by

Consortium Book Sales and Distribution

Phone: 800-283-3572 / SAN 631-760X

Library of Congress Cataloging-in-Publication Data

Names: Kunin, Aaron B., author.

Title: Love three : a study of a poem by George Herbert / Aaron Kunin.

Description: First edition. | Seattle : Wave Books, [2019]

Identifiers: LCCN 2018037459 | ISBN 9781940696829 (trade pbk.)

Subjects: LCSH: Herbert, George, 1593-1633. Love. | Herbert, George,

   1593-1633—Criticism and interpretation. | Christian poetry,

   English—Early modern, 1500-1700—History and criticism. |

   Power (Social sciences) in literature. | Sex in literature.

Classification: LCC PR3507.L68 K86 2019 | DDC 821.3—dc23

LC record available at https://lccn.loc.gov/2018037459

Designed and composed by Quemadura

Printed in the United States of America

9 8 7 6 5 4 3 2 1

First Edition

This book is a few different things:

a study of George Herbert's seventeenth-century devotional poem "Love" (3);

an essay on eroticizing power;

and a memory palace of sexual experiences, fantasies, preferences, and limits, with Herbert's poem as the key.

Each numbered section is a restatement of Herbert's poem. First I paraphrased the poem, then I tried to see what my paraphrase missed, then I studied what other critics had written, and finally I wrote about the poem through my sexual history.

I tried to avoid references to outside sources. Interested readers will find a complete bibliography and notes with page citations at the end of the book.

This book is for Michael Clune.

Love Three

Try to think of it as a third kind of love. The first
kind is nice. The second kind is nasty. Another
kind is nice because it's nasty. Love three.

Love bade me welcome: yet my soul drew back,
                    Guiltie of dust and sinne.
But quick-ey'd Love, observing me grow slack
                    From my first entrance in,
Drew nearer to me, sweetly questioning,
                    If I lack'd any thing.

A guest, I answer'd, worthy to be here:
                    Love said, You shall be he.
I the unkinde, ungratefull? Ah my deare,
                    I cannot look on thee.
Love took my hand, and smiling did reply,
                    Who made the eyes but I?

Truth Lord, but I have marr'd them: let my shame
                    Go where it doth deserve.
And know you not, sayes Love, who bore the blame?
                    My deare, then I will serve.
You must sit down, sayes Love, and taste my meat:
                    So I did sit and eat.

What makes Love so attractive?

What powers does Love have and what powers do I give?

Love is not the kind of god who is everywhere and doing everything. I witness Love's power only as power over me, knowledge of me, presence in my company.

Love forces me to eat the food that is served.

Love knows what I am thinking.

Love answers my objections. Always has the last word.

Do I know anything about Love's other powers? Love's history? I seem to have heard something about Love "bearing the blame" for my faults. I confirm a report of creation that says: Love made

me. Nothing about creating the rest of the world.
Do I think all this trouble is for me?

Mainly Love dominates me verbally.

3

"Sweetly questioning." Love is a sweet voice. Love is a questioning voice.

The speech tag partly obscures the exact wording of the question. You are asking me if I lack anything. It's a merchant's question. "What do you lack?" "What will you buy?"

Does the sweet tone modify the aggressive nature of the question?

What would be a less sweet way of asking the question?

"Do you have a problem?" The kind of emphatic question used to start a fight.

"I said is there a fucking problem?"

4

"You must sit down and taste my meat." I don't think there could be a less polite way of saying that.

What Love says could be written in a toilet stall. It could be a line in rap. It could be dirty talk. It could be assault.

Why doesn't it sound like any of these things?

Herbert writes with a consistency of style that can accommodate basically any material.

A consistency of which I as a writer am incapable.

And which I value somewhat grudgingly.

I like too many effects made possible by inconsistency.

Herbert's style covers the aggression of the penultimate line so that many otherwise careful readers hear only the sweet tone. Sweetness that overpowers every other suggestion.

You could underline the message by adding a rude word. "Bitch, you must sit down and taste my meat." "You must sit down and taste my meat, shithead." The expletive would intensify the harsh language that you were already using.

Is sweetness the same as politeness?

When I put it like that, my way of thinking about sweetness seems obviously incomplete.

Politeness could mean a set of conventions. Formulas that you memorize and apply for no reason other than your training. "Sir, you do me honor." "No, sir, the honor is mine." Because that is what your people say.

Or politeness could mean devices that you invent in new situations to make people feel comfortable. You investigate the cause of their unease and you try to fix the problem.

The second kind of politeness is more aggressive. One thing sweetness has in common with politeness is that both can be done aggressively.

Or politeness could mean an attitude. You try to divine what people are feeling. This is the ethical meaning that empathy has unfortunately acquired. The idea seems to be that empathy is a solid foundation for decent behavior. That you would be incapable of harming a person whose feelings you could imagine as your own. (As though successful military operations did not depend on the tool of empathy. As though "Know your enemy" were not a motto of empathy.)

Like Socrates, Love makes unanswerable arguments in the form of questions that I try to answer until there's nothing left to say.

With all three kinds of politeness, the most effective device is often just the visible fact that you are making an effort to be polite.

6

What other attributes does Love have? What do I love about Love?

It's clear enough that Love is masculine. A lord.

Is a lord always a man? Pretty much. Later I will try to flesh out an alternative.

What kind of man? Lord is a feudal title. Someone who has property and vassals. Which is sort of what I am: a vassal.

What does Love's voice sound like? This I know. It's sweet. It has a sweet sound. It takes the bitterness out of asking questions. Or maybe the pleasant tone of voice reminds you that the questions are kind of unpleasant.

What does Love's face look like? All I know are the eyes. Having "quick eyes" could be a visual characteristic. A feeling of life, strength, and energy in your look. Or your eyes darting back and forth. Shining.

Or "quick-ey'd" could be your temperament. You are curious. Always investigating. You see things that would be invisible to most people. Something I don't show in my face, something I don't say, something that comes and goes in the blink of an eye: you see all of it and respond.

Love also has meat. The meat could be an alienable property, a piece of meat on a plate, or it could be Love's body. Or meat can be an unmentionable part of Love's body. Love's genitals.

I sort of want to take the modifier sweet and move it here. Love's meat may be sweet. "Sweetly questioning" may be a transferred epithet that properly refers to meat, because sweet is a taste word, not a sound word.

Also they rhyme. Meat, sweet, eat.

What am I like?

I am brutally honest.

I think I am brutally honest.

I think I know what I deserve.

Earlier I said that I was your vassal. That isn't the exact relationship between me and you. My status is probably equivalent to that of your vassals. (Assuming you have vassals in an ordinary sense. They are not evident in the poem.) But it seems I am not part of the local hierarchy. I am "a guest," an unworthy guest. A place I inadequately occupy. You and I are strangers of unequal status.

Do I lack anything?

I'm supposed to say no. A worthy guest would say no. Would profess to be completely satisfied. I'm supposed to say, in the words of the psalm, "I shall

not want," which means that I am declaring my
intention not to want anything. I'm supposed to
say that there is nothing I can imagine wanting.

Or "I shall not want" could mean rejection.
I might want something, but you are the wrong
agent to supply my wants.

I doubt my worth. I doubt that you could want me.
I am certain (I do not doubt) that I can't see you,
that my vision is flawed due to my own sad choice.

Do I exaggerate my faults? Are my doubts
reasonable?

Am I a clever person? I don't know the answer to
this question.

Am I making some good points?

I can't get past the sense that you have done all this work for me. A feeling overwhelms me that I don't deserve your excellent work.

Only sometimes I get the feeling that you are playing to please yourself. Then an adjustment takes place. I want to be part of the experience you're having. I want to contribute to it. Serve it. At least I don't want to get in the way of what you are feeling.

Then I resolve to meet you at the level at which you address me. To be as skilled at submitting as you are at dominating.

The transition involves a token action. Kneeling. Kissing a ring or the hem of your garment. Swearing an oath. Following a simple command. Sit down and taste.

What happens is that you are making the rest of the world fall away.

9

The mistake of paganism is to think of gods as kinds of people. Special people. Fascinating but dangerous. Look but don't touch. To be on the safe side maybe you shouldn't look. Unless this god is going to be offended by your not looking.

To be sexual with a god is not safe. But, really, what are you supposed to do with a god whose unspoken name is Love? How is that not a come-on? A god called Love might as well say, "I am McLovin."

A lot of people do have a sexual relationship with the Christian god. Mary is a complicated example. Saint Teresa is a less complicated one. Donne is an interesting example. Let me try to remember what I think about Donne.

Most religious poets want to be God. Milton tries to imitate God. Which means that he is sometimes competing with God. He receives instructions from God and sometimes follows them and sometimes questions them.

> Doth God exact day-labor, light denied?

Sometimes he turns the relationship around and issues new instructions for God.

> Why was the sight
> To such a tender ball as th' eye confin'd?
> So obvious and so easy to be quench't,
> And not as feeling through all parts diffus'd,
> That she might look at will through every pore?

Donne seems different. He wants to be passive before God. He wants to be overwhelmed by God. He will never be free until God captures him. He will never be chaste until God rapes him.

Carew wrote that Donne's poetry "commits holy rapes upon the will." Rape means nonconsent.

Will means consent. (If it happens in accordance with my will, there's no room left for me to withhold consent.) Holy means that playing with nonconsent happens in a ritual frame.

In his very sexual relationship with God, Donne tops from the bottom. Which means that Donne feels comfortable telling God what to do.

> Batter my heart, three person'd God; for, you
> As yet but knocke, breathe, shine, and seeke to mend;
> That I may rise, and stand, o'erthrow mee, and bend
> Your force, to breake, blowe, burn and make me new.

A do-me princess, he worships God by lying back and making God do all of the work. He tells God how to dominate him.

You aren't doing it right.

This is how to make me submit.

This is the *right* way to surprise me.

Herbert wants something different. He wants to serve Love. "My deare, then I will serve."

After several tries at being rejected, he is finally reduced to offering his services.

He isn't competing for the divine position. He wants to be in the other position. Which is what? The creature. The servant.

11

Why do I say that Herbert isn't competitive? Isn't he speaking on behalf of Love? Doesn't that mean that he is competing for the position of Love?

Do you want me? You're wrong.

I preemptively reject myself. I anticipate your rejection of me. I speak on behalf of your rejection.

Here's another reason why you might not want me.

My way of loving by preferring humiliation is always menaced by the shadow of my possible narcissism.

I want to be humiliated by someone superior to me. I become greater when someone even greater makes me lesser.

I doubt your superiority because you indulge my wants.

If you are a superior being, why are you wasting effort on me?

I suspect that you might not be truly superior.

I examine you for small signs of inferiority.

Your humiliation of me, by gratifying my fantasy, confirms my sense that you are closer to me than a real superior being should be.

But if you do not acknowledge my inadequacy, then you must be inadequate too.

If you were true Love, you would know that I was unworthy.

Your wanting me proves my worth, but you must not be worth much if you want me, so I must not be worth anything at all.

"If you don't believe I love you, look what a fool I've been."

That's the suspicion.

"You don't believe."

I believe you only when you lower yourself.

"What a fool."

"So I did sit and eat." A minor refusal in the last line.

LOVE: "Sit and taste."

ME: "Sit and eat."

Instead of replying I follow the command. I am almost surprised. "I did!" The helping verb "did" is not redundant. Yes, I did what you said. But I didn't lose sight of the difference between us. What you said is what I did but what you said is not quite the same as what I said. I used a different word.

13

I "draw back" without showing it, in my soul.
Outwardly I am moving forward.

You "draw nearer," closing the distance.

The word "draw" looks to be significant. Drawing
back and drawing near. A track connecting me
and you. Maybe our movements are symmetrical
after all.

Maybe I'm slowing down. "Growing slack." Maybe
my body has used up its energy. Maybe I lost my
loving look. Maybe I was turned on and I'm now
turned off.

Detumescent. A vulgar interpretation of slack.
The phrase is "grow slack" but it doesn't mean
grow; it means shrink.

If that's what softness looks like, what does
hardness look like?

Love's quick eyes. Lively, sharp, penetrating. Amazing how you catch me drawing invisibly back. Observant enough to see my very soul.

(Whereas I can't even look at you.)

What is Love? Attention and sweetness. Your two positive qualities. (Technically "sweetly" modifies an action and "quick-ey'd" modifies the actor.)

Quick attention not slow attention. Quickness could entail: impatient, impetuous, fickle. Quick to form attachments and quick to dissolve them. You don't reflect. You see, judge, and act immediately.

In the fullness of divine presence, "Thou shalt look us out of pain." Your look is powerful enough!

Powerful enough to see what I want even when I don't know that I want it. Even when I say that I don't want it.

Possibly Love's smile is a sign of arousal. I never smile. I submit willingly (I think) but not cheerfully. "I will serve" expresses a preference but it doesn't express satisfaction.

You never make me confess my satisfaction. Maybe that is a kind of sacrifice you make for me. You express desire but allow me to remain untainted by desire. You indulge my fear of rejection. You express desire so that I don't have to.

I don't have to risk anything.

14

In *Paradise Lost*, Heaven and Hell are densely populated by angels and devils. The density of their population is not a problem. Their numbers are vast but there is no inconvenient crowding because their bodies can be any size.

Meanwhile the human population is just one, then two.

For the poet Milton, living in modern London, the proportions seem to be reversed: densely populated human world, one god, one devil.

Is that true? The angels and minor devils never went away. "Thousands at his bidding speed." Like Adam and Eve, Milton sees armies of angels and is threatened by legions of devils.

It's not a question of populations but of relations between worlds. At the center of *Paradise Lost* is a strange scene that goes on for several thousand lines where Adam and Eve share a meal with an angel, Raphael, "the sociable Spirit," "the affable Arch-angel." The angel who likes conversation. Someone who, like Gutman in *The Maltese Falcon*, likes talking to someone who likes to talk.

The angel and the people eat the same food. Seated at the same place. (Not quite a table. Not indoors. Not movable. A primitive kind of furnishing. Maybe produced by human ingenuity, maybe not. Nonetheless a kind of table.)

Adam and Eve have opportunities to host representatives of other levels of reality. There are plenty of links between their world and other worlds.

In the seventeenth century, communication between Heaven and London has a single attenuated channel, from God through the Holy Spirit to Milton.

In "Love" (3), you are my host. The relationship between human and divine has been reduced to one-on-one. A private affair. There are no other guests.

No one is technically "worthy to be here." You will have to make do with me.

There is a kind of communication between worlds, but not the companionship or condescension of eating the same food in the same place. Our communication is called service.

15

"First entrance." How many times do I enter?

Maybe we have been through the same process before.

Maybe it happens every day.

Maybe it has to happen every time I sit down to eat.

Crucifixion is missing from "Love" (3). No suffering Christ.

Only this: "my meat." Christ's body treated as meat.

Note that it isn't grain, vegetable, or dairy. The food group is meat. Love isn't commanding me to taste bread that becomes flesh or wine that becomes blood. Divinity is present. We are already communicating. Transubstantiation would be a less impressive miracle.

And I'm tasting, not eating. Not gratifying an appetite. Maybe not fully consuming and digesting. Just a taste. For reasons of curiosity, to see what it tastes like. Or a ritual kind of eating where I eat just enough to represent eating.

I am eating, and you are with me, but we are not eating together. I am eating your food, that is to say, I am eating you. Only you're supposed to be the dominant one. You make the decisions and control the experience. Which makes sense if I'm eating without feeling hungry. My eating feeds your appetite, not mine.

Vulnerability is strength. A Christian paradox. What did Anne Boyer say? "I thought that being brave was mostly just being vulnerable."

In dominating me, you aren't objectifying me. You are turning yourself into an object. I, in tasting you, which you force me to do, am dominated by the object you become. Meat.

Tasting your meat is how I choose you. I express my preference. This seat, this meat.

(Not Herbert's rhyme. Herbert rhymes meat with eat.)

Can I say that "sweetly" is Herbert's rhyme?

"Taste" your meat because the point isn't digestion but flavor. The sweet taste, the spoonful of sugar, is the most compelling argument. You are my god, you are my love, because you taste right.

Or think of it as an obscene remark. "My meat." Something you might say about someone whose body you desire. Or something you might say about your own genitals.

"You must sit down and taste my meat."

Get it while it's hot.

"You must sit down and" eat my dinner before it cools.

"You must" eat my dinner now because it's fresh and it won't keep.

"My meat" will spoil if you don't taste it right away.

We don't have the technology to refrigerate "my meat."

Come and get it or we'll give it to the dogs!

Everything that happens without being said.

"My soul drew back."

"Love drew nearer."

"Love took my hand and smiled."

"I did sit and eat."

The rest is talk.

19

Would it make a difference if Love were a woman?

This isn't a crazy idea. It's an old idea. Classical mythology represents Love as a woman. Alma Venus. Her son, Cupid, is subordinate to her and represents an aspect of love.

Herbert is unclear about the gender of Love. This is true in all three "Love" poems. Apart from the title "Lord," there are no remarkable indications of masculinity. If I am anxious for Love to be either a man or a woman, I am reduced to emphasizing vague associations of personal traits with gender.

Such as the following:

Love's voice has a sweet sound, and sweetness is feminine? Begging the question.

Love has power, and power is masculine? Begging exactly the question that interests me: giving power to a woman.

Love is at home, doing a kind of work that women do, wielding a kind of power that women have, because domesticity is feminine? Begging the question.

Love is like a mother, a feminine role? Begging the question.

None of this is convincing. I don't believe Herbert had any such notions.

Here's something Herbert might have been thinking about. Magdalen Herbert, his mother, was a powerful woman. Both at home and in the public world.

Everyone who knew her was impressed by her authority. People wrote poems about it. Donne wrote that she was "a mother which delights to heare / Her early child mis-speake." He saw her dominating her children verbally, and enjoying it.

The anecdote that most strikes me is that she moved the entire family to Oxford when Edward Herbert, the first son, was a student there. That is the kind of presence she was in the lives and careers of her children.

George Herbert's longest poem, *Memoriae Matris Sacrum*, an elegy in Latin and Greek, says this about Magdalen Herbert's rhetorical force:

No occasion could unnerve her,
And from the start she had it in her grip.
Ah, this very storm, this very grace of speech,
Stern winsomeness, wit
And wisdom mixed! She holds a discourse
On hunting and the care of cattle; or if her duties
Take her for an hour, she eases through
Their twists and labyrinths, better than
Very Catos with her wise maxims.

21

Is power interesting to me only when a woman
has it?

Does Love need to be a woman in order for the
poem to be sexually exciting?

I'm not sure. The answer seems to be no. I find
rhetorical power interesting, and even sexually
exciting, no matter where it appears. When, at age
sixteen, I first read the debate in Hell in Book II of
Paradise Lost, I was so turned on by the idea of
rhetorical manipulation that I had to bring myself
to climax before reading to the end of the book.
Just the idea that Satan and Beelzebub had
shaped the debate to produce the result they
wanted. Although, truthfully, in my fantasy, I
combined this idea with thoughts of women.

Maybe finishing the book and encountering the
sick family romance of Satan, Sin, and Death
would have changed the development of my sexual
interests, or maybe I would have been turned off
by scenes of rape, incest, and mutilation.

But, yeah, the idea of rhetorical manipulation always suggests to me the more attractive idea of a rhetorically powerful woman. My fantasy easily makes the translation. A man's eloquence makes me think about a woman's eloquence. I don't do the same thing with other kinds of power. A violent man doesn't suggest to me a violent woman. Although I can be excited by the idea of a violent woman.

22

Am I trying to tell you no?

How do I say no to my god?

Maybe I am trying to set a limit. But, again, how do I set limits on my god?

I can't say: "This isn't for me. I've made a mistake."

I don't want to offend you.

I want to be polite.

If I don't believe that I deserve you, does that mean I prefer the other thing?

If I have a clear sense of what I deserve, does that mean I am choosing?

Love says, "You shall be he." There is maybe a residual sense of merit. I am not worthy, but through contact with you, I will be. That is your choice.

Love is not a relationship between equals. Silvan Tomkins wrote that "if you like to bite and I like to be bitten, then we may enjoy each other." We "enjoy each other" because we have different things and want different things.

Someone "worthy to be here," someone worthy of you, would be another you. As smart, funny, beautiful, powerful, and sweet as you. Why would you want that? You already have those gifts. You don't need them from me.

I can still give you something. My submission.

Simone Weil treated "Love" (3) like something different from a poem. More like an aspirin. Later like a prayer. She was rewarded as though she had been praying; she was converted. Only she wasn't converted to Herbert's religion.

The poem isn't like a prayer. Unless playing hard to get is a form of prayer. Asking *not* to receive grace.

If I were praying, I might be talking to Love, but I'm not. I only talk to Love in the dialogue folded into the poem (which is most of the poem). I'm repeating the dialogue to a third person.

Who is the listener?

Who could it be? Another god? A different love god? Another kind of god?

Doesn't Elijah tease the priests of Baal when they can't cook their meat by divine intervention?

The Jewish god fed me, what are you going to do for me?

Idea for poem. Write a list of my sexual preferences, interests, fantasies, and limits.

What if "Love" (3) were such a list?

One interest is humiliation.

Some of the humiliation has to come from me. I announce my guilt; I specify its contents. ("Guiltie of dust and sinne." Guilt is specified although sin is vague.) I announce my shame. (Which is not specified. Unless it's the marring of my eyes.)

Here's what I don't say. I don't say that I desire humiliation. My confession of guilt remains innocent of wanting to be guilty. I confess guilt and shame but you leave me the alibi of not getting off on my humiliation.

Nor do I ever express my desire for you. The only one who talks about enjoying this scene is you. Thus you leave me the protection of not wanting you.

Now I understand the worst cliché of dirty talk: "You like that don't you." I see why that's important. A lame attempt to break down the last protection.

Other kinks in "Love" (3)?

Sight restrictions. "I cannot look on thee."

Speech restrictions. My voice taken away, argued away, suppressed, stopped, gagged. Finally I don't answer.

Bondage? "Love took my hand." Bondage is a strange kind of holding. I learn that my body is not mine. And that I am not only a body.

Height restrictions? "You must sit down." Unconvincing. This isn't exactly human furniture, is it? If there's a chair, I have to sit in it. The chair isn't myself.

Pain? I don't think so. Pain and its virtues are topics for other poems by Herbert.

25

Playing with power often seems to involve a lot of expensive equipment. A throne, a crown, collars, cuffs, gags, hoods, frames, cages, devices, pieces of furniture, costumes, leather, metal. Equipment for experiencing or illustrating power.

There's nothing like that here. You and I make power together. Out of ourselves alone. I give you my power and you give me more power to give to you.

There isn't another one of me and there isn't another one of you.

Not simply monotheism and monoculture. One god for one human soul.

We don't need a lot of equipment. Only your body, my body, your imagination, and my fantasy.

We almost don't need bodies. Just eyes, hands, a bit of food, somewhere to enter, and a place to sit down. Otherwise it's just my soul, your voice, and my voice.

26

What about the phrase "my deare"? One of a
number of "my" phrases: my soul, my first
entrance, my dear, my hand, my shame, my dear,
my meat.

All of these possessions still don't add much
to the catalogue of equipment. Nothing costly,
nothing rare, nothing too complicated. Everything
on this list is part of you or part of me.

Or it's all of you—which I address as my most
cherished possession, "my deare"—not just part
of you.

No capital D in dear.

"Dear" by itself can be a pet name. Like baby,
sweetie, honey. A title for a pet who is also a god.

"My deare" isn't a name or a title. I think "dear,"
when used as a substantive, retains a trace of
having been a modifier. My dear friend, dear one,
dear ma'am.

There is something subjective too in this form of address. There is a value I see in you that others might not see. Everyone calls you Lord; I alone call you dear.

Is "my deare" shocking because it's intimate?

Or because it conjoins intimacy with subordination? "My deare, then I will serve."

Service can be intimate. You are mine and I serve you. I possess you and give you power to command me.

"My deare" initiates a turn both times. These are the moments when I turn toward you. In other words, the only times when I'm not talking about myself.

One of the fictional characters I most strongly identify with is Monsieur de Bargeton in Balzac's novel *Lost Illusions*. He never opens his mouth to speak because he is a simpleton. His head is empty; he has no words. Only because he is married to a brilliant woman, he is reputed to be wise.

In my favorite episode in the novel, Madame de Bargeton, in a complicated maneuver to protect her reputation, carefully instructs her husband to challenge another man to a duel. (The other man is spreading a rumor that Madame de Bargeton has been unfaithful to her husband, which is basically true. It hasn't happened but it is going to happen.)

Monsieur de Bargeton does exactly what his wife tells him to do. He practices the two sentences of his challenge so many times that he is able to say them flawlessly. His antagonist ends up looking cowardly and weak, while everyone credits Monsieur de Bargeton with resourcefulness, bravery, and wisdom.

I especially like the dialogue between the de Bargetons when Madame informs Monsieur that he is to fight a duel:

> "I am going," replied Monsieur de Bargeton, taking up his hat and cane.

> "Very good, my friend," his wife said with emotion. "That is how I like men to be. You are a gentleman."

I read this book more than twenty years ago and compared this character to myself and thought about my relationship with my girlfriend at the time. I felt a little disturbed because de Bargeton is not the most appealing character. Why would I want to be like him?

Mostly I felt strange, blissful recognition. I wanted to be like him. I was like de Bargeton in the way that I tended to experience the social world through my girlfriend. Maybe, I thought, that wasn't entirely bad. Maybe I could acquire a kind of secondary intelligence by associating with brilliant people.

28

An early experience that may be related to my interest in bondage.

I always used to sleep with the covers pulled close to my body and over my head. When I was very young, my mother tried to discourage me from keeping my head under the covers. She worried that I might suffocate, she said. I never noticed that I had any trouble breathing.

Why did I start sleeping like this? It seemed to mean a few different things. Sometimes I was hiding. I used to imagine that to another person watching the bed from outside there might not appear to be anyone in bed. Sometimes it was for warmth. Later, like many children who are fascinated by books, I used to have a light under the covers to read by when I was supposed to be sleeping.

I still kind of sleep like this, only I'm careful now to leave an opening around my face for air.

Women sometimes find it amusing. "It looks like you swaddled yourself." "It's like you're wearing a hood." Probably it's the sort of thing that can seem endearing if you really like the person, but can easily appear childish, hopeless, or infuriating if the person is getting on your nerves.

29

This one is more embarrassing. I must have been about nine years old. My family owned three beanbag chairs that were quite large, and I used to like to lie under one of them. It covered my head and most of my body so that I couldn't see, breathe, or move.

My sisters and I invented a game in which we piled up the beanbags, I lay under the pile, and my sisters tried to balance on top, until they slid off, which usually didn't take long. The game was probably my idea. I was the oldest.

The idea was suggested by an episode in the comic strip *Peanuts*. There's a running gag where Lucy sulks in her beanbag chair. I can't find any examples of this image, but I think she sometimes puts the beanbag over her head and sulks in that position. The character of Lucy, the crabby little girl, may also have made an impression on my sexual imagination.

My sisters remember this game. Sometimes they ask about it. For them it seems to have been about watching television, which, I guess, is what beanbag chairs are meant for. They called the game *Tower of Babel, We Love Cable!* (Babel pronounced to rhyme with cable.) The reference to Babel sounds as though it could have been my contribution. I have no memory of this part.

Was the game with the beanbags a kind of sex play for me? I don't remember, but it is disturbingly close to fantasies about human furniture that I entertained later in life.

Politicians are for the most part ambitious people who, in order to take power or maintain power, sacrifice their favorite projects. What they want to do they sacrifice for the position in which they might be able to get it done. Like the American president who is perpetually a candidate for the same office or working on behalf of the party or the successor. First making promises to take power, then balancing competing interests to maintain power.

You sign up for power and discover that your schedule is full of meetings. Your position is one in which you sit behind a desk and people on the other side ask you for things that you can't give. You have found the emptiness at the center of power. It's just important for someone to be seated behind the desk. It doesn't matter that much whether you have the resources to give them what they want.

Imagine if it was like that all the way to the top. You satisfy your ambition to become Love only to find that your new job is mainly ceremonial. Everything you want to do now seems within reach yet you still don't accomplish anything. Your moves are encumbered by red tape. You still lack the power to force the others to do what you want.

And you find yourself doing less loving than before. You probably think less about loving now that you are Love. Most of your thoughts are devoted to keeping your position. Stockpiling forms of wealth other than love. Funding the next campaign. Because you are perpetually competing with other ambitious souls who want to become Love. There are many of them. Donne is one. Milton is another.

Not Herbert. He just wants to know what he can do for Love. How he can pay Love back. He can't think of a thing. There's no possible compensation.

If he could think of something, that might not be a way for Herbert to become Love, but it might be a way to undo the power of Love. He might be making Love's job even more difficult.

Had dinner by myself tonight. Worked in the Lee
House office until dinner time. A butler came in very
formally and said, "Mr. President, dinner is served."
I walked into the dining room in the Blair House.
Barnett in tails and white tie pulls out my chair,
pushes me up to the table. John in tails and white tie
brings me a fruit cup. Barnett takes away the empty
cup. John brings me a plate, Barnett brings me a
tenderloin, John brings me asparagus, John brings
me carrots and beets. I have to eat alone and in
silence in a candle lit room. I ring—Barnett takes the
plate and butter plates. John comes in with a napkin
and a silver crumb tray—there are no crumbs but
John has to brush them off the table anyway. Barnett
brings me a plate with a finger bowl and doily on it—
I remove finger bowl and doily and John puts a glass
saucer and a little bowl on the plate. Barnett brings
me some chocolate custard. John brings me a
demitasse (at home a little cup of coffee—about
two good gulps) and my dinner is over. I take a hand
bath in the finger bowl and go back to work.

What a life!

What I am saying throughout our conversation is that you are powerless.

Your first question is what can you do for me.

I keep saying nothing. You can do nothing for me.

Who lacks anything? You, you are lacking.

"A guest worthy to be here" means that it is not in your power to make me a worthy guest.

I'm so bad that nothing can make me better.

I resist every kind of improvement.

Not even Love has the power to love me.

My inferiority is more powerful than your superiority.

33

It must be kind of frustrating for Love to hear me declaring my imperviousness to love.

It must sound as though I am not only nullifying Love's authority but taking Love's place.

Although not in competition with Love in the field of disbursing love, I am speaking on Love's behalf in judging myself and finding myself lacking.

That might be where the note of impatience comes from in the last words Love says.

Today I seem to be writing "Love" rather than "you."

34

Sometimes it's, "Love said," and sometimes it's, "Sayes Love."

Sometimes Love speaks in the present while Herbert is working on getting the poem written.

Or it's a voice I always have in my head saying these words. Love says, Love says.

The speech tag means that Love is the third person, not the second person. I'm telling someone else, not Love, about Love.

The actual second person, the one I'm telling my story to, doesn't have any lines.

What would the second person say?

Did you ever meet Love?

Are you satisfied with Love?

Did you give your consent to Love?

35

Am I praying or am I swearing?

When I say, "Lord," am I taking the Lord's name in vain?

I curse myself: "Let my shame / Go where it doth deserve."

My swearing would be meaningless, inoffensive, if it could not be prayer. If it were impossible for me to be praying.

It's not impossible. There are third-person prayers. Sometimes in prayer God is not addressed but narrated instead.

"The Lord," third person, "is my shepherd. I shall not want."

The psalm celebrates the fulfillment of my desires. My shepherd takes care of me. Watches over me. Feeds me.

Why does the psalm affect me? Because I hear it in Allen Grossman's voice.

Also because of what I hear in it. "I shall not want." A defiant assertion of plenty, even in a state of privation. "My cup runneth over." I have more than I could ever want. More than I could use. More than my vessel can contain.

Like "Love" (3), the psalm acknowledges my supply of food. My good shepherd not only supplies my food but forces me to take it in. "He maketh me to lie down in green pastures."

36

Imagine "Love" (3) as a post on an online review site where contributors rate different spiritual experiences on a scale of 1–10.

Looking for a spiritual experience right now?

Our search found twenty religions in your neighborhood.

Find the religion closest to you.

What's missing from the poem, in that case, is judgment.

My only judgments are of myself. I'm unworthy, unkind, ungrateful, shameful. By my mere presence I'm insulting you with my dust and my broken eyes.

I never use the language of worth to talk about your customer service.

I don't even say whether the meat tastes good.
I'm tasting it but not judging it.

I don't say:

Love paid attention to me.

Love read my profile carefully and crafted an
experience to my specifications.

Recommended to devout and casual believers
alike.

37

Herbert is attracted to neatness.

If it's an activity, he turns it into a ritual. If it's a
space, he turns it into a pattern.

He likes to keep things neat. If they weren't
already neat, he wants to make them neat.

Listen to how he talks to the "sweet phrases,
lovely metaphors" of love poetry.

> But will ye leave me thus? when ye before
> Of stews and brothels onely knew the doores,
> Then did I wash you with my tears, and more,
>   Brought you to Church well drest and clad.

Yes, he addresses them in the language of erotic
complaint they are used to hearing from the
poems of Thomas Wyatt. Then he washes them.
With his tears!

Bits of poetry came to him crumpled and soiled;
he smooths them and cleans them.

Helen Vendler has a different word for this tendency in Herbert's thought. She calls it a love of order.

The real brilliance of her reading is the next step she takes. The value of neatness becomes a temptation. A lie. An injury to nature, where not everything is neat. Whatever is fine and healthy in Wyatt's language might be spoiled by Herbert's neatening. The world might be spoiled by the imposition of an extraneous order.

In "Love" (3), Vendler sees Herbert challenging himself to avoid the temptation of neatness.

38

I have to sit down to dinner as an honored guest
with the dust of the outside world still on my
clothes, face, and hands.

I feel the insult to my host more than my host
could ever feel it.

Maybe there's no real possibility of insulting you.
Maybe I'm using the wish to avoid insult as a
pretext so that I don't have to reject you.

The dust disturbs me. Because I want neatness
to line up with holiness. Usually they line up and
there's no problem. Whatever is holy also happens
to be neat as a pin. When they conflict, I can't tell
whether neatness or holiness matters more.
I wonder if holiness is holy after all.

39

Dust does something interesting in "Love" (1) and (2). It's destructive. It's violent. It gets in my eyes and blinds me.

> How hath man parcel'd out thy glorious name,
> And thrown it on that dust which thou hast made.
> > ("Love" [1])

> Our eies shall see thee, which before saw dust;
> Dust blown by wit, till that they both were blinde.
> > ("Love" [2])

In "Love" (3), I enter your home, my body covered in abundant dust. What a clod. I'm trailing wisps of time in the air behind me. Tracking spots of death on your carpet.

That is why "I cannot look on thee." That is how I marred the eyes that you made. I loved dust and looked at dust and it got in my eyes and made me blind.

The question is whether the restriction on my sight comes from inside or outside.

Is the dust in me or on you?

Am I distracted by dust because I find it more interesting than the divine being that it obscures?

Or is the layer of dust more like wearing a blindfold?

Why is it important that I came from dust? I suppose because I am not made of something excellent or rare. Saying that you made me out of dust is barely a step above saying that I am made of shit.

Dust makes creation seem miraculous. Out of trash you are making living people. The value in me comes from your skill alone.

The saving grace of dust might be that at least it's dry. It isn't all rotten.

40

The other side of the story is that Love couldn't care less about neatness.

Neatness might not positively count against me. My mistake, when I thought that neatness was a sign of holiness, might not condemn me to Hell. But it was never a point in my favor.

Maybe you are a slob! Although I doubt it. (The poem doesn't say a word about your housekeeping.)

You might prefer a rougher surface. California casual. Maybe you are attracted to slobs.

In one literary tradition of the Renaissance, the lover rejects neatness in the name of sprezzatura, studied carelessness, a subtle kind of order that doesn't look like neatness.

"Still to be neat, still to be drest."

No, that isn't where Love lives.

Instead, "Give me a looke, give me a face, / That makes simplicitie a grace."

Herbert: "Give me simplicitie."

You can't use excessive neatness.

41

Love humiliates me by making me act like a slob.

The deepest humiliation is to make the humiliating impulse appear to come from me.

And that's what excites me. Herbert's neatness is a button, that, when pressed, induces humiliation.

ME: I'm a mess.

LOVE: No, you came here to get messed up.

Then I don't remember what you said but it was something to the effect that I wasn't starting in the worst place. I wasn't completely backward and ignorant.

The point was that neatness was my problem, not yours.

I was using you (my wish not to insult you with my mess) as an excuse to preserve a knot in my own thinking.

At the same time my problem was an opportunity
for you to induce humiliation.

What was the phrase you used? With a grimace,
"It's pretty disgusting."

42

There is an adjustment that I have to make every time.

What sometimes allows me to adjust myself is observing this person managing both her desire and my fantasy with unusual energy and skill.

When she calculates my limit. How much I am capable of taking. How much she is capable of giving. How much she can damage me without being forced to end the scene.

I love when she tells me what I must do. Which I know to be impossible.

She tells me what I am going to do, and her tale scares me, because this thing is beyond my capabilities.

She is reasonable only because she wants to believe that she is reasonable.

Does that sound like a terrible thing to say? On the contrary, to manage one's motives rationally is admirable.

I would not want to see an intuitive, uncontrolled, confused person *such as myself* trying to manage motives of sadism.

43

Scenes of humiliation are characterized by surprising reversals.

Any humiliating task, if done particularly well, becomes a demonstration of mastery rather than failure.

For example, if you force me to sing a silly song to make me look foolish, and my singing voice turns out to be exquisite.

Or if in the face of your attempts to undermine my dignity I maintain an attitude of noble suffering, like a religious martyr, and appear both beautiful and ridiculous at once.

In Balzac's story *The Duchess of Langeais*, a duchess and a general trade places practicing emotional cruelty on each other. Their escalating revenges are always emotional and always a mix of several conflicting emotions. Hot revenge rather than classically cold.

Don't Touch the Axe, Rivette's movie based on Balzac's story, is arguably more interesting in that Balzac's narrator always tells you what the characters' motives are, whereas in the movie it's never clear whether the duchess and the general are sincerely albeit perversely expressing their mutual love or maliciously fucking with each other.

The general is going to brand the duchess as punishment for being a coquette and to avenge the uncompromising denial to which she has subjected him.

He holds the red-hot iron in one hand while with the thumb of his other hand he traces the mark that he is going to make in the middle of her forehead.

She meets the pressure of his thumb and presses back, saying, "MY FOREHEAD BURNS HOTTER THAN YOUR IRON." She doesn't acquiesce silently; she demands that he mark her. And her excitement ruins the fantasy for him so that he can't complete his revenge.

The nobility of her submission has the effect of reversing their roles.

And if it were true, if her forehead were hotter, he wouldn't be able to leave a mark on it. Her head would brand the iron.

44

Herbert's motto, "Less than the least of God's mercies." I quote this motto all the time, not necessarily thinking about Herbert. I say it with pride.

It is a proud motto. It's a superlative. Super-superlative. Less than least. Which is either impossible or it means being excluded from the category of God's mercies entirely.

Herbert has excellent reasons for being proud. Good at school. Good at conversation. Good at oratory. Good at poetry. Favored by mother. Favored by teachers. Favored by Lancelot Andrewes, his teacher in grammar school (who also organized the translation of the King James version of the Bible). Favored by Francis Bacon. Favored by King James.

His motto could be an effort to temper his pride in his achievements and his pride in his recognized abilities and his pride in his undeserved favors. "As a sinner, I am less than the least."

He also has some of the pride of seeking humiliation. The exaggerated superlative makes him special.

"You have mercy on everyone but me." That could be the motto of despair. "You chose me to suffer without possibility of being saved."

Or, "You have so much mercy that there remains a minuscule amount of mercy even for someone like me." Herbert is proud to see that the less-than-least of God's mercies could be receiving more than most of God's attention.

More than most would be a minority position. The majority receive a prescribed quantity of mercy. An elite receive more mercy than that. Better mercy.

Less than least would not quite be a minority. "The smallest minority receive a quantity of mercy, but I, I get nothing. I am excluded."

A paradox of divine omnipotence. Can Herbert's god accomplish the miracle of creating a being less deserving of mercy than the least deserving?

Or an act of mercy smaller than the smallest?

My version of the motto, "The least remarkable object in the room." Bottom of the list. But still on the list.

Herbert. Not even the bottom. "Beneath the underdog" (Mingus).

45

I am a bad person who wants to be a good person.

Being bad, I don't know what good means. I am bad from one end to the other. Even in my best attempts.

I try to be good and I don't know how. Nonetheless I succeed maybe fifty percent of the time.

I try to be good and that's my greatest good. Apart from the aspiration to virtue I am all bad.

I will not be saved by the language of righteousness.

But my fantasy of being one of the righteous might be the best thing about me, and it might make me a little better, at least some of the time.

46

Superliminare

Thou, whom the former precepts have
Sprinkled and taught, how to behave
Thy self in church; approach, and taste
The churches mysticall repast.

Avoid Profanenesse; come not here:
Nothing but holy, pure, and cleare,
Or that which groneth to be so,
May at his perill further go.

The sinners who are unprepared to enter the temple are reminded not to be profane. Which means that profanity is not what disqualifies them.

Their ordinary condition is not profane but sinful. Profanity would be the act of bringing sin into the temple.

Even sinners who cherish their sins are motivated to cast Profaneness out of the temple.

They respond to no other command. They aren't "holy, pure, and cleare," and maybe they don't want to be. They don't "grone to be so." But they share Herbert's core value. They are formalists too. They are drawn to neatness.

All sinners love neatness. They want everything in the universe to keep its place.

47

Three kinds of speech tags.

"Love said."

"Sayes Love."

The third kind of speech tag is no tag.

I have already mentioned the tense change.
Said, says. There are interesting suggestions of
chronology (the poem catching up to the present
in which it is spoken) and immediacy (the poem
bringing readers into its action). I am speaking the
poem while Love is speaking to me.

The syntax and its reversal are hard to explain.
Subject, verb. Verb, subject. I don't think the
reversal can be explained by accommodation
to the meter. I would scan both "Love said" and
"sayes Love" as iambs.

There may be a difference in tone.

"Love said." I am writing a report.

"Sayes Love." I am telling a tale.

To whom am I telling my story? I still don't have a good answer for this question.

One answer could be Herbert's mother. The story about the conversation between the unworthy soul and Love is the story that George Herbert has been telling to Magdalen Herbert since the letter he wrote at Cambridge and maybe earlier than that. It's the story of those two early love poems, then the first two poems called "Love" in The Temple, and now the last poem in the book.

In the elegy for his mother, Herbert suggests that all of his poetry is written in praise of his mother for the simple reason that she taught him how to write:

> Ah, Mother, forever will your mourning child
> Praise you; you taught me how to write,
> That skill owes you praise, that skill, unloosed,
> Floods the paper, having gathered labor's

Finest fruit honoring a mother,
Though those who do not understand will not
    allow it.

"Lord" is the title of his older brother, a baron, and "Love" is the name of the host in the tale he is telling, but the real "you," the "you" he's telling it to, could be Magdalen Herbert. The ancestor and effective creator of George Herbert.

48

Gender is tacit in "Love" 1, 2, and 3. The only clear identification of gender is the title "Lord."

The poems Herbert composed at age 17, in his first year at Cambridge, and sent to his mother Magdalen Herbert, are more explicit.

But I fear the heat of my late *Ague* hath dryed up those springs, by which Scholars say, the Muses use to take up their habitations. However, I need not their help, to reprove the vanity of those many Love-poems, that are daily writ and consecrated to *Venus*; nor to bewail that so few are writ, that look towards *God* and *Heaven*. For my own part, my meaning (dear Mother) is in these Sonnets, to declare my resolution to be, that my poor Abilities in *Poetry*, shall be all, and ever consecrated to Gods glory. And—

My God, where is that ancient heat towards thee,
    Wherewith whole showls of *Martyrs* once did burn,
    Besides their other flames? Doth Poetry
Wear *Venus* Livery? only serve her turn?

Why are not *Sonnets* made of thee? and layes
    Upon thine Altar burnt? Cannot thy love
    Heighten a spirit to sound out thy praise
As well as any she? Cannot thy *Dove*
Out-strip their *Cupid* easily in flight?
    Or, since thy wayes are deep, and still the same,
    Will not a verse run smooth that bears thy name?
Why doth that fire, which by thy power and might
    Each breast does feel, no braver fuel choose
    Than that, which one day Worms may chance refuse?

Sure, Lord, there is enough in thee to dry
    Oceans of *Ink*; for, as the Deluge did
    Cover the Earth, so doth thy Majesty:
Each Cloud distills thy praise, and doth forbid
Poets to turn it to another use.
    Roses and *Lillies* speak thee; and to make
    A pair of Cheeks of them, is thy abuse.
Why should I *Womens* eyes for Chrystal take?
Such poor invention burns in their low mind
    Whose fire is wild, and doth not upward go
    To praise, and on thee, Lord, some *Ink* bestow.
Open the bones, and you shall nothing find
    In the best *face* but *filth*, when, Lord, in thee
    The *beauty* lies in the *discovery*.

It may be said that Herbert's whole literary career comes out of these two mediocre sonnets.

The sonnets arbitrate a conflict between two gods who want to be called Love. For the sake of discussion, one of them is known as Venus and the other is known as the Lord.

Poets have traditionally worked for Venus. We "wear *Venus* Livery," the clothes and the colors of her household. We are her servants. We "serve her turn."

The problem with poets is that we are serving the wrong god. Putting power in the wrong place. In other words, Herbert is talking about the problem of giving power to a god who is a woman.

Are these early poems simple misogyny? Maybe. One argument in both poems is that women have dirty faces. The conflict between two gods called Love is the confusion of the true god's face with Venus's face, which is located in a living woman's face, which is mortal, at first made from dust and at last buried in earth, and "which one day Worms may chance refuse." All women, "any she," may be included in this judgment.

There is also, in the letter, an arrogant refusal of the help of the muses. "I need not their help."

Roses and lilies are not mere emblems. They are vessels of divine immanence. God lives in them.

Really flowers are poets themselves. They address themselves to God. They "speak thee."

To compare flowers to a woman's face, her "cheeks," is worse than a figure, it is "abuse."

Who are the victims of this abuse? The poet's mind? The reader's mind? The woman's face? The cheeks? The flowers? God? (Which god? The old god who is a woman? The new god who is inhuman?)

Maybe the injury to the flowers is how they lose their voices.

Comparing eyes to crystal does them no injury, but it is "poor invention," embarrassing.

Come on guys. Her eyes are crystals? Have you no imagination?

50

Open the bones, and you shall nothing find
   In the best *face* but *filth*.

Another face of another corpse so wretched that the creatures who subsist on decayed things would avoid it.

"Open the bones," perform surgery without medical training.

Destroy the face and it will be destroyed.

Kill the face to expose the trash its bearer shares with all women.

Herbert's poem exposes the vanity of human desire. What is exposed is different from death. Human desire is trash, refuse, that is, the substantive form of "to refuse," what the worms do when they encounter the decayed face of a woman's dead body.

God has no face.

"The *beauty*" of God's no-face "lies in the *discovery*." One of those lines people like to quote where Herbert's sweet tone makes his sadism hard to recognize.

What is discovery? Herbert's violent imagination. It should be contrasted with "poor invention" above.

Poor invention means clichéd comparisons. Take the face apart and replace each piece with a conventionally treasured item, a flower or a crystal.

Discovery means cutting away the face to show blood, sinew, and bone. And they do not appear to be parts of a miraculously functioning organism; they are dead meat. Filth.

Filth is a strong word. For human remains, a very strong word.

The alternative is divine discovery. Destroy the world to reveal the hidden god. Not a human face.

52

What part of the human body do we like best?

If Venus said, "You must sit down and taste my meat," what part of her would we choose?

Are we breast men or leg men or ass men?

Pussy men? Do we think Venus is asking us to go down on her?

We, her servants, have chosen the face. That is where we take our bites. Our heat, our fires, are devoted to cooking the face of a woman. Her face (her eyes are crystals, her cheeks are roses and lilies) is our insufficient fuel.

The wiser worms turn away from women's faces. "Filth." Not good for eating.

Herbert tried them all. Venus's face and other women's faces, including the "best face" and the rest of the faces. He went to every face, took one bite, and was disappointed. The worms were right. Only his god was sweet enough.

Maybe what he discovered was the taboo on cannibalism. Human faces shouldn't look to other human faces for nourishing food. It's better to eat a god than to eat a woman.

That was his discovery. Instead of a face, there was meat.

53

The commitment to divine poetry is a promise he makes not to God but to his mother.

The poems are a way of giving power to a woman who was already one of the most powerful people in the world.

It is conceivable that Magdalen Herbert is a human model for divine love. Also note that in the letter he calls her "dear." "Dear mother."

The possibility of giving power to Magdalen Herbert by fulfilling a youthful promise made to her does not exclude the attitude of misogyny. Herbert first expresses the promise in two poems where he says that women's faces are trash. In general I think it's common for men to say nasty things about women as an adjunct to praise of their mothers.

Wanting to give power to a woman doesn't mean that Herbert is a nice man or that he likes women.

54

For Elias Canetti as well, motherhood is a condition of absolute power over another creature. Part of that story is Canetti's mother, a person of unusual energy, will, and control. Canetti took a degree in chemistry, dedicated years of his life to laboratory science, not because he was personally motivated to do scientific research but because his mother insisted.

I guess what I'm saying is that I should look at my relationship with my mother to explain why I want to give power to a woman.

My mother seems an unlikely figure of sovereignty. Our close relationship (close in temperament, not in time spent or distance) does not appear to be one of domination and submission.

We look very much alike.

There is something in me that seeks her approval. Which means that I give her that much power. This bond has rarely been tested because she always gives me her approval. And she worries.

Alternatively one might ask whether I was looking for signs of strength in other women that I didn't find in my mother. She in her weak way formed me, and I in my weak way imitated her, and I looked in foreign places for women whose natures were foreign.

55

From the perspective of feminist criticism, Herbert's love might already be Bizarro. A love that is really hate. Misogyny.

What does it mean to say that demeaning images in love poetry are a form of hate?

We hate what women actually are. We love an idea of a woman who doesn't exist. Or, if she exists, we created her by degrading actual women until they assumed the shape of our idea.

The poet is not being honest. If he were honest he would say that he hates women. He says that he loves a woman but everything that he uses to express himself other than the word love shows his obvious hate. Maybe he's not aware of it. Maybe our culture hates women, and, no matter how the poet feels, the tradition has only tools of hate.

Or maybe the critic is not being honest. Maybe if critics were honest they would say that they don't like love; they like equality. What love has meant for most of human history is not a relationship of equality. If love is to be salvaged for the critics, its tradition might have to be cut loose.

What if I love hate? What if I am a pervert to whom the only legible messages of love are violent attacks?

Like a cartoon.

Like Bizarro Superman.

Like Krazy Kat.

56

Idea for poem. Compile a list of my sexual preferences, fantasies, and limits.

I am interested in verbal humiliation. I fetishize voice and rhetorical power.

Speech restrictions. Your being able to talk and my not being able to talk.

Because I'm physically prevented from speaking.

Because I can't put my thoughts together to formulate speech.

Because you force me to say something that degrades me.

Because you misunderstand what I'm saying when I try to talk. This is the flip side of verbal humiliation, and it might be the part that feels most humiliating.

Other kinds of restrictions. Movement, height, sightlines, clothing. Things that you are allowed to do that I'm not allowed to do. Anything that suggests a difference in power.

I am also interested in physical humiliations. Slapping. Spitting. I like bondage and other forms of physical helplessness. The idea of breath control is exciting and troubling to me.

I have a strange tendency to see myself as a piece of furniture. Mine is not the kind of human furniture where people want to be treated as objects in the sense of being ignored and allowed to disappear into the background. It's beautiful and inspiring that someone could want to be an object in such a pure way, but that is not really my thing. I want to be more like a sofa or a footrest that you treat unfairly, talk to, and make fun of. If there were such a thing.

There is an interesting kind of humiliation in unfairness. No-win situations. Heads you win, tails I lose.

I fetishize body scents. I used to think that I liked the humiliating associations of uncleanness. Then I discovered that I liked the smells themselves. This preference might be my most ordinary human sexual response, apart from my interest in faces.

Would it make sense to say that I fetishize faces? No. Being attracted to faces is normal.

My interest in pain is hard to define. Some kinds of pain, like the feeling of being slapped or pinched, are maybe versions of humiliation, so it's not surprising that I like them.

I also have experience with more intense pain, whipping, caning, and other techniques of corporal punishment. I don't like the feelings of pain, but I really like the loss of control that goes with them. And I like how intimate pain can be.

Tickling can have a similar effect, but most of the time I am not ticklish enough to appreciate the effect. Pain is more reliable.

Plus I'm attracted to sadists, so I had to figure out a way of liking pain.

My hard limits are blood and shit. (A little surface blood is not a concern—I don't freak out at the sight of blood—but no puncture wounds, no needles, and no deliberate cutting.) Marks are fine. Bruises are fine.

57

I wanted to write about "Love" (3) because I thought people were confused about power. Everywhere I went, I heard people talking about power. They didn't seem to know what power was, and they didn't seem to know whether they liked power. They weren't being honest about whether they wanted power.

No, my friends were not sure whether power was a desirable thing. They were not sure whether they were allowed to say that they liked power.

Our teachers had the same problem. In school I heard so much about power and it never sounded interesting. So much about sovereignty and sex but without making it sound sexy.

What did I learn about power from "Love" (3)?

A love relationship can be founded on inequality.

Power comes from submission as well as domination. When I submit, I am giving you power.

Power is attractive. Being attracted to power can mean wanting someone's power or wanting to give someone power.

58

One lesson from the electrical grid is that power is difficult to store. When released it has to be used right away. It dissipates. If I understand anything about the electrical grid.

Power on the electrical grid can be measured and quantified. People who talk about power in politics and society quantify power often without measuring.

They think they are measuring. Their measure is called history. (What they know about history may be questionable.) The idea seems to be that quantities of power in the present are determined by struggles in the past, which were determined unjustly.

As though history stored power. As though power were inherited.

Is power not inherited?

Can a person not give power to another person? Can powers be granted only by a group, a state, an institution?

What about when you leave your children with a babysitter?

What about when you leave your children alone in the apartment?

Transfers of power from person to person are the most ordinary exchange in life. Barely registering as an event in society.

Or is power mostly lost in these exchanges?

The English system of primogeniture, where property is inherited with restrictions on the freedom to alienate it, attempts to minimize the losses that occur in the transfer of power between generations. The restrictions are severe: the oldest living son can't exchange or give away his property and can't choose who inherits it. Primogeniture is an extraordinary measure that patriarchs can take if they are determined to hold power after dying.

My job in school comes with some power. I know there are powers in my job because some people fetishize it. They fantasize about teacher/student roleplay.

For some people it isn't play. I know some teachers and students who are turned on by pedagogical relationships. Many people who pursue academic careers first got the idea from a fantasy about a particular teacher of theirs. Some teachers and students become sexually involved not in spite of but because of the classroom relationship.

I don't feel morally superior to people who are attracted to their teachers or students. I just have trouble seeing it.

Teaching does not come naturally to me. I am uncomfortable with the constant need for self-display and speaking in public. I don't hide my discomfort, and my awkward manner makes my students feel awkward too.

The same awkwardness that makes it difficult for me to speak fluently can also make me an effective public speaker. It creates a distance and a charged atmosphere around me. Not the same as fear but similar to fear. My students will never be afraid of me but they would never think of me as easy to deal with.

When I was a student (quite a happy student) I was often drawn to teachers who frightened me. There may have been an element of fantasy in my fear.

I sometimes think that school may be a psychic terrain even more dark and mysterious than family.

I sexualize power. Therefore I mystify it. I attribute to it special, private meanings.

The notion of ideology also tends to mystify power. I don't simply believe what I believe; my beliefs are supported by an ideology, which is supported by a social structure that I can't see clearly from inside.

The old meaning of power, the meaning that was current for Herbert, is not mystical. Powers are abilities. If you can sew a button, that is one of your powers; if you can translate Cantonese, that is one of your powers.

This is what Hobbes means when he says that the end of knowledge is power.

This is what Aristotle means when he says that rhetoric is the art of discerning the available means of persuasion in any situation. Each lever of persuasion is a power; discerning them is another power.

Herbert's Lord of Power is a mystical vision only because the poet is having a conversation with God.

> Who would have thought my shrivel'd heart
> Could have recover'd greennesse? It was gone
>   Quite under ground; as flowers depart
> To see their mother-root, when they have blown;
>   Where they together
>   All the hard weather,
>   Dead to the world, keep house unknown.
>
>   These are thy wonders, Lord of power,
> Killing and quickening, bringing down to hell
>   And up to heaven in an houre;
> Making a chiming of a passing-bell.

But the workings of divine power are not mystical. They are natural and empirically knowable (although they might not always be easy to follow). They are making the plant live, keeping it alive, and making it die.

No human being eroticizes ideology.

I might almost say, that is how you can tell that
ideology is inadequate as an account of power.

My teachers and friends, who made power seem
unsexy, I assume were not into it.

No one ever showed me a way to talk about what
was attractive in power.

Not in all their talk about power.

I only knew that rhetorical power, when it
inhabited other people, excited me.

Rhetorical power is interesting to me because, for one thing, it has to be manufactured in situations. In the present. Reputation, which refers to past events, has something to do with it. But even a bad reputation can be used as a tool in the present. If you have a bad reputation, you can use it to terrify me, for example.

In situations, one person may have more power than another. It is a mistake to think that these relationships remain constant. They are frequently reversed.

It is a mistake to think that social status comes with a quantity of strength or weakness.

Even in hierarchical societies, power is not a constant quantity. In hierarchical relationships in my society, where there are no castes and no aristocracy, power is certainly not constant.

The history of wielding power is filled with reversals. Servants and masters switch positions. Victims become victimizers.

If the weak never became strong enough to defeat the strong, hierarchy would be a law of nature like entropy.

If reversals were not possible, there would be no point in resisting oppression.

Canetti sees that reversal is an aspect of power because his concept of power is based on eating. He takes the motto of reversal from a Sanskrit book of ritual sacrifices, the *Shatapatha-Brahmana*: "For whatever food a man eats in this world, by that food he is eaten in the next world."

It might seem obvious that power in eating flows in one direction only. When I seize an object for food and incorporate it into my body, I must believe that I am stronger than my food.

However, when I eat, I am exposing the soft interior of my body to a foreign object. Maybe I am not strong enough to handle it.

Maybe I fail to turn my food into myself.

Maybe my food breaks me down and incorporates me instead.

Canetti started with the question, why do people behave differently in crowds? Why do individuals in a crowd dissolve, abandon their personal traits, and move with the crowd?

Before he wrote his book he wondered why he, Canetti, behaved differently in a crowd. Once, during his student days in Vienna, he joined with a crowd of people who rioted in response to an unjust verdict in a murder trial. He was part of the crowd that set fire to the Palace of Justice on July 15, 1927.

> The fire was what held the situation together. You felt the fire, its presence was overwhelming; even if you did not see it, you nevertheless had it in your mind, its attraction and the attraction exerted by the crowd were one and the same. The salvoes of gunfire by the police aroused boohs, the boohs new salvoes. But no matter where you happened to be under the impact of the gunfire, no matter where you seemingly fled, your connection with others (an open or secret

connection, depending on the place) remained in effect. And you were drawn back into the province of the fire—circuitously, since there was no other possible way.

The first fact in Canetti's social psychology is the fear of being touched. People create boundaries between themselves and other people to avoid being touched. Only, when they enter a crowd, their fear turns into a desire to be so close to other people that they lose their boundaries in the crowd.

Behind both the fear of being touched and the wish to become part of the crowd is a single problem, eating. The goal is, most of the time, to eat other people and not to be eaten by them. In the crowd the goal is to be consumed.

Canetti thinks that most exchanges in society involve people eating other people.

> Anyone who wants to rule men first tries to humiliate them, to trick them out of their rights and their capacity for resistance, until they are as powerless before him as animals. He uses them like animals, and, even if he does not tell them so, in himself he always knows quite clearly that they mean just as little to him; when he speaks to his intimates he will call them sheep or cattle. His ultimate aim is to incorporate them into himself and to suck the substance out of them. What remains of them afterwards does not matter to him. The worse he has treated them, the more he despises them. When they are no more use at all, he disposes of them as he does of his excrement, simply seeing to it that they do not poison the air of his house.

Canetti defines a family not as a biological relationship but rather as people eating together who are not eating one another. This unit is an *exceptional* social arrangement. Ordinarily when people eat together they eat one another. Only families look for sources of food apart from family members.

The exception within the exception of the family is the mother, who offers the product of her own body as food for her children. (Her maternal role is defined not by giving birth but by giving food to her children.) Yet she controls the children who consume her. She both dictates and gratifies their appetites.

Maternity is the closest thing to absolute power in human experience.

Like Love in "Love" (3).

The source of both commands and food.

Crowds and Power is a strange book.

It is obviously a response to fascism but Canetti discusses fascism only in a few places: in a chapter on the Versailles Treaty, and in chapters on Schreber's paranoia.

(In the latter case, Canetti mentions Hitler only to insist that Schreber is a more useful example. "A madman, helpless, outcast, and despised, who drags out a twilight existence in some asylum, may, through the insights he procures us, prove more important than Hitler or Napoleon, illuminating for mankind his curse and its masters.")

The book is obviously a response to psychoanalysis, but, again, Canetti mentions Freud only in a parenthesis about the Schreber case.

His response to psychoanalysis is to replace sex with food. *Crowds and Power* is a total account of human civilization based on food rather than sex.

The passages where Canetti writes about sex are revealing.

In two passages it is apparent that Canetti has no vocabulary to distinguish sex from rape. On the first page of the book, describing the universal fear of being touched, he remarks that "we avoid actual contact if we can. If we do not avoid it, it is because we feel attracted to someone; and then it is we who make the approach."

Wanting to be touched is not humanly possible. Someone might want to touch another person as a preliminary to consuming them, but no one wants to be touched, that is, to be eaten.

In another passage, Canetti tells the story of the rape of Thetis by Peleus, then remarks, "The story of Thetis does not really add anything to that of Proteus [which he has also told on the previous page]. I have quoted it here because of its erotic colouring."

Rape is erotic. The desire to rape is the only kind of desire. An attraction to another person is a desire to touch another person, which can never be reciprocated. No one ever consents to being touched.

There is one last turn in Canetti's view of rape and (therefore) sex.

For Canetti the phallus is not an icon of power. Rather power pertains to the hand, the mouth, and the organs of digestion hidden within the human body.

Penetration doesn't look like an aggressive act to him. It looks like a way of being consumed.

Becoming food. Or becoming a mother. (Since motherhood is defined not by conception or birth but by feeding.)

A mother feeding an infant penetrates the infant.

What if she said to her infant, "You must sit down and taste my meat"?

68

Teaching in the humanities.

For Erasmus, the problem was, "We are teaching them to rule us."

The teacher, who knows the liberal arts that are unknown to the pupils, rules the pupils. The teacher can administer corporal punishment. And the beatings go on all day.

Meanwhile the teacher is giving new powers to the pupils. Making them fit to rule.

For my students, poetry is not a path to preferment. Knowledge of poetry will not help them attract a duchess's attention. Humanistic learning will not qualify them to be ambassadors to the courts of Europe.

For me and my colleagues, the problem is that we are keepers of a treasure no one else wants.

69

There is a strange misconception going around that politics is a noble endeavor. It is not.

One of the best images of political action is the description of preferment at the Lilliputian court in Book I of *Gulliver's Travels*.

> There is likewise another Diversion, which is only shewn before the Emperor and Empress, and first Minister, upon particular Occasions. The Emperor lays on a Table three fine silken Threads of six Inches long. One is Blue, the other Red, and the third Green. These Threads are proposed as Prizes, for those Persons whom the Emperor hath a mind to distinguish by a peculiar Mark of his Favour. The Ceremony is performed in his Majesty's great Chamber of State; where the Candidates are to undergo a Tryal of Dexterity very different from the former; and such as I have not observed the least Resemblance of in any other Country of the old or the new World. The Emperor holds a Stick in his Hands, both Ends parallel to the Horizon, while the Candidates advancing one by one, sometimes leap

over the Stick, sometimes creep under it backwards and forwards several times, according as the Stick is advanced or depressed. Sometimes the Emperor holds one End of the Stick, and his first Minister the other; sometimes the Minister has it entirely to himself. Whoever performs his part with most Agility, and holds out the longest in *leaping* and *creeping*, is rewarded with the Blue-coloured silk; the Red is given to the next, and the Green to the third, which they all wear girt twice round about the Middle; and you see few great Persons about this Court, who are not adorned with one of these Girdles.

The point of the corrosively ironic comment, "such as I have not observed the least Resemblance of in any other Country of the old or the new World," is that these entertainments, leaping and creeping, may be observed in every nation, in every part of the world where people form governments.

Politics in every sense, in all of its manifestations—

Lobbying. Legislation. Activism. Protocol. Conspiracy. Bureaucracy. Subversion.

Countersubversion. Negotiation. Revolution.
Campaigning. Cold calling. Knocking on doors.
Speeches on platforms. Hectoring. Fulminating.
Wheedling. Begging for gifts. Begging for votes.
Forming alliances. Making motions. Making
statements. Making donations. Meeting voters.
Meeting job-seekers. Meeting fellow travelers.
Meeting enemies. Meeting press agents.
Promising. Signing petitions. Signing treaties.
Marching. Printing leaflets. Bumper stickers.
Pinback buttons. Signs posted in the windows
and on the lawns. Whistle stops. Kissing babies.
Kissing rings. Bowing and scraping. Crawling.

Rope dancing. Leaping and creeping.

The single art of ruling and being ruled.

Far from inculcating virtue, far from being
ennobling, it has only dire consequences for the
human soul.

It is degrading.

It is opportunism.

It is seeking favor.

It is the realm of opinion.

It is court life.

Politics,

a second-rate form of human activity, neither an
art nor a science, at once corrupting to the soul and
fatiguing to the mind, an activity either of those who
cannot live without the illusion of affairs or those so
fearful of being ruled by others that they will pay
away their own lives to prevent it.

The assumed moral superiority of weak people
may not be a mistake. It is true that power
corrupts. I think I know how it happens. Those
who enjoy power calculate that their powers
benefit all people. They maintain their position
with its remarkable powers for the good of society.
To maintain their position for the good of society
they compromise themselves.

Everyone makes the same mistake:

No one should have this much power.

But I can do something good with it.

And I would do anything to keep it.

And I don't care what happens to you if you try to
take it away.

Stanley Fish taught me to read "The Flower" as a lesson in monism.

> We say amisse,
> This or that is:
> Thy word is all, if we could spell.

One of those incredible passages in Herbert's poetry where the diction is stunningly plain. Almost all monosyllables. And yet the meaning is obscure.

Fish paraphrased it like this. We flawed human souls speak a language that multiplies distinctions. Our words make divisions in the world. When we speak we turn the same object into different objects. We multiply and arrange levels of reality.

But the world really is a single substance, which is the body of God.

If only we could stop making illusory divisions, "If only we could stop spelling!", we would be seamlessly participating in divine presence. Just like how God acts in the flower.

I think Herbert is criticizing a different distinction. He is thinking about God, and he uses two ways of talking about God to organize the poem. Some of the verses are addressed to the Lord of Power, and the rest are addressed to the Lord of Love.

We call you by two names, power and love, and we say amiss. They are the same thing.

You can control your desires.

A rational attitude, no?

Before you desire something you should calculate what would be the best thing to desire and choose that thing.

Something that you like, something that would be good for you. Something better than all the things that you didn't choose.

The gay liberation movement has found it strategically useful to maintain the opposite attitude. Human sexual preferences are innate. We are born with our desires; we never get to choose them.

Gay activism has obviously had some success with this line of thought.

Yet it might be useful, it might be healthy, to think of sexual desires as personal choices.

This other line of thought might turn out to be a better strategy for defending strange desires.

"We're queer, not because we have no choice, but because it's the best choice."

"We choose objects of desire that are better for us."

There is a big part of sex that is neither innate nor a choice.

All the things I desire that I not only would never have chosen but would never have imagined that someone could desire if someone else had not already established them as things to desire.

A kink can be induced.

Some of my kinks seem to be inbuilt parts of me. I am pretty sure that fetishizing rhetorical power would have been a basic truth about me even if I had never consciously apprehended it.

Then there are kinks that I would never have invented if someone else hadn't invented them first but they nonetheless became important to me. They developed in me because I associate them with a good experience or a person I like.

La Rochefoucauld writes about people who "would never have fallen in love if they had never heard of love," which is rather damning but also sort of interesting and creative.

There is something embarrassing about the fact that I did not make up my sexual preferences entirely out of myself.

75

It's strange what you find and what you invent. It's just as strange now that my fantasies include a lifetime of remembered experiences. It's strange what you remember.

My sense is that I discovered masturbation late.

I have a few early memories of touching myself and my parents noticing what I was doing; they laughed gently while I struggled to answer and weakly denied that I was doing anything notable.

This is probably how they agreed to teach me normal behavior. They weren't forbidding what I was doing but trying to show that it was a funny thing to do when other people were around to see it. I wonder if this reaction could have taught me to associate arousal with humiliation.

My parents owned some books on child development. I used to read them to compare my experiences to the theoretical models.

Around age eleven I remember reading about boys my age discovering masturbation. Nothing like that was happening to me. I thought that maybe I was different from other kids. That seemed fine. Masturbation sounded messy.

I started consciously masturbating a year or two later than the books led me to expect. I did it by pressing myself against the bed one morning after waking. When I felt the wonderful climax I knew that I was masturbating although I was humping the mattress rather than using my hand as the literature described.

My fantasies were about elaborate bondage but they didn't involve any of the traditional bondage equipment that I came to know much later. No handcuffs, chains, leather, sleepsacks, hoods. Instead I thought about ropes. Nets. I believe these images came from school. Gym and recess equipment.

In one fantasy I was elaborately mummified in rope, the wrapping so overdone that I became almost like a ball of yarn. Then dangled from a scaffold.

Sometimes the fantasies involved the threat of pain or punishment or, alternatively, rape. This part of the fantasy was almost an afterthought. The girl who was putting me in immobilizing bondage would talk about other things she might do to me. But this was only a way of talking that excited me. The focus of the fantasies was always bondage.

I didn't have the word bondage. The words I knew were the nouns ropes and knots and the verb to tie.

I didn't use the word fantasies. I called them thoughts.

I didn't usually think about girls I knew or scenes from movies or other images. The visual and narrative components of my fantasy life have always been minimal.

Does "visual" mean what you see when your eyes are open? In that case my inclinations are not predominantly visual.

Sometimes the sound of a voice would be important. It might be the voice of someone I knew.

I sometimes have sexual dreams about a woman I know. Just a brief vivid scene or a suggestion of something exciting. The dreams always make me feel warmly toward the woman. Even if it's someone I don't like. We have shared an intimacy.

Are you sure that you would be able to recognize my pornography?

I should write about the backpack in my attic room and the things I kept there. This would have been late adolescence, around ages sixteen, seventeen, eighteen.

A paperback translation of the complete works of de Sade that I lifted from my parents' bookshelves. I now judge it to have been a poor translation. Even at the time I noticed some questionable choices.

A French magazine. It contained nothing obviously sexy, only journalism and advertisements. I don't think there were any naked bodies in the advertisements.

Possibly a copy of *City Pages* or was it *City Reader*? The weekly newspaper of Minneapolis that occasionally published personals related to BDSM.

Remember my sexual response to the debate in Hell in Book 2 of *Paradise Lost*. Rhetorical power was one of my favorite things from the beginning. That should go into the backpack too.

Remember the cartoons I saw long ago. "Mickey's Nightmare." "Bimbo's Initiation."

The women's army in *The Marvelous Land of Oz*.

Barbara sermonizing in *Major Barbara*.

Jean Simmons slapping Robert Mitchum in *Angel Face*.

How does anyone know what my pornography looks like? One of our legal definitions of pornography is that you know it when you see it. But you really don't know.

The backpack also contained some belts, cords, straps, and I seem to remember a nylon leash and collar that I used to practice binding myself. I have written about these experiments and their abrupt end elsewhere.

What an arbitrary, meager collection.

I remember how difficult it was to masturbate with Sade.

Part of the trouble was that I sometimes got interested in the writing. I would get caught up in the story about Justine or the crazy ideas of her persecutors and forget that I was trying to think sexually.

Part of the trouble was that a lot of the sex was boring or repulsive. My real sexual interests were represented in a few passages from *120 Days of Sodom* but I had to pick and choose carefully. The parts about bondage and torture were interesting to me but I was indifferent to the vanilla sex acts, disturbed by the mutilations, confused by the emphasis on blasphemy, and turned off by the scenes with shit.

There was one "passion" that I used to enjoy reading where I liked the idea of being dominated by a woman but I had to ignore what she was doing. Whipping, sucking, and shitting.

Other passions that I remember include an appeasement scene where a man has to degrade himself to attain forgiveness by eating snot or licking the bottom of a woman's shoe. He also has the option of receiving fifty cane strokes if he refuses any penance as too disgusting.

There was another passion where a man is inescapably bound and a woman pinches him, scratches him, and burns him. I knew that burning would be a limit for me.

Later I had a French edition and I used to pretend to be uncertain about the meaning of *brûler*. Maybe it meant bite.

Sometimes I would read the final "devil's passion" but not if I wanted to masturbate afterwards.

I felt some intellectual curiosity regarding the blasphemous passions. I don't think they had a sexual meaning for me. It still seems strange to me that anyone could be sexually excited by desecrating the wafer.

Sade and Herbert might have had an interesting debate on this topic.

But isn't it inspiring how imaginative some people are. The unlikely things they choose to be turned on by. A very smart woman once told me, "This is the most advanced sexuality on the planet."

The French magazine was banal general interest but a photograph in an advertisement for luggage interested me. It showed a woman's back. She was wearing summer athletic clothing. What interested me was her hair, which was gathered in a braid, and the curve of her ass in khaki shorts.

This image seems worth recalling because there was a time when I did not know that a woman's ass could be interesting. It was not a prominent fact in the popular culture of the time.

When this fact was acknowledged, for example in *City of Women*, or in Robert Crumb's cartoons where it was exaggerated beyond human possibility, I found it perplexing. Why does Snaporaz care about asses?

Even as I was starting to see the interest in this shape, it did not seem more interesting than the shape of the hair.

I don't think my ignorance would have been possible in a young person growing up in any city in the United States after the 1990s.

In *Fallen Angel*, Linda Darnell eats Dana Andrews's hamburger and then makes him pay for it with his last dollar bill.

Nothing personal. She doesn't know him or care about him.

This isn't her coffee shop so the money isn't for her. She doesn't want his money; she wants him to have no money.

The hamburger looks so good. It has onions and "the entire state of California" on it.

He wants the sandwich and doesn't get it and has to pay for it; she wants it and gets it. Something for everybody. Or maybe what I mean is everything for somebody.

I'm not sure which one I want to be. Andrews, Darnell, the hamburger?

I think of the ways you humiliated me with food.

Once you pissed into my food.

Another time you chewed my food before I ate it.

Another time you sneezed while chewing a gummy worm and had me eat the fragment of candy that you had sneezed.

We were eating the same food but you did something to it to underline the difference between your status and mine.

Humiliation meant something different each time.

Chewing and spitting the food was surprisingly dainty and caring, whereas sneezing the gummy worm was exactly the opposite, crude and uncaring.

Imagine "Love" (3) as a manual of conventions for a relationship between host and guest.

By convention I am reluctant to accept your hospitality. That makes me ungrateful but it also makes me a good guest. A worthy guest. The kind of guest who follows the manual.

I can't call myself a worthy guest. It may be part of the pattern of a worthy guest to question one's worth.

And to speak of oneself in the third person.

Isn't that a strange thing to say? "A guest worthy to be here."

If I were truly worthy I would already be here. You wouldn't have to welcome me. I wouldn't be a stranger.

If I were worthy of your help I wouldn't need help.

Modern households are less concerned with hospitality. Taking strangers into the household seems too big a risk.

The oldest conventions of hospitality are ways of keeping society together without a government or polite formulas.

Hospitality goes deeper than polite formulas. The oldest households had no use for polite behavior. A stranger wouldn't know the formulas anyway.

Being a stranger, not knowing the rules, earns me a temporary place in your household. A traveler in a strange land, I am vulnerable to you, my host. And to the world.

You are at home but your home becomes vulnerable to me.

Neither of us has any privacy.

We have to be vigilant.

Love's hospitality is not symmetrical like that.

You welcome me in words that are spoken according to ritual.

I "draw back," not in words but in "my soul." In words, according to ritual, I accuse myself of lacking the qualities of a worthy guest.

You "take" my hand. Not a gesture of extension in two directions. You reach for me and take me; I am pulling away.

I always misremember this line as, "Love held my hand." No, it's, "Love took my hand." Not holding but taking.

My hand isn't mine. You have it.

But it's still called "my hand." It remains my own to that extent. You take me while I'm resisting. I'm separate enough to resist.

You look at me. I look away. Unlike your quick eyes, mine are "marr'd." They "cannot look."

A nonpenetrating vision. A slack vision.

The lack in slack (Herbert's rhyme) is a want of life. I can't do anything with conviction. I enter but there's no life or energy or sharpness in my step.

I can't look at you. I can't meet your gaze. I can't look at any part of you.

I refuse the food that you offer.

I can't sit down and eat your food until you tell me to do it and force me to do it and stand there to watch me doing it.

We are not eating the same food. I am eating and you are not eating; you are talking.

You tell me to do it and I do it.

Is that symmetry?

No. That's discipline. Saying it and making it happen.

The asymmetrical relationship at the heart of many of Herbert's poems is sacrifice.

I can compensate for almost any gift. I can give something back; I can give thanks. But I can offer no return for the gift of Christ's crucifixion.

> I will do for that—
> Alas, my God, I know not what.

Herbert avoids thinking about sacrifice in "Love" (3). There is one mild reminder of Christ's suffering, "who bore the blame."

That half-line is enough to finish my objections.

"I will serve."

This is a funny kind of service, isn't it?

You are serving me. I am sitting and eating while you serve.

You are enjoying the power of hospitality while I am reluctantly accepting the privilege of being served.

Maybe service is Herbert's paradox of consent to divine power.

Vaguely corresponding to the fantasy of rape in Donne's "Holy Sonnets."

I serve, which means that I accept your hospitality. I worship you by allowing you to feed me.

In rituals of courtesy, Michael Schoenfeldt argues, "Victory is achieved not by mastery but by submission. He who wins is he who most effectively serves and obeys the other, since in doing so, he places the other in his debt."

Schoenfeldt is commenting on a dialogue from a courtesy manual, which he compares to "Love" (3).

> *The Mirror of Complements*, a seventeenth-century courtesy book, discloses the manner in which such protracted displays of deference can become expressions of social aggression. The following dialogue, entitled "To entertaine a friend that comes to visit us," suggests that the contest of courtesy between the speaker and host of "Love (3)" is actually a battle for political superiority:
>
> . . .
>
> I see that you will conquer me with courtesie, but if it please you to sit, wee shall discourse more at leisure.

I thanke you sir, it needs not; besides, it were undecent for mee to be first in place, but if it please you to sit, I shall keepe you company.

Then I pray you sit there.

It shall be then to obey you.

Sir, I am your servant.

Sir, it is I that am yours, and the most affectionate of all your servants.

The host and the guest in the model dialogue are competing to outdo each other in feats of modesty. By accepting the host's gifts with supreme modesty, the guest confers an obligation on the host. By forcing the guest to occupy the seat of honor, the host humiliates the guest.

The speaker in "The Thanksgiving" might be trying to do something like that. To outdo the generosity of his god.

Surely I will revenge me on thy love,
  And trie who shall victorious prove.
If thou dost give me wealth, I will restore
  All back unto thee by the poore.
If thou dost give me honour, men shall see,

> The honour doth belong to thee.
>   I will not marry; or, if she be mine,
>   She and her children shall be thine.

For every one of your gifts, I find a suitable return. Only in the last couplet I have to admit that we are not on a footing of near equality that would make our exchange competitive.

> Then for thy passion—I will do for that—
>   Alas, my God, I know not what.

You saved me. How can I save you so that we can call it even? Or so that you can be in my debt?

What's the phrase in my head? "Thy modestie, / Which conquers all." In "To Camden," trying to force William Camden, his teacher in grammar school, to accept a compliment, Jonson says that Camden's modesty "conquers all." That is how aggressive modesty can be. It conquers not just other modesty, but everything else, "all." It takes over the world.

These scenes suggest some of the power involved in the act of submission, and the reversals that characterize hierarchical relationships. Giving rich gifts can be done aggressively, but giving thanks can be just as aggressive. The right expression of gratitude can overpower the giver.

After you, my dear Alphonse.

No, after you, my dear Alphonse.

The point of comparing the foregoing routines should be that they are not remotely similar to "Love" (3). Here's why.

I frankly confess that I am unworthy.

How do you know that I am speaking frankly? How do you know that I'm not being strategic, angling for a better favor or to put you down?

Readers should know that I'm being frank because I confess my unworthiness to them before I confess it to you. I tell them that I'm "guiltie of dust and sinne." Unlike the model dialogue from *The Mirror of Complements*, the poem doesn't consist only of the exchange of polite formulas. Behind the formulas, I give an account of my motives too.

And you see, before I confess my unworthiness, that I believe myself unworthy. You know me from inside. You read my image from my soul.

If you can read my mind, if you know all of my responses before I experience them, your knowledge puts us in a scene utterly different from that of *The Mirror of Complements* where the rivals attempt to master each other in displays of modesty.

Modesty? You aren't playing any such game.

You never try to outdo me in modesty. Never question being in the position of Lord or Love.

You never worry about the unfairness of the hierarchy or acknowledge that I have any worth.

Would you want me if I were worthy?

A worthy guest would be a competitor. One of those other poets.

The language of worth is all mine. You never judge me in these terms.

Herbert wrote a book called *Outlandish Proverbs*.

Some of the proverbs are in use today and some appear in Herbert's poems and other writings. They are pieces of practical advice but not practical to implement all at once because not mutually consistent.

They are English proverbs but he calls them outlandish.

Does that mean the proverbs are ancient (whether classical or biblical)? Is Herbert treating common phrases as remnants of another age?

They might be outlandish only from the point of view of scholarship. Herbert might have been engaging in the strange activity of an antiquarian like John Aubrey, collecting "antiquities" that no one else wanted. They were old but in common use, underfoot, trodden into the dirt.

Or like Samuel Pepys collecting, binding, and preserving ballads and tracts. Printed matter that lots of people bought but no one else wanted to keep. Why did he do it? Because he thought they were historically interesting and he liked the music. He loved singing, even common ballads.

The first proverb is, "Man Proposeth, God disposeth."

I wonder if Herbert collected proverbs locally. Could the meaning of outlandish include his home? Did he think that his parish was an out-of-the-way place? (Bemerton. Near Salisbury cathedral. Sounds like a busy crossroads.)

Maybe the proverbs were not specific to any place. Maybe they were proverbs that Herbert didn't often hear.

"223. In the house of a Fidler, all fiddle."

Outlandish. Foreign or ancient or unusual. Somehow uncommon. At the same time they are proverbs. Maybe the title means, "Common language not in common usage." One of those sharp, nearly paradoxical titles, like *The Bourgeois Gentleman* or *The Fair Jilt*.

The real significance of the existence of this book is this. Herbert's interest in plain language is a matter for study and art. He is fascinated by plain language. He approaches plainness as an intrinsically interesting object. He collects examples of it. He appreciates it even apart from the wisdom it communicates. He likes the sound of proverbs.

In *Outlandish Proverbs* he is trying to figure out plainness. He is studying its effects and practicing how to imitate them. He wants to be able to drop some of this homely language unexpectedly into a line.

No one seriously questions Herbert's intelligence and artistry. Nonetheless they are qualities worth remembering. And they can be underestimated if readers think they are incompatible with holiness and simplicity, the first traits they associate with Herbert.

88

Were the proverbs rules of conduct? A hilarious
and impossible idea.

You couldn't conform your conduct to every
proverb in the collection. The proverbs don't fit
together. Some of them are descriptive rather than
prescriptive.

How are you going to live by, "In the house of a
Fidler, all fiddle"?

I like to think that Herbert was struck by the same
proverb and felt the same ambivalence.

He adapts the proverb for use in his treatise *The
Country Parson, His Character*.

> As in the house of those that are skill'd in Musick, all
> are Musicians; so in the house of a Preacher, all are
> preachers.

Everyone in the fiddler's house knows how to play
the fiddle. Is that because the children pick it up
naturally, because fiddles are nearby? Or is it

because the fiddler has a distorted perspective on the importance of fiddling, and expects all of his children to carry on the family business, regardless of their interests or aptitudes?

The idea of a rule is important.

Herbert likes rules because they are rules.
Because rules are neat. That is what appeals to
him.

He likes knowledge in the neat form of a proverb.
Even silly, contradictory proverbs. Even if they are
outlandish.

I'm like that too.

I am not pretending to have a lot in common with
Herbert, but this is one thing.

I like a code of conduct because it's a code.
Herbert likes it because of its neatness.

He values it as wisdom, maybe he even values it
as conduct, simply for the neatness of correction.

What was Herbert's relationship to the courtesy manuals?

He loved neatness. But it wasn't his favorite thing. He did not value all codes of order and hygiene.

> In another walk to Salisbury he saw a poor man with a poorer horse that was fallen under his load; they were both in distress and needed present help; which, Mr Herbert perceiving, put off his canonical coat and helped the poor man to unload, and after to load his horse. The poor man blest him for it, and he blest the poor man; and was so like the good Samaritan that he gave him money to refresh both himself and his horse; and told him, "That if he loved himself, he should be merciful to his beast."—Thus he left the poor man, and at his coming to his musical friends at Salisbury, they began to wonder that Mr George Herbert which used to be so trim and clean came into that company so soiled and discomposed; but he told them the occasion; and when one of the company told him he had

disparaged himself by so dirty an employment, his answer was, "That the thought of what he had done would prove music to him at midnight; and that the omission of it would have upbraided and made discord in his conscience, whensoever he should pass by that place; for, if I be bound to pray for all that be in distress, I am sure that I am bound so far as it is in my power to practise what I pray for. And though I do not wish for the like occasion every day, yet let me tell you, I would not willingly pass one day of my life without comforting a sad soul or showing mercy; and I praise God for this occasion: and now let's tune our instruments."

The famous anecdote of Herbert's "music at midnight" is premised on his refusal to conform to rules of courtesy.

He shows up late for music practice. His clothes disordered. Dirty. His appearance an insult to the other musicians. He who "used to be so trim and clean"!

That is what Herbert thinks of courtesy.

Why did Renaissance courtesy manuals give so much power to the question of who sits first at dinner?

No writer is better than the Victorian novelist Anthony Trollope at depicting momentary exchanges in power that occur by a word, a gesture, or a glance. His discussion of the rule of precedence in *The Last Chronicle of Barset* is instructive.

Here the hostess at a dinner party makes a mistake, giving her arm to the ratfink Crosbie, a secretary, to precede the other guests in sitting down to dinner.

> Having married an earl's daughter he was selected
> for that honour. There was a barrister in the room,
> and Mrs Dobbs Broughton ought to have known
> better. As she professed to be guided in such matters
> by the rules laid down by the recognized authorities,
> she ought to have been aware that a man takes no

rank from his wife. But she was entitled I think to merciful consideration for her error. A woman situated as was Mrs Dobbs Broughton cannot altogether ignore these terrible rules. She cannot let her guests draw lots for precedence. She must select someone for the honour of her own arm. And amidst the intricacies of rank how is it possible for a woman to learn and to remember everything? If Providence would only send Mrs Dobbs Broughton a Peer for every dinner-party, the thing would go more easily; but what woman will tell me, off-hand, which should go out of a room first; a CB, an Admiral of the Blue, the Dean of Barchester, or the Dean of Arches? Who is to know who was everybody's father? How am I to remember that young Thompson's progenitor was made a baronet and not a knight when he was Lord Mayor? Perhaps Mrs Dobbs Broughton ought to have known that Mr Crosbie could have gained nothing by his wife's rank, and the barrister may be considered to have been not immoderately severe when he simply spoke of her afterwards as the silliest and most ignorant old woman he had ever met in his life.

The vertical organization of nineteenth-century England is even more finely articulated than that of seventeenth-century England. One chart from a nineteenth-century courtesy manual divides the male guests at a dinner party into sixty ranks and degrees! Mrs. Dobbs Broughton must remember all of them, and their exact order, if she hopes never to be mistaken about precedence.

Trollope thinks that precedence is kind of funny. He also thinks that Mrs. Dobbs Broughton is kind of funny for not understanding the rule that she professes to follow.

His amusement and her ignorance might suggest that precedence is silly. Arbitrary. Unimportant.

Exactly the opposite is true. Trollope's point is that mistakes are inevitable not because there are no rules, and not because the rules are unwritten, but because every member of society contributes to them without understanding them completely.

Thus, even in patriarchal societies, even in the English way of doing primogeniture, there are situations where a man takes rank from his wife.

Trollope is in the same position as Mrs. Dobbs Broughton. They give power to a rule to which they hope to conform their behavior although they can never master it in their knowledge.

We are in a different position. We live under the same mysterious power, only we have no rule.

92

Is it really that hard to imagine the power of precedence?

Remember how difficult it can be, if you enter the coffee shop behind your friend, to pay for your friend's coffee. That's a minor effect of precedence.

Or think of children, brothers and sisters, wanting to ride shotgun in the family car. Each one wants to sit in front of the others. Because the front seat is better! There's more room to stretch your legs. It's easier to talk to the driver.

The rival siblings are not giving power to precedence arbitrarily. They are taking advantage of the real power in precedence.

They are seeking rules for managing a mysterious power in their lives.

Theirs is a reasonable attitude. It's rational to fear a power that you don't fully understand.

We who have no rules for managing precedence laugh at the old rules because we don't understand them. They who wrote the courtesy manuals feared what they did not understand. They may have been putting power in the wrong places when they wrote their manuals, but their attitude was saner than ours.

93

Ten years ago I heard one of Stephen Booth's lectures in an introductory literature course for undergraduates.

The lecture had already started when I came in. The students were not looking at Booth but at their personal copies of the text, *Go, Dog. Go!*, a picture book by P. D. Eastman.

At the front of the lecture hall, Booth stooped over a microphone, speaking quietly, patiently, as he described each page of the book in numerical order.

At the turn of each page, he remarked a new set of facts, relationships, patterns, and effects, and he tried to describe them in simple language.

The caption tells the dogs to go. Most of them are going but this one is stopping.

The dog's fur has the same color as one of the cars.

The dog keeps asking, "Do you like my hat?", always using the same words to ask her question.

The implication was that we could do what he was doing. We didn't know. The students in the class were maybe eighteen years old and they didn't know, and I was maybe twice their age and I didn't know.

To see what was in front of us was not impossible. The work we had undertaken was possible and beautiful and difficult. A worthy ambition. That was what Booth was trying to teach us.

One of the most profound, humbling experiences of my reading life.

Booth has this to say about "Love" (3):

"The word 'host' never appears in the poem."

And yet, he proposes, "host" might be the most important word in the poem. The very idea of the poem might be a pun on host as dispenser of hospitality and Host as sacrament.

This is a beautiful idea. A dormant pun. Somewhere in the poem Herbert planted a bomb. Then he exited the poem without detonating it.

It would have been the easiest thing in the world to say the word "host."

Schoenfeldt has another idea. He turns the tacitness of the pun into allegory. The pressure of the unspoken word "host" on the spoken words is a figure for the real presence of God in the wafer.

I don't think it's true that an unspoken pun is the basis for the poem.

Herbert was thinking about hospitality. He considered using the word "host," noted the pun, thought it was a cheap trick, made a face, and did his best to keep it out of the poem.

He didn't use the word because he didn't want the pun.

There is a better reason why Herbert didn't want a pun on "host."

Because he wanted to avoid the confusing suggestion of transubstantiation.

Because "Love" (3) is not about Communion.

Although, yes, it's about eating the body of God.

Eating God happens as part of Communion. In the ritual that Herbert performed in the church at Bemerton, Communion is a series of transformations. Wine turns into blood. Bread, which is called the Host, turns into flesh.

In the poem, I don't need another host. I don't have to wait for your presence in the wafer to change the wafer into your flesh. My food supply has a more direct route.

Why would I care about real presence when I have your meat?

You are present to me. Your flesh appears to me as meat. I taste the meat that comes from you.

You show amazing tact in handling crucifixion. No tact at all about what you are having me eat.

"Meat" isn't the English word used in the ceremony.

Your word is culinary rather than ritualistic.

> Who knows not Love, let him assay
> And taste that juice, which on the crosse a pike
> Did set again abroach; then let him say
> If ever he did taste the like.
> Love is that liquour sweet and most divine,
> Which my God feels as bloud; but I, as wine.

That also is not transubstantiation.

Christ doesn't transform wine into his blood. He suffers on the cross while I put my mouth to his chest and drink the liquor flowing out of his body.

The liquor doesn't change. What changes is the unique feeling. The sweet taste. The like.

What it's like to me is not what it's like to you. You feel it one way (blood); I feel it another way (food).

As though Christ's words were not magic but perception.

"Take, eat; *I feel* this is my body. Drink ye all of it; *I feel* this is my blood."

And I know what my god is feeling.

My love is a kind of pleasure that I take in mere appearances.

With the following strange refinement.

My pleasure in how something appears to me mixes with my pleasure in knowing how the same object appears to you.

I guess the important part of "Superliminare" is "the churches mysticall repast."

I say that because of Herbert's obsession with food.

And because this is the first poem in the book and he makes you wait until the last poem for the promised taste.

I'm surprised by the word "mysticall."

An odd word to find in a mystical text.

"Mysticall repast" sounds as though he is talking about transubstantiation. A reference he usually avoids.

"Mysticall" appears in the place where I might expect Herbert to say, "Sweet."

A modifier that suggests a flavor. What kind of taste is it going to be?

He is finally going to share a meal with God, which is not really the same as mystical union with God where there is no distance. Even if God is the meal.

You know, it just occurred to me, what's great about calling Herbert's book *The Temple* is that the temple in question could be a place of worship for practically any religion.

If anything, "temple" has a slightly Jewish flavor.

It must be said that "Love" (3) is not a very Christian poem. In fact there's nothing in the poem that points strongly toward Christian meaning or ritual.

Instead Herbert might want to suppress all references to the Eucharist. He might find the idea vulgar. Barely tolerable.

He hopes that you can read the poem without thinking about it.

That is also why Love shows such tact in saying, "Who bore the blame." Herbert is trying to mute any references to crucifixion.

Let's not make this poem too Christian in other words.

Elsewhere Herbert celebrates crucifixion, the suffering body of Christ, the rituals of the English Church, the smells and bells, in explicit language.

This time he doesn't talk about any aspect of God or any part of sacred history.

This time his language doesn't tend to make biblical or ecclesiastical allusions.

You might say that the poem relies on the idea that God is Love. But where is God in this poem?

What is available to the senses?

This is a tricky question because some abstractions have a bodily existence.

Love is an abstract concept with whom I am involved in a physical relationship.

Love is a person with hands that hold me. Eyes whose look I feel as a physical weight on my face. A mouth that smiles.

And an otherwise unimaginable body.

My soul is neither abstract nor vague. It's known to both of us, individual, recognizable, but invisible. Perhaps you see it better than I can.

Dust and sin are not abstractions, no, but dust may be a symbol, representative of abstract concepts such as time, death, and vanity.

Sin is vague.

"A guest," not merely an existential relationship, and "worthy to be here," which means that something specific is intended. There are recognized traits of worthy guests.

Here's an interesting one. "My shame." Is that sensuous or not? "My" makes it a lot less vague. It could be code for part of my body. It might refer to genitals. It might refer to eyes which refer to genitals.

What about "the blame"? I would call that a euphemism. A vague representation of a well-known, painful punishment. A polite way of mentioning something that you don't want to depict in sensuous detail.

Herbert sometimes likes to dwell on the event of crucifixion. He likes to imagine it vividly. He likes to rank it in comparison with other events, feelings, gifts, griefs.

> Shame tears my soul, my bodie many a wound;
> Sharp nails pierce this, but sharper that confound;
> Reproaches, which are free, while I am bound.
>   Was ever grief like mine?

Always concluding that it is incomparable.

I want to avoid debasing Herbert's religion. Not degrading the poem or turning it into blasphemy even when writing about degradation and blasphemy.

Some readers look for sexual meanings in Herbert's language.

A weak objection to the excavation of codes for sex in "Love" (3) is that Herbert could not possibly intend them.

To which the response would be that Herbert obviously did intend them in the two early "Love" sonnets written to his mother. Which he was still thinking about when he wrote the three later "Love" poems.

And if he was not thinking consciously about sexual meanings, he was thinking about them unconsciously. Part of his greatness as a poet is how he lets in the unconscious. Empson said that.

I also think the excavation of these sexual meanings is weak.

For example: "*Serve* has a bawdy meaning."

True. But look at the word people use for the code words. "Bawdy." That word tells you the whole story.

Anyone who uses the word "bawdy" doesn't believe the poem is about sex either. Bawdy is a formula to avoid paying serious attention to sexual language.

The codes are gratuitous anyway. What are these ingenious studies of secondary archaic sexual meanings good for? I don't need them.

The whole point of Herbert's poem is to define love as domination and submission. That is the primary meaning of the poem. The fact that service has a secondary sexual sense is interesting but gratuitous.

The bodies in "Love" (3) are secondary at best. Herbert isn't trying to show you the eyes, the face, the hands.

Nonetheless I want to write about these subjects. The romance one can have with the shapes of bodies. Their smells. Parts of bodies.

How do I write about early memories and fantasies?

I'm not into telling secrets. I especially don't want to tell someone else's secrets.

Isn't my interpretation of "Love" (3) a secret?

This is something about the poem that I know and no one else does.

My secret is that what the poem says is what it's about.

Maybe the model of affirming that the poem is about what it says it's about suggests a way of writing about my own life. The most obvious facts about me are true ones.

Here is a person who isn't comfortable with the sound of his own voice. That might be the first thing anyone would notice about me.

Here is someone whose sexual fantasies are about having his voice taken away.

102

Something else from elementary school that I wondered about later.

Two classes, fourth grade and fifth grade, formed lines and went back into the school building from recess.

I remember we filed past two girls at the entrance. They were younger, not part of our class. Barely able to stand, completely out of control, as though visitors from a world of all recess and no classes, they were laughing, kissing, falling over each other, and yelling, "We're lesbians!"

Did that happen? Did they say those words? I can picture them vividly and I remember my reaction too. "How immature," I thought. I probably didn't use the word immature but I remember feeling superior. I get the sense that I was a few years older than they were.

Maybe I didn't like the word lesbian. Maybe it was the first time I heard the word lesbian. I don't think I knew what it meant but I felt that it was a bad word.

Or maybe I knew exactly what it meant. Maybe I was unhappy hearing them declare that they were lesbians when I did not know how to avow my own attraction to women.

We walked past them in a line. None of us said a word. There was a feeling that the two girls were on display. To me their performance felt like a warning. "Keep it together! Or else see how low you might sink."

I wonder if this memory is accurate in any way.

103

This one is about humiliation.

I think it's about humiliation.

Age six. I was attending summer day camp. We had gone on a field trip to see a waterfall. Most of the afternoon we spent playing in the creek upstream from the falls. First wading a few steps to feel the current. Then diving into the center of the stream and letting the current carry us.

We must have been far enough from the falls that no one was worried, but we were close to some choppy, rapidly moving water. I remember being impressed by the force of the current when I was in it.

At the end of the day, when it was time to get out of the water, I did something strange. Once out of the creek I immediately stripped out of my bathing suit. Then I looked up and saw that the other kids were staring at me. The boys on the near side of the creek, the girls in a line on the opposite side. I pulled my bathing suit back on, burst into tears, and ran away.

I'm not sure how to explain what happened. The way I remember it, what happened is that I got confused. I wasn't paying attention to what I was doing, and through force of habit a bodily memory took over and guided my actions. After swimming, you take off your swimming trunks and change into dry clothes.

I might be capable of that much confusion. I can be absentminded. There have been times in my adult life when I have felt the pull of a similar confusion. Once, entering a classroom on a cold day, I took off my coat, folded it, and caught myself as I was starting to take off my sweater too. What if I had continued, and removed every article of clothing before remembering that I was there to teach a class on Renaissance poetry?

It's possible that I was kind of clueless at age six. My parents had always treated nudity casually. They didn't go around naked all the time but they didn't allow themselves a lot of private space. They treated it as not a big deal if they happened to be naked. They weren't off-limits when they were getting dressed. Maybe I didn't know that it was inappropriate to dress or undress in front of other people.

I am not sure if these explanations are on the right track. Could I have been so absentminded or clueless? Maybe those are just stories that I tell myself.

Another explanation has occurred to me. Maybe I was intentionally exposing myself. Maybe nudity in public was something I really wanted to do.

Maybe I was testing myself to see what I wanted. Maybe, if the result had been different, I would have done it again. Maybe it would have become my sexual preference.

In that case I'm grateful to have gotten a result I disliked enough that I learned never to do it again. And, at the same time, I'm grateful that I later learned to eroticize humiliation, an ability that has enriched my life.

Age eleven, I think. Sixth grade. Bored in study hall, I started writing descriptions of the different kinds of shoes that other kids were wearing. Any shoes that I could see from where I was sitting.

I don't remember the details of what I wrote, but I remember emphasizing the variety of different kinds of shoes. Sneakers, shoes with heels, cowboy boots, skateboard shoes, loafers, saddle shoes.

I typed my piece and sent it to the school newspaper. It was, I guess, my first publication. I also remember the school principal commending my piece in an assembly later that year. Shoes were probably the sort of benign topic that he thought appropriate for a middle school newspaper.

I don't remember having any sexual feelings when I was studying the shoes of the other kids. Still, thinking back on this episode, I wonder, why is this child so interested in shoes? Maybe there was a latent fetish in me that never blossomed.

In my period of self-experimentation, roughly between ages 14–16, I practiced binding myself with a small collection of belts and cords.

Similar experiments are common among bondage enthusiasts.

One morning I tied myself up and couldn't free myself.

I got scared, struggled, and one of my movements pulled lightly on a collar around my throat.

That sensation turned me on, and my response to that response was total panic. I remember thinking, this must be exactly what happens to those poor kids who die from autoerotic asphyxiation!

Contorting my body, I finally managed to work myself out of the bondage.

After that I stopped experimenting. Seemed too dangerous. Never touched my collection of belts and cords again.

Too bad. If I had continued I might be more proficient today.

There are three questions in "Love" (3). Maybe four.

The first one is what do I lack? Do I lack anything?

What's the answer?

I'm supposed to say that I lack nothing. You have supplied everything. I am more than satisfied. There is nothing I could want. My cup runneth over.

If I'm trying to be courteous, I'm probably supposed to resist your generosity. Oh, no, I couldn't accept such a generous gift. Thank you, no, I'm good.

Is there a rule of courtesy that prescribes a self-deprecating answer such as the one I actually give? Yes, I do lack anything. I lack everything, to be frank. I lack even myself.

Unless I'm trying to be rude. What I bring is insufficient, but you, too, are insufficient. You can supply nothing that I lack.

Or maybe I'm trying to imitate you.

I see that you are a host, and I want to be like you. Now I need to find someone to be my guest.

107

The second question is mine. "I the unkind, ungrateful?"

Is that a question?

I'm answering your first question by asking if you know me.

Are you talking to me? Surely you mean someone else?

(Did God's phone call me by mistake?)

One answer to my question is no. I'm neither unkind nor ungrateful.

Another answer is yes. Unkindness and ingratitude are within my limits. I can be those things.

You might even be attracted to my unkindness.

Third question. "Who made the eyes but I?"

This question includes its answer. It depends on my acknowledging you as my creator.

What if I don't?

What if someone else made the eyes?

"Who made the eyes but I?" "Prove it."

I'm not looking at you, so how do I recognize you? How do I know that you have the right credentials?

It's one thing to have faith in the existence of a divine creator. Worshipping a manifestation that I take to be my creator is something else.

My answer is that I waive discussion. "Truth," you made me, "Lord." In accepting you as my creator, in accepting your account of a creation that I did

not witness and do not remember, I seem
remarkably trusting.

Do I worship absolutely anyone who claims to be
my creator?

Your question has another strange premise.

You made the eyes, so the eyes should be able to look at you. Why is that?

In "Longing," the speaker asks, "Shall he who made the ear / Not hear?"

Ah but that's different. Your involvement in making the ear gives you undeniable expertise in the physical act of hearing; your involvement in fabricating me and my personal ear gives you an interest in what happens to me, and an obligation to pay attention when I complain to you.

By the same logic, you made the eye, therefore you can look at me. You should be looking at me. You know how to look, it's your right to surveil me, and it's your duty to take care of me.

None of those facts about you is a fact about me. I didn't make your eyes and I didn't make my eyes. My eyes are broken. How can I use them to look at you?

Your question presumes that my eyes are always in contact with you, whether looking directly at you or looking away. That my eyes retain the virtue of your touch. Simply because the mechanism of seeing was originally one of your gifts.

Not a democratic notion. (Not, "A cat may look at a king.")

My eyes touched you when you made them. Why shouldn't they look at you now? Looking is more distant than touching anyway.

Who made me?

God made me!

The first question and the first answer in the catechism.

"Who made the eyes but I?" A version of the same question. And the same answer.

Fish's paraphrase: "You cannot escape me because you are of my substance." (Turning Herbert's language into Milton's ontology. The world is a single substance which is the body of God.)

That isn't what the line says! Okay, you made me, you made my eyes, and, okay, you might still control my eyes, but that doesn't mean we are the same substance.

If Fish is right, if Love and I have the same substance, that would explain why I can't look at Love, because seeing usually requires some distance.

Last question. "And know you not who bore the blame?"

Possible answer: I don't know.

Possible answer: Who?

Possible answer: Yes. I know. It's my own fault. I want to take the blame.

It isn't good for me to let someone else be punished for my faults.

Your love is oppressive. You restrict my ability to choose for myself.

Your question does not include its answer but reminds me that I already know the answer.

Your question is not really asking who bore the blame. You are asking, what do I know? What are the contents of my head?

If you bore the blame, then why do I think it's my sin?

If you really bore the blame, wouldn't it become your sin?

What I trust least in my early memories is the spectacular aspect. Some of my clearest memories show up in my mind as pageants.

The memory of two girls laughing, collapsing, kissing, announcing, "We're lesbians!" That could have happened.

The girls could have been caught up in their play while the other kids were getting in line. The teachers might have had enough to do to corral the kids and might not have noticed two who escaped the dragnet. We in our orderly line filed past this vision of anarchy and sex.

What seems impossible when I try to consider my memory objectively is for the other kids to have treated the two girls as a spectacle. The scene I remember has an unusual formality. The girls laughed and shouted, "We're lesbians!" No one else said a word. No one stopped for too long. The line moved slowly past the girls, and each kid took a moment to stare and consider what was being demonstrated and what was being said, maybe learned a new word, and then walked on without comment.

That's what I don't believe. How did the line stay together? How could some of the kids not have stopped, laughed, shouted, gotten involved? How could there not be a disruption?

My memory of this incident feels like an item from the lesson plan of the day. We seemed to be looking at something we were supposed to see. Yet we were a far more respectful audience than we usually were in the classroom or at a museum.

113

The same aspect of pageantry makes me distrust my memory of the strange incident of my self-exhibition at day camp.

This certainly happened but I don't think it could have happened the way I remember. My motives are questionable.

I don't trust the memory of how this scene was staged. My memory puts the girls, every girl I knew at the time, on the opposite side of the creek silently staring at me. I don't think it's natural for kids to do that.

Even if you tell a group of kids that they have to stand in line quietly it won't be easy to keep the line together or maintain silence. Especially if you show them something weird or funny or different. A lot of the kids are going to want to talk about it. Or say something to it. Or laugh.

I wonder why my memory puts the girls on one side of the creek and the boys on the other side. Maybe the camp counselors separated the kids by gender.

I do think it's natural for kids to stare. That probably happened.

The strange formality of the scene is probably how my memory feels about sex.

114

First word, love. Last word, eat.

First act, welcome. Last act, forced eating.

Between welcome and eating, resistance.

What happens when we run the tape backwards?

Food comes out of my mouth. I stand. I pledge my service. You ask who is to blame. I take all the blame on myself and invite punishment. You remind me that you created me. You release my hand. I say that I can't look. I accuse myself of ingratitude and unkindness. You affirm that I am an unprecedented mixture of ingratitude and perversity. I summon a worthier guest. You ask if anything is missing. You move toward me and I respond by moving away inwardly. My soul draws back. You greet me warmly.

Backwards, "Love" (3) becomes a poem of liberation.

The story of my freedom could be pointed in various ways.

It could be about emancipation from service. I pledge my fealty and am released from my oath.

It could be more about the rejection of my offer. My dismissal from service due to failure and general unworthiness.

Or the point could be damnation. Repeating Satan's motto, "I will not serve," and his banishment from Heaven.

Back to front, the scene resembles an exorcism. Starting with vomit. My body rejects the demon that possesses me. Finally my soul moves away from it too. Get thee behind me. Like an octopus sending its guts out of its body. The guts remain in place while the body swims backward.

"Also it is written," in *Paradise Regained*, Christ, tempted, stands, "Tempt not the Lord thy God; he said, and stood," while Satan falls.

115

I wonder how much I repeat myself.

I wonder how much I contradict myself. My first act is a kind of contradiction. Entering with my body, drawing back in spirit. An action that my soul contradicts. Doesn't feel right to me. I can't accept what I am doing.

The whole poem describes my reversal. What I am saying changes from "I cannot" to "I will."

Did I change my mind? Did you convince me?

Probably we agree that I am not worthy. There was never a disagreement about that. You had a better sense than I did of what I was capable of. How much I could take.

I repeat, "My dear," to introduce the two statements that reverse each other. My dear, I cannot. My dear, I will.

Put together like that, "My dear" sounds more like the convention of saying, "Yes, sir," or, "Yes, ma'am," to a superior.

I repeat, "Love bade," "Love took," "Love says." Also, "Love," at some distance, "drew." Love is the subject. Out of this syntax the poem is built.

"Unkind, ungrateful," repeating "un." One of Herbert's revisions. A place where you can see him writing the poem. Leaving a variant inside the line.

Unkind, I don't do what I am supposed to do. Ungrateful, I don't want what I am supposed to want. My will does not support my obligations.

Another usage of mine. I repeatedly use helping verbs as intensifiers. Really to pad the line. Slow it down. This usage builds a bridge between, on one side, my speeches addressed to Love, and, on the other side, my utterance of the poem, which is addressed to an unidentified person.

The intense "did" in the final line is how I express surprise. I really did it!

"Doth" seems to express something more like certainty. My unworth is indisputable. You can't credibly say otherwise. I will not allow you to contradict me. (You will force me to contradict myself.)

Love repeats, "You shall"; commands, "You must."

And questions, "Who but I?", and repeats, "Who," also implying, "but I?"

I don't see that you ever contradict yourself.

Your love isn't modest. You are always reminding me of your achievements. It seems to embarrass me to hear them. It would almost be impolite to acknowledge them.

The scene begins in line one. The conversation begins in line five.

The first stanza turns over a few times. Yet, but. Welcome, yet drawing back. Drawing back, but drawing nearer.

As though we are having a dialogue before we start talking. The conjunctions mark shifts between actors. You do something, then I respond, then you, then me.

There is no possibility of the two of us acting simultaneously or talking simultaneously.

Does the scene end with the last line? Probably not.

Does the conversation end with the last line? Possibly I stop talking with, "I will serve." I serve and am silent.

Possibly you keep talking while I am eating.

Beauty asks Herbert, "Whose hands are these?"

Beauty is an interesting kind of unfairness.

It isn't fair to me that all the world's beauty is concentrated in you. It isn't fair to you that I am able to enjoy the visual effect of the world's beauty; you can't see it because you live inside it.

Your beauty draws me to you and delivers my body, represented by my hands, to you.

Herbert's loyalty does not belong to the visible power that commandeers his hands but rather to the unseen power that commandeers his voice.

His answer is to defer his answer to the voice of the unseen power who never speaks in the poem: "But thou shalt answer, Lord, for me."

"In no society do people talk all the time."

Richard Bauman makes this simple, profound observation in an anthropological study of the speech behaviors of seventeenth-century Quakers.

What makes Quakers a fascinating case study is the unique value they discover in silence. Their practice of silent group meditation irregularly punctured by "openings," speeches that occur whenever a member of the congregation is inspired to assume the role of minister, is supported by a theology that understands silence as communication with God, speech as communication with the world.

However, Bauman continues, although Quakers rate silence higher than speech, they are not silent all the time. Just as people in societies that prefer speech to silence do not talk all the time.

Quakers rely on speech to communicate with fellow believers and to convert nonbelievers to Quakerism. Speech diminishes the communication that occurs in silence but it is an inevitable practical concession to the church's evangelical work.

119

When Voltaire met the Quaker Andrew Pitt, he was unnerved by Pitt's silence. And by the plainness of the few words Pitt spoke.

Voltaire was chagrinned to discover how many of his own words were either compliments or oaths.

The Quaker's muted speech seemed to impel the philosopher to appeal vainly to God and to recite extravagant compliments to fill the silent spaces in their exchange.

120

In Errol Morris's interview with Donald Rumsfeld,
many viewers want to see a confrontation.
Rumsfeld's deceptions should be exposed. He
should be forced to admit his guilty actions—
Rumsfeldian actions which not even their
ostensibly positive outcomes could justify. Or
he should defend them, fail, and be reduced to
silence.

It's easy to see how, in an encounter with a sheet
of paper, a sharp pair of scissors would make a
cut, and, in repeated encounters, go on cutting
until the bits of paper were too small to be
divided further. It's just as easy to see how a
hard rock would blunt, mangle, and crush the
scissors.

The power of paper to cover rock is more
mysterious. You might assume that rock would
defeat paper—weighty and jagged, the rock would
tear the paper's surface—but this isn't so.

If the paper were a document, covered with writing, its threat of coverage might be understood as a power of representation. To render the image of the rock in a different medium.

That doesn't seem right to me. The point, I believe, is that the paper creates a boundary. Its power is to frame the rock. To determine how it is going to be framed. To display or obscure it.

Paper covers rock. In this rule, a profound idea that everyone knows.

Rumsfeld has the same idea. Talk is a contest in which the prize is to take everything, give nothing. How deep can this attitude go?

For him withholding information is a way of life. His is a luminous intellect resolved not to turn the sword of its own wit on itself. Not to cut itself on its own sharpness. Thus not to examine itself.

Finally, in Morris's view, this attitude causes the greatest possible injury: Rumsfeld's wits become dull. He is so advanced a practitioner of the techniques of dullness that he can no longer be considered an intelligent creature.

I see a different, happier story.

Is there not something incoherent in the very idea of self-deception? "You're deceiving yourself." "You're fooling yourself." Doesn't that sound unlikely? If one part of the intellect is fooled by another, controlling part, then the controlling part should stay intact and undeceived.

Can I keep my wits together without ever using them on myself? Yes! One can't, after all, dull the wits entirely. They still operate in sudden flashes and lunges.

Imagine an exquisitely refined society, the Heian court in Japan or the court of Louis XIV in France, where etiquette required that every utterance had to be preceded by a ritual confession of the speaker's improper credentials.

The rule is that I begin by confessing my bad faith.

Every circumstance of my social position that makes what I am going to say inexpert, insincere, suspicious.

"As a veteran,"

"As a queer femme of color,"

"As an ex-con,"

"As a single mom,"

I might as well not finish the sentence.

Subject position means that I am inexpert in other people's stuff.

Ideology means that I am inexpert in my own stuff.

Thus disqualified to make any statement beyond identification of my subject position.

A double move. A Till Eulenspiegel prank.

Notice how efficiently Herbert's "Dialogue" creates a convention and breaks it.

> Sweetest Saviour, if my soul
> Were but worth the having,
> Quickly should I then controll
> Any thought of waving.
> But when all my care and pains
> Cannot give the name of gains
> To thy wretch so full of stains,
> What delight or hope remains?
>
> *What, Child, is the ballance thine,*
> *Thine the poise and measure?*
> *If I say, Thou shalt be mine;*
> *Finger not my treasure.*
> *What the gains in having thee*
> *Do amount to, onely he,*
> *Who for man was sold, can see;*
> *That transferr'd th' accounts to me.*
>
> But as I can see no merit,
> Leading to this favour:

So the way to fit me for it
    Is beyond my savour.
As the reason then is thine;
So the way is none of mine:
I disclaim the whole designe:
Sinne disclaims and I resigne.

That is all, if that I could
    Get without repining;
And my clay, my creature, would
    Follow my resigning:
That as I did freely part
With my glorie and desert,
Left all joyes to feel all smart—
    Ah! no more: thou break'st my heart.

The dialogue consists of two exchanges. First voice, second voice, first voice, second voice. Each voice is granted a complete stanza in which to speak.

The last line breaks the form. The first voice stops the second voice. "Ah! no more: thou break'st my heart."

Is Herbert running a test for "Love" (3)?

In "Love" (3), Love takes the speaker's voice away and the poem ends. In "Dialogue," the first, human voice interrupts the second, divine voice and ends the conversation.

In "Love" (3), vaguely recalling the crucifixion shortens the exchange and leads to the speaker's silence. In "Dialogue," the reminder of crucifixion is so painful that the first voice doesn't want to let the second voice talk further.

The interjection does not interrupt the patterns of rhythm and rhyme.

Right. But something is broken. The speaker's heart breaks. The pattern of the exchange breaks.

Nothing unusual in that. Nothing we haven't seen in other poems.

But here's the thing. The speaker is rude. The first voice interrupts the second voice. That's not neatness.

The first voice can taste the second voice.

What does it taste like? "Sweetest," of course.
First word in the poem.

What the first voice can't taste is part of himself.
That would be "beyond my savour." This is
something that either has no taste or there's
nothing in his palate that corresponds to the
taste.

He can't taste what he tastes like to the second
voice. Whatever makes him attractive to the
second voice. His "treasure."

"Finger not my treasure," says the second voice.
Another one of those lines that have an obscene
suggestion although "finger" wouldn't have the
vulgar meaning for Herbert that it would have for
William Burroughs.

The obscene suggestion would be masturbatory. The second voice accuses the first voice of a bad kind of self-touch.

And that's important. Touching rather than tasting.

Finger not rather than lick not.

Mild humiliation in a medical setting. A dialogue.

—Anything else?

—Well there is one thing. I have water in my right ear. This happens to me sometimes from swimming. A little water gets into my ear canal, sloshes around, and won't come out. Then, usually, it works its way out after a few days. Only now, this time, the water has been in my ear for a long time, more than three weeks.

—Can you hear out of that ear?

—Sound comes through kind of muffled, like being underwater.

—Any ringing in your ear?

—No. And there's no pain.

—Fever?

—No.

—Vertigo? Dizziness?

—No.

—Probably nothing serious. For how long did you say?

—A few weeks . . . Since September 17.

—How did it happen?

—I'm not sure. Well actually I do remember. It isn't water. I mean, it's mostly water. It's urine. That doesn't make it more serious, does it, if it's urine rather than water?

—Medically, no, that doesn't make it more serious.

(An inquiring look.)

—A woman pissed on me. It was consensual.

The first two "Love" poems are about jealousy.
Maybe "Love" (3) is too.

Herbert's god is a jealous god.

Everyone is worshipping the wrong god. Poets are
writing poems to praise the wrong god. They are
using the holy name of Love for someone who
does not deserve to be called Love. They practice
idolatry. They are taking the name of Love in vain.

What if their idolatry is a strategy to activate the
jealousy of a jealous god?

How do I get you to care about me? By making you
jealous. I burn incense at other altars.

Herbert's god sometimes thinks like this. The
divine strategy in "Rest" is to withhold rest with
the idea that restlessness in life may finally
bounce the wandering human soul into God's
embrace when life is done.

What happens in a relationship where both parties play hard to get?

Donne never does that. When he pursues a woman, he is "naked first." When he pursues God, he explains how God is to pursue him. Break me, blow me, etc. He is waiting for you before you get there. "Hard to get" in a different sense is a feature of figurative language. Donne's thought is hard to follow. His meaning is hard to understand. He can be easily seduced but his wit can be hard to grasp.

Herbert is not simply the opposite. (Which would make him hard to seduce but easy to understand.) He shares with Donne a feeling of impatience with the classical pantheon. He is cooler than Donne to be sure. He is outspoken in denouncing figurative complexity, "decking the sense," he calls it, "as if it were to sell."

To an extent he substitutes other complexities. Sound and shape. Rhyme schemes so complicated you can't pick them out by ear; you have to look at them if you want to observe the pattern. When you look, the shapes of his poems never appear simple. Even a couplet has two different left margins. The shapes of a few poems are icons. Wings. A column. Silhouettes of their subjects. Other poems create shapes of still greater complexity.

His figurative language does not evade understanding. It doesn't send messages "at two removes." But he does use figurative language more than he acknowledges. A big part of his plainness is propaganda.

Paradoxically, "hard to get" may be what gives the impression of piety, simplicity, and plainness in Herbert's poetry. He's cool. He doesn't get overexcited.

That's what piety is supposed to look like. He's calm. He has inner peace. He embodies the Anglican compromise. Pleasant afternoon church services in novels by Barbara Pym. God wonders if he really cares.

Sometimes I think sweetness might be the antonym of plainness. Plain fare would have no flavor at all. Or it would have the flavor of meat, vegetable, bread, without seasoning. Herbert loads every dish with sweeteners. He's the Chinese stereotype of the English sugaring their tea.

The first sign of Herbert's approaching death is
the loss of eloquence.

As the tools of rhetoric take their leave he
assaults them with the highest concentration of
sweet diction in all of his poetry.

> Farewell sweet phrases, lovely metaphors.
> But will ye leave me thus?
>   . . .
> Lovely enchanting language, sugar-cane,
> Hony of roses, whither wilt thou flie?

Sweet and lovely and lovely and enchanting and
sugarcane and honey. And the honey comes from
roses. A lot of sweet words and sweet things.

Herbert's soul, parting from his body, is his
rhetorical faculty. A place where sweetness is
made into images, "a box," another poem says,
"where sweets compacted lie."

When eloquence goes, it leaves behind a short
phrase, "Thou art still my God." A phrase lacking
the seasoning of sweetness.

Herbert's gifts (his intellect, his rhetoric, his language, the magnificent English language—all sweet things) have been taken from him. Or returned to him in a muzzled form.

Or his gifts were muzzling him. The sweetness was a muzzle.

Can Herbert live with a sweetness that is only embellishment?

The loss of words, figures, phrases, and voice is not supposed to be felt as deprivation. For all their sweetness, the tools of rhetoric add nothing to the knowledge that remains in a vocabulary of five words. Farewell sweetness, "for, *Thou art still my God*, is all that ye / Perhaps with more embellishment can say."

Yes. Herbert can live with that. In fact he can't live without it. This embellishment is the sweetness of living; its loss is fatal.

Herbert matures.

As he matures, he grows into plainness.

Herbert wrote poems aspiring to plainness and if he had lived longer might have written the most beautiful plain poems in history.

Or Herbert is regressing, and, as he regresses, his mastery of language leaves him. Words escape him. He descends into muteness.

The speaker seeks the silence before the poem. The point where he was an infant. A time before language.

The infant's relationship to language is that grownups have it. Mother has it. The infant can imitate it, which means that language is being measured in small nonsignifying units. Sound by sound.

Does this process (whether of maturity or regression) occur in the life narrative of Herbert's career?

Does it occur in the arrangement of poems in his book?

Does it happen more than once and not always successfully?

Does it succeed at all, even as an emblem, or is the process impossible and unending?

The process is difficult because Herbert is no child. And because he's a very verbal person.

What comes easily to him is rhetorical complexity. He feels at ease in language. Muteness is difficult.

The process is difficult because Herbert loves eloquence.

He loves sweetness, and there's nothing sweeter than tropes, words, sounds.

Edward, Lord Herbert of Cherbury, reports that his younger brother George was "not exempt from passion and choler."

"Not exempt" is a way of saying that George is human and has human feelings.

Or, better, Edward and George are brothers, and the feelings involved in that relationship may differ from those in George's relationships with other people.

With everyone else he might be "holy and exemplary." He might seem inhumanly virtuous.

Edward brings out unholy behavior in George. They regress in company with each other.

Edward is tired of people saying, "Why can't you be holy all the time like your brother?", and he wants to say, "If only you knew what George was really like." Remembering a stupid argument from twenty years ago.

It would be interesting if anger drove George Herbert. And if his aspirations to plain style were reacting against the inwrought figures of traditional poetic language.

There's a difference between power and class privilege.

George Herbert's career is a good example. The younger brother of a baron, he was expected to live as a member of an aristocracy and maintain the honor of his family without possessing the resources that would help to fulfill the obligations. The family's property belonged to his older brother Edward.

George Herbert's social status prohibited a career in trade. (His privilege as a son of the Herbert family was not to participate in commerce. Which is to say that his obligation was not to participate in commerce.) He spent years waiting for the political preferment that his family connections and brilliant career at school seemed to have prepared him for. An ambassadorship or secretaryship. Which he never got. All those years spent memorizing proverbs in foreign languages and he never had the opportunity to travel to foreign lands. With no other options, he dedicated the last few years of his life to the Church of England.

Privilege is a form of obligation. You make and do nothing. Your advantage is no prize claimed by your personal power. It comes from privilege.

What if the poem were about the problem of loving something familiar? "I cannot look on thee," because everything on you is already intimately known. My guilt is not what I brought to the relationship but what I created in the existing relationship. Which means that your greeting is not our first encounter. (Not love at first sight.)

Shouldn't that be obvious? The poem can't possibly begin at the start of the relationship. The idea of the thunderclap belongs to the other tradition, classical love, mythological love, all false loves. You and I have been together for a long time when this poem comes to be. Long enough for there to be love.

Familiar becomes strange. And the strangeness is either a new reason to fall in love or a sign of falling out of love.

You can still surprise me, you're wonderful!

Ugh, I never really knew you.

Maybe my guilt is because the thrill is gone.
I'm avoiding you, and that makes me guilty, and
guilt makes me avoid you. Or I'm pretending, and
that makes me guilty. Or I'm not pretending well
enough, and that makes me guilty.

Or my guilt is that I'm unfaithful. And lying. I put
my love into mythology. You're at home keeping
my dinner warm while I'm out having adventures.
Worshipping strange gods.

A commercial expression: "Sweetly questioning, /
If I lack'd anything." The question that peddlers
call in the streets. The question that drawers ask
in the taverns. The question that pimps ask on the
streets and in the taverns.

What do you lack?

Synonymous with, what will you buy?

They ask the first question at Bartholomew Fair
and the second question at Vanity Fair. In *The
Pilgrim's Progress from This World, to That Which
Is to Come*, the answer is, "We buy the truth."

I doubt that "Love" (3) is about buying and selling.
I don't think that's a credible interpretation. But
it's about exchange. What do you want from me,
what do I want from you, how can I stop worrying
about my personal issues long enough to give you
satisfaction and be satisfied myself?

Imagine Love as a sex worker. A brilliant sex worker. A committed emotional manager. Dedicated to forging a personal connection with every client. Which could mean, finally, reversing the client/server relationship. Love serves the client by demanding the client's patronage as a form of service.

The client's guilt could be a response to the stigma of paying for sex. It could imply a judgment of Love. I feel guilty being with you because my status is mirrored by anyone with whom I am intimate, and I am intimate with someone who is a social outcast. A creature of the demimonde.

I feel that I am part of the same world. I can slip off my mask and be comfortably my true self only in your world.

My instinctive response would be gratitude. As long as we agree that I am undeserving of you, I will be immensely grateful for your overindulgence of my small worth. As long as I believe that you are worthy of something better than my unworthiness.

But this response could easily turn into its opposite. I become "unkinde, ungratefull," for example, if I decide that you are unworthy.

I am grateful for being overcompensated. But my gratitude can lead me to wonder if I am being undercompensated. Why are you giving me more than I'm worth? What if you're taking advantage of me? What if this exchange exploits an angle that I can't see? What if you are getting a better deal?

Your association with me can only feed these suspicions. If you are with me, and I am undeserving, and my social status is mirrored by those with whom I am intimate, then you are no better than you should be, no better than I am, and no more deserving. If you actually enjoy being with me, and I am "unkinde, ungratefull," then the time we spend together is work that I'm doing for you. Only you're the one being paid for it. Now I feel cheated and enraged. I lack the self-respect to price my services so that I can make a profit. I'm a *cheap* whore!

There could also be a suspicion of involvement in other invisible relationships. I'm paying you, but whom are you paying? Who gets the money finally?

There could be similar problems for a sex worker who has romantic partners. You find yourself using the same techniques on romantic partners that you use with your clients. And you find that the responses of your partners and clients are exactly the same in every way.

My notes yesterday assumed that society in "Love" (3) would stigmatize sex work much like Herbert's society or mine.

What if it didn't?

What if Love were an ordinary merchant?

What if society stigmatized every kind of commerce *except* selling love?

What if it stigmatized every kind of love except the love exchanged for money?

I'm trying to imagine a society where everyone agreed with Herbert. Merchants and consumers on the love market would not be guilty creatures. Society would honor them.

Guilt would have to come from a different place. Not because society did not sanction the exchange but because something in me did not approve it. My guilt could come from conforming to social expectations despite my personal inclination. It could come from a disavowal of my inclination.

I feel bad for not wanting what I'm supposed to want. I feel bad for not wanting what society says I should want. What you say I should want. What I say I want.

Love tells me to want love.

In Herbert's society, the convention is for
marriages to be arranged by a third party, a parent
or guardian or marriage broker. (Herbert's marriage
was brokered.) The traditional explanation for this
practice is that arranged marriages have a better
rate of success than marriages where the partners
choose their own partners. Because love that
grows out of an arrangement is more durable than
love that grows out of romance.

Tocqueville argues that the practice is correct
but the explanation is only partly correct. The
conventional arrangement succeeds because it is
conventional. The romantic partnership runs into
trouble because it is unconventional. The problem
with people who marry for love rather than
because their parents tell them to get married is
that they are nonconformists. Which means that
they are probably going to be unhappy no matter
what they do.

The conformists who marry according to the
dictates of society and their parents, in addition to

whatever good feeling they create together within the confines of the marriage, enjoy the additional good feeling of positive reinforcement from the rest of society and their elders.

The nonconformists, in addition to their other burdens, must bear the disapproval of society and their elders. It's truly the nonconformists, and the love they create for themselves, fighting against the rest of the world.

In this account Tocqueville invents the first move of sociology. The fact of society itself. The strong action of society on its members. The pressure on the minority to conform to the expectations of the majority.

This analysis is supported by the fact that in my society the convention and the explanation are reversed. For us the cliché is that romantic partnerships are more durable than arranged marriages. Those who marry into arrangements devised by third parties are the nonconformists.

A different account, also in the spirit of Tocqueville, would be to say that the nonconformists are those who are more likely to be made happy by resisting social pressures. They enjoy not conforming. They experience their elders' outraged looks as incentives.

The partners would also exert pressure on each other. And that would be closer to a description of "Love" (3).

There is no social context in "Love" (3). No other members of society to speak of. No one else to talk to.

Society is what you and I do.

134

My sister Natasha, who is a social worker, once spoke to me about the interesting fact that I was not bullied in school.

I at first was not willing to admit that it was true. School seemed to me to be pretty awful. Since I have sifted my memories for examples of possible bullying, and since I have witnessed actual bullying and I know how much worse school was for some kids, I can admit that Natasha was right. I do not have a history of being bullied.

Natasha's first attempt to explain how I protected myself from bullies was, "Social skills." "You weren't bullied because you had social skills."

This is the answer you would expect from a social worker. Children who avoided becoming victims of bullying must have learned social skills to defeat bullies.

A funny answer in my case. Because I possessed nothing that could truthfully be called a social skill. Maybe I still don't.

When my social behavior is correct, it's because I have successfully disguised myself as a normal person for five minutes. It's probably because I asked a normal person what a normal person would do.

In my childhood I lacked even the self-consciousness to impersonate a normal human being.

Part of Natasha's premise, the reason why her question is interesting, is that I was seemingly an excellent candidate for being picked on.

A strange kid who wears a bowler hat and other old-fashioned clothes, isn't interested in computers, likes books, and likes to read out loud and sing.

Natasha's second explanation is that I didn't care what other people thought of me.

Bullies rely on weaknesses in their victims. Wanting to fit in. Wanting to be liked. I didn't give them a handle.

This theory is not as ridiculous as Natasha's first idea.

Maybe I had unrealistic notions of what kind of thing might impress people.

I was proud. I still am.

It was never true that I didn't care what other people thought. But I may have given the impression that I didn't care. Maybe my notions of what people should care about were so alien that my friends thought I was joking.

I never saw peer pressure in the actions of my friends. I thought peer pressure was their excuse for doing what they enjoyed. I thought peer pressure was a myth, and this belief saved me from it.

And perhaps because I recognized no peer, I felt no pressure.

How does this sense of self-satisfaction evolve in one who is otherwise such a worrywart?

135

In fourth grade we had to write an essay on "the most interesting person you know."

Half of the kids, including me, wrote about one of our grandparents.

My grandfather Fred Schwalen fascinated me because of his wartime experiences and especially because of his stories about his childhood.

Years ago I lost the beautiful letter he wrote about his intelligent dog and the house where his parents lived. Maybe his work in the war was interesting too because I liked secret codes and that is what being a cryptographer would have meant to me.

The other half of the fourth graders wrote about me. Was there anything interesting about me? I was a funny kid. I liked old stuff. I read books obsessively.

The kids thought I was interesting because I didn't like computer games. They told stories about how I went to their houses and didn't want to play computer games. Or they had a birthday party at a video arcade and I didn't want to play.

That was unusual enough to be the most interesting thing in their experience and worthy of a school composition.

I remember feeling disappointed that Shelly wrote about her grandfather. I wasn't the most interesting person she knew.

136

I had some confusion early on about the concept of art.

Art was a period in school. It was a room where we went to draw, paint, work with clay, glue things to paper. It was those activities.

The art teacher's name was Mrs. Arneson. The source of my confusion was the similarity between art's name and her name.

Was it called art because her name was Arneson?

Was she called Arneson because she taught art to kids?

Why was her name Arneson? Shouldn't it have a t instead of n? Arteson?

I was never sure how to pronounce her name. I wanted it to sound more like art.

It never occurred to me that art might be pronounced differently. I mean, I never made the mistake of calling it arn.

137

It has taken me a long time to see Herbert as one of my favorite writers.

And I'm not sure that I would ever have said that "Love" (3) was one of my favorite poems. Although I'm sure I would have said that it was one of the most beautiful poems in the universe. I might have agreed with Weil about that.

When I read Adam's essay on "Love" (3) I felt vaguely frustrated.

He saw it as a poem of sweetness and patient understanding. Nothing but nice.

Adam had studied the poem with me, and it isn't my goal as a teacher to have my students read exactly the way I do, but it bothered me that he had taken nothing from me. He wasn't even writing against me. He didn't see my interpretation as something to write against.

Adam's essay told me that I knew something about the poem that other people did not know. That even my students did not know.

That made the poem mine.

The most important part of the story, though, is how the sentence, "Ah my deare, / I cannot look on thee" became meaningful.

I associate this line with a particular desire. The desire, my most perverse, inexplicable desire, to be forbidden the sight of your face, the face I most want to see.

138

What makes them our favorite books?

We are responding to a consistency of style.

The effect is consistent in every phrase.

A truly consistent style can incorporate any
material.

Cut into it at any point—the same richness, the
same depth.

There were no interruptions in its consistency
until you made your cut.

139

The energy of a consistent style is when it touches stuff that seems contrary to the writer's sensibility.

Henry James writes about war?

Frances Burney wrote a tragedy in verse?

I have never learned to achieve such consistency.

That's the weakness of my style when it can't handle material of a certain type.

Maybe I don't want it. Some effects are lost by consistency, like the effect of pulling out all the stops of the organ.

140

Most of "The Quidditie" is about what verse is not.

Sort of like negative theology, where I approach
my god by deleting everything that is not divine.

But that isn't what the poem does. The poem
starts with "My God." God is a given and does not
need to be approached indirectly.

> My God, a verse is not a crown,
> No point of honour, or gay suit,
> No hawk, or banquet, or renown,
> Nor a good sword, nor yet a lute:
>
> It cannot vault, or dance, or play;
> It never was in *France* or *Spain*;
> Nor can it entertain the day
> With my great stable or demain:
>
> It is no office, art, or news,
> Nor the Exchange, or busie Hall;
> But it is that which while I use
> I am with thee, and *most take all*.

What the poem struggles to define by erasing everything in the world is not God but poetry.

"A verse is not a crown." Crown means a piece of jewelry and also the form of government it represents. A verse is not a king. A verse is not a state.

A verse can't "entertain the day." The day is a guest. The day is a friend for whom I wish an impressive horse and land well stocked with game.

Because the poem negates so many things, actions, and institutions, the world starts to seem full. Its cup runneth over.

Poetry falls out. Poetry passes through the net. Everything else, everything in the world, is caught in the net.

Poetry is in the world and it makes a hole in the world through which you go somewhere else.

141

Buried in "The Quidditie" is a strange denial of art.

"It is no art."

Is poetry not an art? What does Herbert mean?

There's an argument about that in Plato's dialogues. Poetry is not an art because it doesn't know anything.

Ion tries to convince Socrates that poetry is the same art as war. The best rhapsode is also the greatest general. I don't think that's what Herbert means.

Herbert might be thinking of art in the limited sense of visual art. I doubt that. Poetry used to be more of an art than painting or sculpture. Poussin, Herbert's contemporary, could only call painting an art by analogy with language arts such as poetry and rhetoric.

Herbert probably doesn't mean the otherworldliness that art has for romantic poets. He probably means something closer to what Plato would mean. Knowledge. Skill. Plastic manipulation.

The best hypothesis is probably that Herbert wants to distinguish spiritual practice from art.

Maybe art in the old sense of plastic manipulation is a human province. Something I can do or know or have without divine intervention. And Herbert means the opposite of that. Verse is not a human province but a place where he is most "with" his god.

142

Helen Vendler thinks that Herbert talks to God in the same way that he would talk to a friend.

I guess the first question would be how does Vendler talk to her friends?

Does she call her friends Lord?

Does she call them Master, and does she take pleasure in saying the words?

> How sweetly doth *My Master* sound! *My Master!*
>   As Amber-greese leaves a rich sent
>   Unto the taster:
>   So do these words a sweet content,
> An orientall fragrancie, *My Master*.

Does she call her friends Love?

Even names can be misleading. In Baltimore everyone is called Hon. In London everyone is called Love. Outsiders make the mistake of thinking this usage is too intimate when they hear it at the grocery. It is casual and indiscriminate.

278

I believe sometimes this casual usage can be pointedly used to cross distances, test listeners, or to make outsiders uncomfortable. It can have a few different tones. It can be menacing. It can be spoken like a tape recording. And, even then, it can make me feel better.

I find usages like this very appealing. I like that nonintimate relationships use intimate language. A formal use of informal address. A low-stakes love exchanged between strangers.

That would be the easiest way to understand the relationship in "Love" (3). You and I are strangers. I am a stranger brought into the household but not adopted into the family. We rely on ancient conventions of hospitality to survive our time together.

Guest and host don't have to be strangers. A guest can be a friend. Having a friend as a guest can relieve some of the pressure of hospitality. A friend may be more forgiving of the deficiencies of the host. Sometimes you have to remind yourself not to take your friend too much for granted. To treat a friend as well as any strange guest.

Assuming that Herbert addressed God as a friend, why would that be unusual?

Isn't that what Donne is famous for?

> Thou hast made me, And shall thy worke decay?

Donne is far more informal than Herbert in talking to God. Sometimes aggressive in the way that friends can be. Informal or complaining or teasing. Taking the piss, busting chops. Like a friend to a friend. Conversation poems.

I don't think that's how Herbert talks to God.

> Me thoughts I heard one calling, *Child!*
> And I reply'd, *My Lord*.

He is a child. He is a servant.

Does he ever call God a friend? Does he have a friend in Jesus?

Can we be friends if I am obsessively fixated on your death by torture?

Vendler calls Herbert's god an "intimate friend."

> Herbert suggests that to be an intimate friend is to answer, with improvements, a speaker's questions, using, to his surprise, his own syllables to do so.

Does Herbert suggest that? Is the word "friend" one of "his own syllables"? Not that I can see.

Friendship means a relationship of equality. Both friends have the same status. "Adult to adult," in Vendler's phrase.

Intimate means mutual and symmetrical. Both friends bring the same things to the relationship and take the same things out.

This interpretation seems so wrong to me that I wonder how a reader as sensitive as Vendler could maintain it.

Here is her astonishing example: "Thy power and love, my love and trust / Make one place ev'ry where."

Her comment: "The word 'love' here stands for an identity of feeling." I think she means that the speaker and the addressee are both feeling love.

I don't think the loves are identical. It's "thy love" and "my love." Two loves, not one love.

The crux of my disagreement with her might be the phrase "make one place ev'ry where." Maybe she thinks that "one place" becoming "ev'ry where" makes for a uniform surface. From place to place, all experiences are converted into the same monotonous routine.

I think just the opposite. I think the different values we bring to the relationship (power, trust, and love) make for an endlessly changing, surprising, and fascinating surface, so that, while remaining in place, we seem to go everywhere, and, out of ourselves alone, receive all experiences.

This is the lesson of consensual sadomasochism for students of human relationships: compatibility is more important than mutuality.

You bring power to the relationship and I bring trust, and we both bring love.

There is a difference between our loves, and the difference *on which our loves depend* is a vertical one.

145

Compatibility is more important than mutuality.

A corollary to this lesson is that compatibility is not given. It has to be found. It can even be created.

This doesn't mean that lovers fall magically into place with their lovers.

It doesn't mean that anyone can be anything for anyone.

I mean that two people, if they are sufficiently motivated, can probably find a way of being sexually compatible.

With some sexual partners I had nothing in common. Not even communication or understanding. Not even kinks.

Nonetheless, if we were interested in each other, we found a way of being sexual together.

Leo Bersani:

> If it is time to sing the praises of the penis once again, it is not only because a fundamental reason for a gay man's willingness to identify his desires as homosexual is love of the cock (an acknowledgement profoundly incorrect and especially unpopular with many of our feminist allies), but also because it was perhaps in early play with that much-shamed organ that we learned about the *rhythms* of power, and we were or should have been initiated into the biological connection between male sexuality and surrender or passivity—a connection that men have been remarkably successful in persuading women to consider nonexistent.

I never like how Vendler opposes power and sweetness.

She thinks that "Love" (3) is all sweetness and no power. Sweetness so overpowers power that, in the end, "pure sweetness returns forever."

Really there isn't a lot of sweetness in the poem. Only the questions are said to taste sweet. Meat rhymes with sweet and eat, but no one says a word about its flavor. Or how long the flavor lasts for that matter.

About "Vertue" she says that the "strength" of the virtuous soul is "taking precedence, visibly, over its sweetness."

> Sweet rose, whose hue angrie and brave
> Bids the rash gazer wipe his eye:
> Thy root is ever in its grave,
>   And thou must die.

The sight of the sweet rose is painfully beautiful.

It presses on my face and makes tears come out.

Then there is a counter-pressure. My soul has its own strength. Virtue. A species of sweetness that resists.

Vendler can hear this strength in the voice that speaks the words of the poem. "This is a voice which 'never gives.'"

The incompatibility of power and sweetness makes Vendler question whether the rose is sweet after all. The first word in the verse is "sweet," but then Herbert must have decided that the rose was not sweet and described it in non-sweet language, "angrie and brave."

If the rose were truly sweet, it couldn't be angry and brave, because sweetness is weakness, whereas anger and bravery are strengths.

I am not convinced. It looks to me as though Herbert thought that an object could have all of these qualities. Sweet, angry, brave.

It also looks to me as though Vendler's reading depends on sweetness wielding some strength.

A better way of making her point would be to say that no one else would have said that the rose poking him in the eye was sweet, but Herbert said it was sweet.

148

Why would anyone expect me to feel grateful when I follow your instructions?

I don't express gratitude. I don't use the polite formulas.

The poem ends with eating, not with, "Thank you."

I would give thanks for a gift. But your meat isn't a gift. You aren't doing this to be nice.

There is no way to repay you. Whatever I give you was already "your own works." A piece of yourself that you see in me.

— Do our works deserve nothing then at God's hand?
— No: for they are his own works in us.

Which means that it would be as nonsensical for you to feel gratitude as it would be for me.

"Thank you" isn't the ritual form even in the highest protocol of BDSM, although it might be appropriate to give thanks for punishment, humiliation, or favors.

In response to a command, I carry out the command. Maybe I add, "Yes, ma'am."

149

I have done almost no writing about my own history with sexualizing power.

My usual policy is that I want to be as open as possible with my own stuff and as careful as possible with other people's stuff.

By my own stuff I mean my interests and preferences, including the ones that disgust me.

Do I mean my experiences? Not easy to talk about them without talking about some women.

I am sure that I want to write about my early experiences.

The bedcovers, the beanbag chairs, undressing at Minnehaha Falls, looking at shoes in study hall.

"Mickey's Nightmare," the women's army of Oz, the Circe chapter in *Ulysses*.

150

Bondage is freedom. A lot of religious poetry is about this. Donne commands his god to enthrall him so that he can be truly free. I am just starting to see what that could mean.

I was originally interested in bondage as a kind of humiliation. My attitude seems to be unusual. Most bondage enthusiasts don't seem to get humiliation out of it.

My fantasies about bondage always begin as physical demonstrations of power.

You can do whatever you want with your body, and you also control my body, making me move however you decide or restricting my movements. When you immobilize me, you can do other things to me that underline the difference between your strength and my helplessness.

Humiliation is one of the things that bondage makes me feel. But bondage is much bigger and more complicated and mysterious than that. It may be as big as sex itself.

In a cage or a sack, I'm being held; you're taking care of me. There are feelings of security as well as vulnerability. That's one paradox.

Another paradox is that, immobilized, sacked, hooded, fixed to a platform, I have been reduced to my body, while at the same time most of my senses—the basis of my bodily experience—have been taken away.

I feel like I am only a body.

And I feel like I have been taken out of my body.

Therefore I'm not just a body! Part of me is something else. And that is where the feeling of freedom, the biggest paradox, comes from.

There is a moment of adjustment where I feel that my body no longer belongs to me. Is no longer me.

I remember that I am part of something bigger. Something I want to be part of.

Bondage is freedom. Bondage is one of my sexual preferences, so it's sexual freedom, but, more than that, it includes its opposite.

151

My first entry into pain was as a kind of humiliation. I wasn't excited by pain itself but I was attracted to sadists and I liked the loss of control that pain entails.

Being destroyed and putting myself back together and being destroyed and not able to put myself back together.

Then you showed me how intimate pain can be. I always feel close to you when you beat me.

I feel your wonderful analytical mind reaching out to me, judging my reactions, and deciding what I can take.

I love being able to put both fear and trust in the same place.

I forget about my false issues when you are beating me. I stop being nervous about the ways in which I disappoint you.

Then I started feeling sentimental about marks.
I never used to feel that way.

Being marked wasn't a limit for me but I never
used to enjoy lingering pain and the inconvenience
of not being able to sit comfortably or wanting to
go for a swim and having to put it off until my body
was no longer covered in bruises.

Now I like being able to see and feel the evidence
of your effects on me. Marks help me to remember
you. I'm sorry when they fade away.

Finally I learned to like being made to ask for pain
or to express enjoyment in pain. This is forced
speech, a kind of humiliation that I love.

This kind of forced speech is also exciting because
it allows me to play at being a masochist.

Afterwards my clothes and things have an
uncertain appearance. My hands start toward my
glasses, which have the look of costume pieces,
like mine, but used for a different purpose.

152

A woman told me, "I think you might be a masochist."

She was wrong. We went further with pain than I was ready for.

I avoided pain for a while after that.

Another woman called me a heavy player.

She said that I could really take a beating, for someone who wasn't a masochist.

She called me a goody two-shoes.

Another woman said that I was a true submissive.

Another woman said, when beating me, that it made sense to treat me like a masochist, even though she knew I wasn't one.

Another woman described me as a submissive with very few limits.

She said that I was 50 percent submissive,
30 percent fetishist, 10 percent vanilla, and
10 percent vintagist.

I would describe myself not as a real masochist
but rather as a submissive who can sometimes
sexualize pain by processing it as humiliation.

I would say that I am pretty good at taking pain.
Somewhat to my surprise.

153

Sex with women (in the sense of fucking) is something that I almost never think about.

Even when I was a teenager practicing tying myself up and imagining women overpowering me and tying me up, I didn't think much about fucking.

There have been times in my life, with certain women, when I really got into fucking.

Today, at this point in my life, I don't think about it. Mostly I think about power, humiliation, objectification, pain, and bondage. That's the meaning of sex for me now.

Romance is a different question. About romance, I'm ambivalent. There are kinds of love, trust, vulnerability, and intimacy that may only be possible in romantic relationships. There is also a kind of sanity that belongs to cohabitation with someone you love.

I miss all of those things. I both want them and don't want them.

Not knowing what one wants is dangerous!

Perhaps more dangerous than wanting dangerous things.

Are they considered brave who risk social diseases and pregnancy?

We who fetishize distance may be spared those risks. Pain may leave scars but playing with pain is unlikely to lead to systemic illness.

Not to mention those who fetishize chastity.

The risks of vanilla sex may actually be greater than the ones associated with sexualized pain.

I have done some things that most people would not do.

A few things I have done that probably no one should do.

No one should play with breath. The risks are too great. Too unpredictable. Everyone who has studied human physiology agrees that there is no way to reduce the risks. No matter how careful we believe ourselves to be.

No one should take blows to the head. A real hard slap in the face risks damaging teeth, jaw, eyes, spine, and brain. The risks are at least predictable.

My rule, I am embarrassed to admit, is that I only do these things with a woman I really trust.

My second rule, which is far more embarrassing, is that I only do these things with a woman who I think is lucky.

I believe your luck protects me. But only to the extent that nothing too terrible is going to happen through you.

At least, if something terrible should happen, you would not be blamed.

How do I justify using Herbert's poem to write about eroticizing power?

Herbert and I do not put power in the same place.

There's just one thing we both like.

We invest power in talk. We like to give power to someone who takes our voices away. Love is someone who takes our voices away.

We eroticize humiliation, and we are especially interested in verbal humiliation.

My speech controlled by another voice. My speech answered with ridicule, finality, and triumph. My speech unanswered. My speech silenced.

I look for a woman to do that. Herbert looks for a god who, some readers think, has feminine attributes.

157

I am not writing from identity.

My claim is not that my sexual preferences give me a special insight into the nature of power. They don't even give me a special insight into sexualizing power.

Rather my claim is that sexualizing power is a fine thing to do. It has an appeal that anyone should be able to understand.

158

How do I defend my desires?

Is humiliation okay as long as we both consent?
Is desiring humiliation okay as long as my desires
are part of human nature?

These are weak defenses. Consent is weak
because it's a minimum requirement. Consent
means that at least no one is committing assault
or rape.

(In Herbert's poem, I *don't* consent.)

The defense based on human nature is vulnerable
to the objection that some desires, although
innate, are impossible or reprehensible.

Everyone has heard this objection. It's an old
argument against tolerating homosexuality. If sex
between men is okay because the desires are
innate, then what's wrong with desiring children

or dogs? What's wrong with incest and rape? What's wrong with treating human flesh as food? For some people these are innate desires.

Bigots who ask these questions view gay sex as morally equivalent to pedophilia or bestiality or rape or cannibalism. They are wrong. But they are pointing out a weakness in the liberal argument for tolerating whatever acts are consensual, whatever desires are innate.

I want to say that masochism is morally equivalent to homosexuality and morally superior to cannibalism, pedophilia, and rape. And it's easier to make that distinction if you treat sexual preferences as choices rather than inner drives.

The strongest defense of desiring humiliation is to say that desiring it is desirable. A choice.

A good choice. The best choice.

I am not saying that I know something about power because I am a masochist.

I am not saying that Herbert knew something about power because he was a masochist.

There are plenty of masochists in the world who are hopelessly confused about power.

Nor am I saying that Herbert was a masochist.

I am saying that Herbert knew lots of things because he was a very smart person. Some things he knew about power. Some things he knew about masochism.

He knew those things because masochism is a human possibility.

I know them because Herbert wrote about them. I see them in his poems because I am a good reader of poetry.

Herbert's thing with power is not exactly the same as my thing.

But when I put my thing, my human possibility, alongside Herbert's, I can see a little better.

Standing next to each other, we disclose our interests clearly.

How would I want to change Herbert's poem?

The first change is that Love would be a woman.

Maybe that isn't a change. The only obstacle is the masculine title "Lord." But I have a pretty good argument for seeing Love as a woman, and this interpretation turns out to be a commonplace of the critical tradition.

Another change is that I might want the difference in status to be more explicit.

In this regard my fantasy is the same as the speaker's.

Many of the restrictions in the poem come from the speaker. They are the fantasy he brings to the scene.

He wants to look at Love. Even more than that he wants a rule that will prohibit looking at Love.

He wants to serve; he wants to kneel. Love forces him to sit at the table like a member of the human race.

He is uncomfortable with his grubby appearance, with the apparent lack of structure in the scene, and with the lack of apparent hierarchy. He might prefer a higher protocol.

At last he is compelled by the force Love uses and by the fact that she is using force.

He can feel more comfortable being grubby if his personal appearance is outside of his control.
If his appearance is something she does to him.

The speaker worries about making a mistake, and his worrying only creates new opportunities for mistakes to happen; when inevitably he makes a mistake, he keeps worrying about it. The mistake doesn't necessarily lead to other mistakes but he can't let go of it.

She impatiently takes the worry away from him.

So far I'm finding that I don't want to change anything.

I wouldn't touch the display of rhetorical power. A verbal confrontation in which Love is victorious at every step of the exchange is exactly my thing.

The speaker scores no points at all.

Love is always right and always says it better.

Until finally the speaker can't say anything. There's nothing left to say and his mouth is stopped.

The part about food is less interesting to me.

Would I want to change that? Change to something sexually exciting?

Sweetness might not mean to me what it means to Herbert.

161

Love humiliates him by taking away his favorite posture of submission, kneeling.

He has a favorite signal for giving up control. Love takes it away.

Then he gives power to food. Love humiliates him with food.

Love gives him, at the table, a position of honor that makes him uncomfortable.

Love takes away his voice and gives him food. You could almost say that Love replaces his voice with food. "Eat."

One humiliating implication of this line is unfairness. At this point in the poem Love is still talking and the speaker isn't.

Love can talk and the speaker can't talk.

What Love says has a sweet sound, although some of the words are harsh. Love gets away with vulgarity only because of who Love is.

162

Does Love know my name?

Does Love think my name is Love?

Why would anyone accept love from someone not named Love?

Of course that's more a problem for you than for me.

I know where I'm going to take love from. I don't have much of a choice. You don't give me a choice. Not because it's a good offer, not even because it's the only offer, but because it's not really an offer.

I'm a cheap imitation. My name isn't Love. Are you going to accept love from me? Maybe that would be better than taking love from the false prophets who illegitimately call themselves Love. At least I'm not guilty of false advertising. Report the merchants of sleaze to the Better Business Bureau and accept my poor substitute for love. What choice do you have?

Or take love from everybody, even the sleaze merchants. That is what the speaker says you do in Donne's "Holy Sonnets." Your goal is to make your love "embrac'd and open to most men."

Am I guilty of false advertising? One of the distinct tendencies of my submission is a funny kind of innocence. Funny because it's the opposite of innocent. It's disingenuous.

My instinct is to submit. Because my desire is to submit. But I don't acknowledge the desire. I don't admit knowledge of what I am here for. I take the information from you, which means that I make the information come out of you. I manage the information, and I manage my speech and your speech, to support my fantasy of innocence.

You make me do it but you don't make me say that I want it. Thus you play into my fantasy of innocence.

I enter and say: It's not because I believe myself worthy of you that I came here.

I'm not here for love.

In other words I don't know why I'm here.

I don't even acknowledge that I'm here.

Is that disingenuous? Maybe it's polite. Some would say that's how you ask for something. (What moronic code of polite behavior would require me to ask for something, to say I want something, by accusing myself of being unworthy of receiving it? This requirement goes far beyond praising your magnanimity, "If you would be so kind . . .")

At last you require me to acknowledge something in you. You gently press, "And know you not," on my disingenuousness. You are forcing me to admit that I know part of your history. I know what you are and by implication why I am here.

One of the kindest, and, at the same time, most manipulative things someone I love can do is to create an opening for me to declare my strong feelings. Or, if necessary, force me to declare, "I love you." The words, familiar as they are, can be powerful if I haven't said them before, if I haven't thought about saying them, if I haven't allowed myself to say them, even to myself.

My other distinct tendency as a submissive is a more credible form of innocence. To press the point, I might even call it ingenuousness. Not only do I do whatever you say, I believe whatever you say. I always believe your whoppers.

My second submissive trait could be viewed as a trusting nature. An unquestioning willingness to enter into whatever you say. A seriousness in handling figurative language, exaggerations, jokes.

What did I mean when I told her, "You have to trust me"?

I meant that she had to decide whether to trust me or not. I had done as much as I could to prove my love, but no proof was sufficient. Finally our relationship depended on whether she was willing to trust me.

At first I found it hard to trust her because when we first met she extinguished a cigarette on my thigh. I still have the scar.

Was she careless? No, we were communicating poorly, that's all.

She was trying to impress me. That was the real trouble. She was competing with what she thought was my vast experience. Although by any objective standard her experiences were more numerous and varied.

Her major problem with trust was the source of my minor problem with trust. First it made her want to impress me, then it made her disbelieve that she could make an impression on me.

You shouldn't trust me.

I am given to complaining about folks called Love.

Everyone else with your name I exposed as a fraud. "Love" (1): inadequate, doesn't deserve to be called Love. "Love" (2): inadequate, doesn't deserve to be called Love. I will probably do the same to you too.

How am I going to keep love a secret from Love? Maybe I want you to know only I don't want to tell you.

Maybe I am reluctant to admit my love for you because that would seem to cast doubt on my love for previous partners. My use of the concept of love in poetry has been so free that further repetitions seem insincere.

Is it true that Love expresses love? It's true that I leave all expression of desire to you. But are you any more explicit than I am?

No one says love in "Love" (3).

No one says, "I love you."

Notes

1

Unless otherwise noted, quotations from Herbert's
   English poems follow the text of *The Works of
   George Herbert*, edited by Hutchinson.

5

Herbert: "Love's a man of warre" ("Discipline").

On the limits of empathy as a tool of warfare, compare
   Grant: "Oh, I am heartily tired of hearing about what
   Lee is going to do. . . . Go back to your command,
   and try to think what we are going to do ourselves,
   instead of what Lee is going to do." Quoted in Foote,
   The Civil War, 3.185.

7

"I'm supposed to say . . ." Psalm 23. Herbert's translation of this psalm appears in *The Temple*.

10

"Doth God exact . . ." Milton, Sonnet 19.

"Why was the sight . . ." Milton, *Samson Agonistes*,
   93–97.

"Commits holy rapes . . ." Carew, "An Elegy." Quotation
   slightly altered.

"Batter my heart . . ." Donne, Holy Sonnet 14.

11

"If you don't believe . . ." Memphis Jug Band, "Stealin',
Stealin'."

13

"Thou shalt look . . ." Herbert, "The Glance."

14

On populations in Milton's universe, see Glimp, *Increase
and Multiply*, 152–161.
"The sociable Spirit . . ." Milton, *Paradise Lost*, 5.221.
"The affable Arch-angel . . ." *Paradise Lost*, 7.41.
On communication between worlds, see Calasso,
The Marriage of Cadmus and Harmony, 53.

16

In the seventeenth century "meat" was often used as a
general term for food or for the edible part of a food
object—"meat" as opposed to rind, shell, stone, or
bone. There are also many examples in seventeenth-
century literature of "meat" being used as a synonym
for flesh. Since eating a divine or human body is one
of the subjects of Herbert's poem, "meat" implies
flesh.
"I thought that being brave . . ." Anne Boyer, unpublished
essay, quoted with the author's permission.

20

When her first husband died, Magdalen Herbert remarried and took a new name and title, Lady Magdalen Danvers. I am using the name she shares with her son and by which Donne addressed her.
"A mother which delights . . ." Donne, "To Mrs. M. H."
"No occasion could unnerve her . . ." Herbert, *Latin Poetry*, 127.

22

"If you like to bite . . ." Tomkins, *Shame and Its Sisters*, 4. Quotation slightly altered.

23

On Weil, see Rees, *Simone Weil*, 58.

25

The items on this list are "entrails of power" (Canetti, *Crowds and Power*, 201–224).

27

"I am going . . ." Balzac, *Lost Illusions*, 135.

31

"Had dinner by myself . . ." Truman, quoted in McCullough, *Truman*, 751.

35

"The Lord is my shepherd . . ." Psalm 23.

37

"But will ye leave me thus? . . ." Herbert, "The Forerunners."

On order, see Vendler, *The Poetry of George Herbert*, 59–
60, 92.

40

"Still to be neat . . ." Jonson, *Epicœne or The Silent
Woman*, 1.1.91–92.

"Give me a looke . . ." Jonson, *Epicœne*, 1.1.97–98.

"Give me simplicitie . . ." Herbert, "A Wreath."

43

"MY FOREHEAD . . ." Balzac, *History of the Thirteen*,
261. Quotation altered.

46

"Avoid Profanenesse . . ." Hutchinson introduces a
comma after "Avoid" to support a reading of the
poem in which the speaker apostrophizes Profaneness. I have deleted the comma because I prefer
Fish's reading in which the poem demarcates classes
of readers (those who are prepared to enter the temple and those who are not) and then undoes the clas-

sification (Fish, *The Living Temple*, 129–130). Hutchinson's note supporting his emended punctuation appears in Herbert, *Works*, 484.

47

"Ah, Mother . . ." Herbert, *Latin Poems*, 129.

48

"But I fear the heat . . ." Herbert, *Works*, 363.

61

"Who would have thought . . ." Herbert, "The Flower."

64

"For whatever food . . ." Canetti, *Crowds and Power*, 324.

65

"The fire was what held . . ." Canetti, *The Torch in My Ear*, 249–50.
On "fear of being touched," see Canetti, *Crowds and Power*, 15–16.

66

"Anyone who wants to rule . . ." Canetti, *Crowds and Power*, 210. On family and motherhood, see Canetti, 220–21.

67

On the Versailles Treaty, see Canetti, *Crowds and Power*,
179–183.

"A madman, helpless, outcast . . ." *Crowds and Power*,
448. The allusion to Freud follows on 449.

"We avoid actual contact . . ." *Crowds and Power*, 15.

"The story of Thetis . . ." *Crowds and Power*, 345.

68

"We are teaching them . . ." I am paraphrasing Correll's
essay, "Malleable Materials, Models of Power," 254.

69

"There is likewise . . ." Swift, *Writings*, 22.

70

"A second-rate form . . ." Oakeshott, "Introduction to
Leviathan," xliv. Oakeshott deleted this sentence
from later editions.

72

"We say amisse . . ." Herbert, "The Flower."

73

This argument was suggested by Sedgwick, "How to
Bring Your Kids Up Gay," and Nunokawa, *Tame Passions of Wilde*.

74

"Who would never have fallen in love . . ." La Rochefoucauld, *Maxims*, 5.136.

77

I wrote this section from memory, without consulting
120 Days of Sodom.

79

I wrote this section from memory, without viewing
Fallen Angel.

84

"I will do for that . . ." Herbert, "The Thanksgiving."
When I first read "Love" (3) I assumed that the speaker
was serving Love by following the command to eat.
Most modern readers of "Love" (3) agree that the
speaker of the poem isn't allowed to serve; instead
Love insists on serving the speaker. One notable
exception is Allen Grossman, *Summa Lyrica* 22.1
and 30.9 (*The Sighted Singer*, 256, 288–89).

85

"Victory is achieved . . ." and "*The Mirror of Complements*
. . ." Schoenfeldt, *Prayer and Power*, 205–206.
"Surely I will revenge . . ." Herbert, "The Thanksgiving."
"Thy modestie . . ." Jonson, "To Camden."

87

"Man Proposeth . . ." Herbert, *Works*, 321.

Hutchinson: "The title *Outlandish* is more fully justified than might have been expected until an analysis was made of the collection. I have found French, Italian, or Spanish originals or equivalents of more than six-sevenths of *Outlandish Proverbs*" (*The Works of George Herbert*, 573).

Amy Charles suggests that Herbert associated collecting and trading proverbs with his brother Henry (*A Life of George Herbert*, 79).

"In the house of a Fidler . . ." Herbert, *Works*, 328.

88

"As in the house . . ." Herbert, *Works*, 240.

90

"In another walk . . ." Walton, *Life of Herbert*, 303–304.

91

"Having married an earl's daughter . . ." Trollope, *The Last Chronicle of Barset*, 238.

The reference to the Victorian manual of etiquette is from Gilmartin's footnote in her edition of *Last Chronicle*, 872n2.

94

"The word 'host' . . ." Booth, *Shakespeare's Sonnets*.
For Schoenfeldt's response, see "The Real Presence of
Unstated Puns," 77.

95

I agree with Strier that the poem is not "primarily
Eucharistic in reference" (*Love Known*, 78).

96

"Who knows not Love . . ." Herbert, "The Agonie."
On pleasure in mere appearance, see Terada, *Looking
Away*.

97

"The churches mysticall repast . . ." Herbert, "Superliminare."

99

"Shame tears my soul . . ." Herbert, "The Sacrifice."

100

For the argument that Herbert could not have intended
sexual meanings, see Vendler, *Invisible Listeners*, 87.
On the unconscious, see Empson, "George Herbert and
Miss Tuve," 737.

For Schoenfeldt on bawdy meanings, see *Prayer and Power*, 257–261.

110

"You cannot escape . . ." Fish, *The Living Temple*, 133.

114

"Also it is written . . ." Milton, *Paradise Regained*, 4.560–61.

115

Vendler discusses Herbert's tendency to incorporate revisions within lines in "Alternatives: The Reinvented Poem," chapter two of *The Poetry of George Herbert*, 25–56.

117

"Whose hands are these? . . ." Herbert, "The Quip." Quotation altered.

118

"In no society . . ." Bauman, "Speaking in the Light," 145.

120

For the interview, see Errol Morris, *The Unknown Known*.

122

"Sweetest Saviour . . ." Herbert, "Dialogue."

125

"Naked first . . ." Donne, Elegy 19.

"Decking the sense . . ." Herbert, "Jordan" (2).

"At two removes . . ." "Jordan" (1).

126

"Farewell sweet phrases . . ." Herbert, "The Forerunners."

"A box where sweets . . ." Herbert, "Vertue."

127

This section is a dialogue between Vendler, who tells
a story in which Herbert matures into plainness,
and Colie, who tells a different one in which Herbert
regresses into muteness. Vendler, *The Poetry of
George Herbert*, 267–68; Colie, *Paradoxia Epidemica*,
190–215.

128

"Not exempt . . ." Quoted in Schoenfeldt, *Bodies and
Selves*, 110.

131

"We buy the truth . . ." Bunyan, *The Pilgrim's Progress*, 139.

133

On love by arrangement and by romance, see Tocqueville, *Democracy in America*, 699–702.

Elster discusses Tocqueville's chapter in *Nuts and Bolts for the Social Sciences*, 5.

142

For Vendler's argument about friendship, see *Intimate Listeners*, 9–30.

143

"Thou hast made me . . ." Donne, Holy Sonnet 1.

"Me thoughts I heard . . ." Herbert, "The Collar."

Does Herbert ever call God a friend? He does, for example, in "Jordan" (2). He does not do so in "Love" (3) or in Vendler's other examples.

144

"Herbert suggests . . ." Vendler, *Intimate Listeners*, 21.

"Adult to adult . . ." *Intimate Listeners*, 16.

"Thy power and love . . ." Herbert, "The Temper" (1).

"The word 'love' . . ." *Intimate Listeners*, 15.

146

"If it is time . . ." Bersani, *Homos*, 103.

147

"Pure sweetness returns forever . . ." Vendler, *The Poetry of George Herbert*, 24.

(I prefer Strier: "The toughness makes for the sweetness." *Love Known*, 77n37.)

"Strength takes precedence . . ." *The Poetry of George Herbert*, 23.

"This is a voice . . ." *The Poetry of George Herbert*, 19.

Although I do not agree with some of what Vendler says, I have to admit that this chapter, "A Reading of *Vertue*," is one of the best pieces of criticism I have ever read.

148

"Do our works . . ." Quoted in Fish, *The Living Temple*, 135. Quotation altered.

162

"Embrac'd and open . . ." Donne, Holy Sonnet 18.

Bibliography

Balzac, Honoré de. *History of the Thirteen*. Herbert J. Hunt, trans. New York: Penguin, 1974.

———— *Lost Illusions*. Herbert J. Hunt, trans. New York: Penguin, 1971.

Bauman, Richard. "Speaking in the Light: The Role of the Quaker Minister." In *Explorations in the Ethnography of Speaking*. Bauman and Joel Scherzer, eds. Cambridge: Harvard University Press, 1989, 144–160.

Bersani, Leo. *Homos*. Cambridge: Harvard University Press, 1995.

Booth, Stephen. *Shakespeare's Sonnets, Edited with Analytic Commentary*. New Haven: Yale University Press, 1978.

Bunyan, John. *The Pilgrim's Progress*. Roger Sharrock, ed. New York: Penguin, 1965.

Calasso, Roberto. *The Marriage of Cadmus and Harmony*. Tim Parks, trans. New York: Vintage, 1994.

Canetti, Elias. *Crowds and Power*. Carol Stewart, trans. New York: Farrar, Straus, Giroux, 1984.

———— *The Torch in My Ear*. Joachim Neugroschel, trans. New York: Farrar, Straus, Giroux, 1982.

Carew, Thomas. *Poems 1640* [facsimile edition]. Menston: Scolar Press, 1969.

Charles, Amy. *A Life of George Herbert*. Ithaca: Cornell University Press, 1977.

Colie, Rosalie. *Paradoxia Epidemica: The Renaissance Tradition of Paradox*. Princeton: Princeton University Press, 1966.

Correll, Barbara. "Malleable Materials, Models of Power: Women in Erasmus's 'Marriage Group' and *Civility in Boys*." *English Literary History* 57:2 (1990), 241–262.

Donne, John. *The Poems of John Donne*. Herbert Grierson, ed. Oxford: Oxford University Press, 1968.

Drury, John. *Music at Midnight: The Life and Poetry of George Herbert*. Chicago: University of Chicago Press, 2013.

Elster, Jon. *Nuts and Bolts for the Social Sciences*. Cambridge: Cambridge University Press, 1989.

Empson, William. "George Herbert and Miss Tuve." *Kenyon Review* 12:4 (1950), 735–738.

Fish, Stanley. *The Living Temple: George Herbert and Catechizing*. Berkeley: University of California Press, 1978.

———*Self-Consuming Artifacts: The Experience of Seventeenth-Century Literature*. Berkeley: University of California Press, 1972.

Foote, Shelby. *The Civil War: A Narrative*. New York: Vintage, 1986.

Fox, George. *The Journal*. Nigel Smith, ed. London: Penguin, 1998.

Glimp, David. *Increase and Multiply: Governing Cultural Reproduction in Early Modern England*. Minneapolis: University of Minnesota Press, 2003.

Grossman, Allen. *The Sighted Singer: Two Works on Poetry for Readers and Writers*. With Mark Halliday. Baltimore: Johns Hopkins University Press, 1992.

Herbert, George. *The Latin Poetry of George Herbert: A Bilingual Edition*. Mark McCloskey and Paul R. Murphy, eds. and trans. Athens: Ohio University Press, 1965.

———*The Works of George Herbert*. F. E. Hutchinson, ed. Oxford: Clarendon Press, 1941.

Jonson, Ben. *The Works of Ben Jonson*. C. H. Herford, Percy Simpson, and Evelyn Simpson, eds. Oxford: Clarendon Press, 1970.

Kerrigan, William. "The Outside of Herbert's Poetry." *Psychiatry* 48:1 (1985), 68–82.

La Rochefoucauld, François de. *Maxims*. Leonard Tancock, trans. London: Penguin Books, 1959.

McCullough, David. *Truman*. New York: Simon and Schuster, 1992.

Memphis Jug Band. "Stealin', Stealin'." Memphis: Victor, 1928. Audio recording.

Milton, John. *Complete Poems and Major Prose*. Merritt Y. Hughes, ed. Indianapolis: Odyssey Press, 1957.

Mingus, Charles. *Beneath the Underdog: His World as*

Composed by Mingus. Nel King, ed. New York: Vintage, 1991.

Morris, Errol. *The Unknown Known*. 2013. Film.

Nunokawa, Jeff. *Tame Passions of Wilde: The Styles of Manageable Desire*. Princeton: Princeton University Press, 2003.

Oakeshott, Michael. "Introduction to *Leviathan*." In Thomas Hobbes, *Leviathan*. Oxford: Blackwell, 1946.

Rees, Richard. *Simone Weil: A Sketch for a Portrait*. Carbondale: Southern Illinois University Press, 1966.

Rivette, Jacques. *Don't Touch the Axe*. 2007. Film.

Schoenfeldt, Michael. *Bodies and Selves in Early Modern England: Physiology and Inwardness in Spenser, Shakespeare, Herbert, and Milton*. Cambridge: Cambridge University Press, 1999.

———*Prayer and Power: George Herbert and Renaissance Courtship*. Chicago: University of Chicago Press, 1991.

———"The Real Presence of Unstated Puns: Herbert's 'Love (III).'" In *Shakespeare Up Close: Reading Early Modern Texts*. Russ McDonald, Nicholas D. Nace, and Travis D. Williams, eds. London: Arden Shakespeare, 2012, 76–83.

Sedgwick, Eve Kosofsky. "How to Bring Your Kids Up Gay: The War on Effeminate Boys." In *Tendencies*. Durham: Duke University Press, 1993, 154–163.

Siegel, Jerry. *Tales of the Bizarro World*. New York: DC Comics, 2000.

Stein, Arnold. *George Herbert's Lyrics*. Baltimore: Johns Hopkins University Press, 1968.

Strier, Richard. *Love Known: Theology and Experience in George Herbert's Poetry*. Chicago: University of Chicago Press, 1983.

Swift, Jonathan. *The Writings of Jonathan Swift*. Robert A. Greenberg and William B. Piper, eds. New York: Norton, 1973.

Terada, Rei. *Looking Away: Phenomenality and Dissatisfaction, Kant to Adorno*. Cambridge: Harvard University Press, 2009.

Thorpe, James. "Reflections and Self-Reflections: *Outlandish Proverbs* as a Context for Herbert's Other Writings." In *Illustrious Evidence: Approaches to English Literature of the Early Seventeenth Century*. Earl Miner, ed. Berkeley: University of California Press, 1975.

Tocqueville, Alexis de. *Democracy in America*. Arthur Goldhammer, trans. New York: Library of America, 2004.

Tomkins, Silvan. *Shame and Its Sisters: A Silvan Tomkins Reader*. Eve Kosofsky Sedgwick and Adam Frank, eds. Durham: Duke University Press, 1995.

Trollope, Anthony. *The Last Chronicle of Barset*. Sophie Gilmartin, ed. New York: Penguin, 2002.

Tuve, Rosemond. "Herbert and Caritas." In *Essays: Spenser, Herbert, Milton*. Thomas P. Roche, ed. Princeton: Princeton University Press, 1970, 167–206.

———*A Reading of George Herbert*. Chicago: University of Chicago Press, 1952.

Vendler, Helen. *Invisible Listeners: Lyric Intimacy in Herbert, Whitman, and Ashbery*. Princeton: Princeton University Press, 2005.

———*The Poetry of George Herbert*. Cambridge: Harvard University Press, 1975.

Walton, Izaak. *The Compleat Angler*. John Buxton, ed. Oxford: Oxford University Press, 1982.

———"Life of Herbert." In *George Herbert: The Complete English Poems*. John Tobin, ed. New York: Penguin, 1991, 265–313.

Acknowledgments

Drafts of a few sections of this book originally
appeared in two essays: "Careless Talk," *English
Language Notes* 50:1 (2012); and "Tantali Umbra,"
in Hannah Whitaker's catalog *Peer to Peer* (London:
Mörel Books, 2015). Thanks to Julie Carr, Jon Cotner,
Andy Fitch, and Hannah Whitaker.

For twelve years I have been studying Herbert's poetry
in classes at Pomona College; my readings of the
poems have been influenced by my students, including
Leyla Akay, Andrew Carlson, Hunter Dukes, Nur Aliza
Lalji, Daniel Lipson, Adam Plunkett, Aaron Sharper, and
Sophie Zagerman.

I first tried out some of my ideas in correspondence
with Joshua Beckman, Anne Boyer, Michael Clune,
Ofélia del Corazon, Marcie Frank, Peter Gizzi, James
Kuzner, Ben Lerner, Trisha Low, Jacqueline Waters, and
Audra Wist. Their responses helped to shape this book.

Helpful questions and suggestions came from
audiences at the Poetic Research Bureau in Los
Angeles, the Claremont Colleges working group in Renaissance studies, the Drawing Center in New York, the

poetics group at the University of Chicago, and a seminar at the American Comparative Literature Association conference; my particular thanks go to J. K. Barret, Peter Coviello, David Diamond, Jeff Dolven, Lori Anne Ferrell, Joe Jeon, Elaine Kahn, Jordan Kirk, Andrew Maxwell, Julie Orlemanski, Chicu Reddy, Colleen Rosenfeld, Jen Scappettone, David Scher, Richard Strier, Daniel Tiffany, and Lynn Xu.

Thanks to Heidi Broadhead, Jeff Clark, Blyss Ervin, Ryo Yamaguchi, and the staff at Wave Books for their work on this book.

Finally, I gratefully acknowledge the contributions of a few correspondents whose names I can't publish.

ghosts and haunts
of Tennessee

Christopher K. Coleman

JOHN F. BLAIR
P U B L I S H E R
1406 Plaza Drive
Winston-Salem, North Carolina 27103
www.blairpub.com

Manufactured in the United States of America

Library of Congress Cataloging-in-Publication Data
Coleman, Christopher Kiernan, 1949-
  Ghosts and haunts of Tennessee / By Christopher K. Coleman.
    p.   cm.
  ISBN 978-0-89587-389-7 (alk. paper) — ISBN 978-0-89587-512-9 (ebook)
  1. Ghosts—Tennessee. 2. Haunted places—Tennessee. I. Title.
  BF1472.U6C6479 2011
  133.109768—dc22
                        2010046596

DESIGN AND COVER ILLUSTRATION BY DEBRA LONG HAMPTON

To my beloved wife, Veronica,
for her love and support now and in the past,
and to my daughter, Boo,
who chases the wolves back into the forest

Contents

"Though a good deal is too strange to be believed, nothing is too strange to have happened."

Thomas Hardy

Preface

Although graced by the hand of God with an abundance of natural wonders, Tennessee is also a land where strange tales of supernatural wonders abound. The mountains of East Tennessee have long had a reputation as a repository of supernatural lore. But truth be told, the entire state is full of such stories. From the haint tales of Appalachia to uncanny encounters in Middle Tennessee's limestone-lined river valley and highlands to the supernatural stirrings in the rich red-clay cotton fields of West Tennessee, the state boasts all manner of weird and uncanny phenomena: haunted houses, phantoms, witches, events that defy all reason, uncanny creatures that should not exist.

It has been over a decade since I first chronicled the ghostly tales of Tennessee—"the Dark and Bloody Ground" of Native American prophecy. Even then, I realized that the state's haunted heritage could not be encompassed in just one book. Far too many weird and wonderful things exist in Tennessee to be surveyed between the covers of a single tome. Nor should this volume be considered the final word on the subject.

Moreover, much has changed since I previously chronicled the Volunteer State's ghosts. For one thing, people are far more willing to discuss their local haunts with outsiders. When I first wrote, I encountered reluctance among some to relate what they knew—more so if they had actually experienced hauntings themselves. Some folks may be unwilling to discuss such matters for fear of public ridicule. Others may not want to talk out of religious scruples. Understandably, many deeply religious folks are hesitant to come forth with their experiences of the supernatural, lest those happenings somehow conflict with their faith. In such cases, accurate information about supernatural encounters can be hard to obtain.

Over that last decade, however, attitudes have changed. For one thing, interest in the paranormal has grown and become a matter of open discussion. Many people are now more willing to discuss what they know about particular hauntings. Moreover, many hotels, restaurants, historic sites, and other places that previously refused to discuss their ghosts for fear of frightening the public have come to realize that telling their stories is likely to attract visitors. Now, many such places openly admit they are hosts to ghosts.

The last decade has brought an explosion of interest in the paranormal and media coverage of it. Not just books and magazines but radio, film, the Internet, and especially cable television have served to heighten public awareness of the paranormal. My first book, in fact, was the basis for an excellent documentary, *The Ghosts of Music City*, produced by Greystone Productions.

Not just legitimate documentaries on the paranormal but a slew of so-called reality shows have explored just about every nook and cranny of the uncanny. Although some programs seriously investigate legitimate hauntings, one has to question the value of shows in which people with no knowledge of what they're doing run around with flashlights on their faces pretending to be scared for the camera, with nary a genuine ghost in sight. It must be concluded that there is very little reality to such reality shows.

The days when the dedicated academics from the Duke University

Parapsychology Laboratory were the lone wolves of serious paranormal investigation are long past. Today, just about every town has at least one group of homegrown ghost busters with the latest in high-tech gear.

Although I wish each and every such group well, my own approach to the subject is totally unscientific. I prefer to rely on eyewitness testimonies, folklore, local history, and sometimes just sheer hearsay. The truth is that, even with state-of-the-art electronic equipment, no one can really prove—or disprove—that ghosts exist. Do I believe that such things can be? Yes! I think the evidence for ghosts and other such phenomena is overwhelming. But sadly, evidence is not proof—at least not scientific proof. People who have encountered ghosts and other paranormal phenomena for the most part know what they have experienced. However, no amount of gadgetry will convince the scientific community—and it certainly will not sway professional "debunkers," who already have their minds made up.

Nowadays, some ghost tours "guarantee" their customers will see an apparition. The truth is that genuine paranormal activity is unpredictable. Persons may live or work for years in a spot that is genuinely haunted but never experience anything. Other persons who may not even believe in ghosts might encounter supernatural phenomena in the same place. Is one person right and the other wrong? The truth is often more elusive than the ghosts themselves.

For those fascinated with the supernatural but who are disinclined to traipse about musty old mansions and stumble through graveyards in the dark, *Ghosts and Haunts of Tennessee* can serve as an armchair tour of the state's haunted heritage. For those bold souls who crave firsthand frights, I have provided information on places in the book that are open to the public and even on some haunted places to spend the night.

All across the Volunteer State, readers can find a host of ghosts that may lack the star power of famous spirits such as the Bell Witch but have nevertheless given locals quite a fright. I have been told that my prior chronicling of Tennessee's haunted heritage has sometimes caused readers to leave their lights on long after they ceased reading for the night. If after enjoying this present collection you feel uncomfortable in the dark, then I'll know I've done my work right. By all means, leave a light burning to ward off the shadows, lest they start moving on their own. Good haunting!

Acknowledgments

I wish to thank the entire team at John F. Blair, Publisher, for their efforts in helping me bring this present work to press. I also wish to thank the many individuals and institutions who through the years have been helpful in gathering the material included in this book. Their assistance has allowed me to see, however dimly, through the veil of reality to the greater reality beyond.

I
Appalachian Apparitions

Haints of East Tennessee and the Smokies

Big Orange Hauntings

If Knoxville is famous for one thing, it is the Big Orange. For the uninitiated, Big Orange stands for the University of Tennessee—and the University of Tennessee stands for football. On select weekends in the autumn, Knoxville comes to a virtual standstill as fans fill Neyland Stadium to watch the Big Orange play—and win.

For some Big Orange fans, it may come as a surprise to learn that something other than sports goes on at UT. The University of Tennessee in fact possesses many outstanding academic departments and programs. Less publicized, however, is the fact that the UT campus is also possessed of something else—possessed of the spirits of the dead. The home of the Big Orange is haunted—quite haunted, in fact.

Now, in fairness, UT is far from unique in this regard. Many colleges and universities, especially those of long standing, have accumulated various and sundry ghosts. As Betsey Creekmore, an associate vice chancellor at the university, once observed, "A campus as old as ours . . . would not be much of a campus" if it didn't have ghosts. A campus ghost or three is as much a part of many schools' traditions as, well, football. Freshmen at UT are often instructed as to such hallowed traditions on—when else?—Halloween.

Far and away the best-known and most commonly encountered ghost on campus is Sophie. Sophronia Marks was born in Shelbyville, Tennessee, in 1817. After marrying Dr. Joseph Strong, a Knoxville physician, at age sixteen, she spent most of her married life in the city, raising twelve children before dying in 1867. It was not until 1915, however, that her son Benjamin gave the tract where the family home once stood to the university. He donated the property in his mother's memory with the proviso that a women's dormitory be built on the spot and that it should always have a flower garden in front—a tribute to the "June roses" residing within, no doubt. (A "June rose" was a young lady of quality who was graduating—more commonly from finishing school in those days.)

Sophronia Strong Hall was constructed during the early 1920s. By 1925, the first female students began to take up residence there. It was not long before the ghost nicknamed "Sophie" began to make her presence known.

When Strong Hall opened, each room featured a full-length mirror, so the young ladies could make sure they were properly groomed and attired. In the dormitory's early days, one resident was brushing her hair before the mirror when she saw Sophie standing behind her. When she turned, the ghost was gone. Ever since, on the anniversary of her birthday—February 17—Sophie appears in dormitory mirrors, all dressed in white.

Each new generation of students encounters her anew. Most commonly, Sophie makes her presence known by means of poltergeist-like pranks played on dorm residents. Girls planning to go out for a night on the town may suddenly find themselves locked in their rooms. Coeds needing to go to the toilet may discover that the bathroom stalls are all locked, even though empty. Cups and glasses move about on their own, as if by an unseen hand.

Such manifestations are commonly attributed to Sophie's desire to make sure the hall's residents behave like proper young ladies. Sophie is frequently in evidence when tempers flare between coeds; she has even been reported to have forcefully intervened to break up arguments.

Similarly, Sophie seems concerned about the residents' morals; some of her actions seem directed at female students maintaining their chastity.

While Sophie has been seen all over the building, one room in particular seems to warrant her special attention. The resident assistant's quarters on the fourth floor are commonly called "Sophie's Room," and whoever is posted there is referred to as "Sophie's roommate." It is rare that any resident assistant assigned to the room lasts long, so intense are the paranormal phenomena they are subjected to.

While meeting Sophie for the first time may be scary, most who have encountered her agree that she is more maternal than malevolent. Late at night, it is not uncommon for Strong Hall residents to see something float by in the corridors. Some describe it as a light and others as a diaphanous, glowing cloud, but everyone knows it is Sophie. As one alumna put it, "When you live in Strong Hall, you *will* see Sophie before the year is up."

Two blocks from Strong Hall on Cumberland Avenue sits Hoskins Library, the favorite haunt of another campus ghost. What her actual name in life may have been is unknown, but the ghost is generally referred to by students and staff as "Evening Primrose." The library's elevators have been known to travel from floor to floor without any riders, while books in the stacks are prone to removing themselves from the shelves and falling to the floor. At other times, people in the library hear the sound of footsteps behind them. Turning to find out who it may be, they see no one at all. Sometimes, library staff even report smelling the distinct aroma of fresh cornbread throughout the building, although nary a square of bread is in evidence anywhere. Presumably, Evening Primrose loved her cornbread.

The specter inhabiting Hoskins is definitely female. She is generally thought to be the ghost of a graduate student who, having been told by her faculty adviser to rewrite her massive doctoral dissertation for the hundredth time, camped out in the library in order to finish that last, worst hurdle on the road to graduation. Evening Primrose died in the stacks, her frail frame slumped over a pile of dusty tomes. Apparently, nobody paid attention to the deceased doctoral candidate, assuming her to be just another pallid grad student burning the midnight oil. So Evening Primrose wanders the corridors of Hoskins Library, forever doomed to be ABD (All But Dissertation).

Across the street from Hoskins rises an acclivity simply called "The Hill." Although a cluster of academic buildings encircles The Hill, the eminence itself is of most interest to ghost hunters. On the steps leading up The Hill and around the knoll itself, visitors may encounter the spirit of a young man dressed in garb that is strangely out of date. He wears a bowler hat and an old-fashioned removable celluloid collar.

This odd young man is commonly encountered pacing, head bowed, hands behind his back, as if deep in thought. The story goes that at some time in the 1930s, he was a student at UT. The earnest young scholar was in love with a girl. Thinking she felt the same way about him, he had intentions of making her his wife. It came as something of a shock, therefore, when she eloped with another man. Worse still, she ran off with a Yankee from Boston!

In a fit of despair, the young man took a revolver to his temple and blew his brains out one moonlit night on The Hill. Ever since, it is said, he paces the place of his demise. Mostly, he ignores passersby. Occasionally, however, he politely tips his bowler hat. It is then that visitors may see the gaping hole in his skull where his temple should be.

Another apparition is also said to inhabit The Hill. But this is an entity of a far more sinister sort. On rare occasion, visitors encounter a large, ominous-looking black canine. It has glowing red eyes, like two coals. Its long, sharp fangs drip a slimy goo as it bares its teeth at passing pedestrians.

The black dog that haunts The Hill is no stray pet but what is called a barghest—not like Lassie but more of a hound of the Baskervilles sort. This hound from hell howls a ferocious cry at all hours of the night, prompting calls to the campus police. But when a patrol car arrives, the beast has vanished into the dark.

Whence the creature came, no one knows, but it seems tied to The Hill, rather than any specific building nearby. Some have theorized that the spectral hound is the ghost of Bonita, a beloved family pet buried on the grounds of Tyson House, several blocks away. That seems unlikely, as the black hound of The Hill was never anybody's pet. It is commonly believed that just looking upon it will bring misfortune or even death.

The canine apparition may in fact date to before the creation of the university. Numerous prehistoric Native American graves are known to have existed on campus. Some are still untouched, but many have been desecrated over the years. It has been theorized that the beast could be a protective spirit summoned by some dead Indian shaman to watch over the skeletons of his ancestors and prevent them from being further disturbed. If that is indeed the case, then giving this dog a bone may not be the wisest thing to do.

Just down from The Hill and nestled next to Neyland Stadium is the Alumni Memorial Building, the abode of one of UT's more famous ghosts. To most on campus, the phantom of Alumni Memorial is known simply as Fannie.

According to tradition, Fannie was a beautiful young coed from the 1920s who had aspirations of movie stardom. The young lady's dreams seemed to be coming true when a moving picture was shot in Knoxville and Fannie landed a small role in it. The producers took notice and offered her a movie contract if she ever showed up in Hollywood. Sadly, before she could take the film moguls up on their offer, Fannie contracted tuberculosis and died.

Ever since Fannie's death, her unfulfilled acting ambitions have caused her spirit to haunt UT's theaters and auditoriums. Fannie's first phantom abode was the old Science Hall, which once held an auditorium used to stage plays in the 1920s and 1930s. Fannie had performed in various productions there in life, so it was understandable that her shade should continue to haunt its footlights.

Alas, in 1967, Science Hall, a landmark since 1894, was torn down to make way for campus improvements, and Fannie was left homeless. But soon after the theater in Science Hall was razed, students and staff in the Alumni Memorial Building began to report uncanny occurrences in that building's theater.

Campus productions are frequently rehearsed in Alumni Memorial's theater today. It is at such times that Fannie's presence is most in evidence. The pallid apparition is strongly attracted to the roar of greasepaint and the smell of the crowd (as it were). UT's thespians have become used to Fannie's occasional antics. She haunts the wings like some eager understudy hoping for the leading lady to *really* break a leg. Being a theater ghost, after all, is a role to die for.

The campus home of the Big Orange has many other apparitions, to be sure. A Civil War battle fought virtually on the campus may account for several sightings of ghosts in Yankee uniforms, for example. And Reese Hall, the General Counseling Center, and Tyson Hall all claim resident specters. Still, for sheer devotion to her avocation, none of them can beat UT's Fannie.

Chapter 2

Gatlinburg Ghosts

Time was, Gatlinburg was a sleepy little village far removed from big-city trappings. Today, as the center of Great Smoky Mountains tourism, this scenic Appalachian community has plenty of hustle and bustle. It also has plenty of ghosts.

Visitors by the hundreds of thousands descend on the area every year to play. With the Great Smoky Mountains National Park just around the corner and many other scenic wonders nearby, they hang their hats at one or anther hotel, motel, or resort in Gatlinburg. In fact, some become so attached to the place that they stay around forever.

The Greenbrier Restaurant is one such place where folks like to hang out. Sitting astride a winding mountain road just outside downtown Gatlinburg, the Greenbrier has been a popular haunt for decades. Locals wanting slow-cooked prime rib or a good Smoky Mountains strip steak that's been marinated for days know where to go—the cozy log lodge that houses the Greenbrier. Little wonder that regulars often linger over dinner and drinks until closing time.

And then there is Lydia. Before the Greenbrier was a restaurant, it was an inn—the Greenbrier Lodge—where a raven-haired lady named Lydia lived. Lydia was young and deeply in love. In due course, she became engaged to a young man from town. On her wedding day, Lydia dressed in a long white gown and went into town to meet her lover at the church. She stood at the altar waiting for her fiancé—and she waited, and she waited. The appointed time came and passed, and still no beau.

Finally, Lydia returned to the Greenbrier Lodge unmarried, brokenhearted, and alone. She climbed the stairs but never made it to her room. On the second-floor landing, Lydia tossed a rope around a stout wooden beam and, still clad in her nuptial gown, hanged herself. Needless to say, she is still hanging around to this day.

A caretaker who lived in the lodge some years back was constantly awakened in the middle of the night by Lydia's pitiful cries. Night after night, he heard her moaning, "Mark my grave, mark my grave!" Finally, the caretaker had enough. Having grown up in Gatlinburg, he knew exactly where Lydia lay buried. So, one moonlit night, he made his way down the mountainside and put up a marker over Lydia's grave. From that night on, the caretaker slept undisturbed.

When the Hadden family bought the Greenbrier in the early 1980s, locals told them about Lydia. At first, they dismissed her story as just a typical tale that came with an old house. But as the Haddens renovated the log building and transformed it into the scenic restaurant that welcomes guests today, each member of the family became aware of Lydia's presence.

Becky Hadden, who manages the lounge at the Greenbrier, tells of the time her young son called out, "Daddy! Dad!" When his father turned around to see what was disturbing the preschooler, the boy exclaimed, "A girl was there, but now she's gone!" The restaurant was closed at the time, and no one was present but staff. Becky is convinced her son saw Lydia. Nor was he the only one. Oftentimes, Lydia is seen on the second-floor landing where she died. Patrons have witnessed her small, sad figure wandering the lodge. Others have felt a chilling presence without actually seeing her.

Like Lydia, many of Gatlinburg's other ghosts seem to have been lodgers in the city's many inns and hotels. Far and away the most active hostelry in terms of ghosts is the Garden Plaza Hotel. Formerly known as the Holiday Inn Sunspree, the Garden Plaza is one of the more venerable resort hotels in Gatlinburg. For decades, this four-hundred-room hotel has accumulated specters and restless spirits.

The Garden Plaza actually consists of two buildings—a main structure referred to as "the Holidome" and an addition called "the Tower." Both have unique resident spooks.

The oldest phantom in the hotel is named Alvin. Alvin was a long-time employee who worked as a cook from the time the resort opened. In recognition of Alvin's many years of service, the original owners gave him a brand-new boat as a birthday present. Tragically, the first time Alvin took his boat onto the lake, it sank. Unable to swim, he drowned.

Ever since then, employees in the hotel's two kitchens have had to share their workspace with Alvin's ghost. In the early-morning hours, cooks have reported an unseen entity that whispers their names. At other times, dishes fly across the kitchen and break against the wall. The faucets also turn on and off by themselves. Old Alvin is apparently fond of playing pranks on his fellow cooks.

Room 413 has a reputation as the most haunted room in the Holidome. Back in the late 1970s, two young women were murdered by a stranger they'd picked up in a bar. The stranger drowned one girl in the bathtub. He strangled the other, then dragged her body onto the roof, where he dumped it. Ever since then, members of the housekeeping staff have had chilling encounters while cleaning Room 413. Maids often report noises coming from the bathroom. Objects in the room mysteriously move from one place to another.

Several more ghosts are known to abide in the Tower. Room 471, for example, was the scene of a suicide in the late 1990s. A businessman, upset over personal disappointments, killed himself with a .357 Magnum. Allegedly, he left a $3.57 tip on the night table. Various people have seen his shadow facing the pool at night. Others have encountered him in his room.

The seventh floor of the Tower was the scene of a mass murder when a crazed scoutmaster slaughtered several members of his Boy Scout troop. In later years, an employee on the seventh floor when all the rooms were vacant heard running feet and bloodcurdling screams. Alarmed, the worker investigated but found nothing. Someone on the seventh floor is not a happy trooper.

For scenic haunts, it is hard to beat the Edgewater Hotel along the banks of the Little Pigeon River. The bridged main entrance to the eight-story hotel looks like a medieval drawbridge over a moat. The haint here was the victim of a domestic tragedy.

In 1972, a husband and wife were staying in the Edgewater with their seven-year-old daughter. The girl fell off their room's balcony and plunged to her death in the rocky river below. At first, police thought it was just a tragic accident. But upon further investigation, they determined that the father was responsible for the girl's death. The couple fled, only to have their car flip over while rounding a curve. They, too, plunged down a steep cliff into the cold waters of the Little Pigeon River and died.

Every year on the anniversary of her death, the little girl stands in the mountain stream, silently pointing up to the balcony from which she was thrown. Local residents have become familiar with her annual visitation, but tourists continue to be disturbed by the sight of her pallid, pathetic ghost.

In your haste while rushing from one attraction to another, you may scarcely notice Gatlinburg's ghostly goings-on. Local folks are far more aware of them. If you are curious, Gatlinburg's citizens are more than willing to direct you to other local haunts—provided you don't mind a serious scare or three.

Greenbrier Restaurant
370 Newman Road
Gatlinburg, TN 37738
(423) 436-6318
www.greenbrierrestaurant.com

Edgewater Hotel
402 River Road
Gatlinburg, TN 37738
(866) 602-2618
www.edgewater-hotel.com

CHAPTER 3

Round About Midnight
The Haunting of the
Baker-Peters Jazz Club

Along the Kingston Pike in Knoxville sits the Baker-Peters Jazz Club. The trendy nightclub is housed in an old building where most any night patrons can enjoy hot jazz while sipping cool drinks. At no additional charge, they are often served an extra treat: a spirited encounter with the ghosts of the building's original owners.

The first hint that something is different at Baker-Peters is the chap in a photograph hanging behind the hostess station right where guests enter the club. A close inspection reveals it to be a picture of the building's windows with what looks like a face—the face of a resident ghost—peering from one of them.

Employees and patrons alike have a storehouse of tales of their experiences with the nightclub's phantom residents. Although general manager Ann Brown has never actually witnessed any specter with her own eyes, she has at various times seen the lights go off and on with no one near the switches and heard glasses crash to the floor for no apparent reason. Others claim to have heard voices whispering and seen objects move all by themselves. At other times, ghostly footsteps have been heard inside the club. There is even one account of an amber-colored light moving from room to room, as if an old-fashioned whale-oil lantern was traveling about the house.

In the old days before the jazz club, a chandelier graced the dining room. On one occasion, all the candleholders attached to the chandelier were found twisted upside down—a rather acrobatic feat for anyone trying to pull a prank.

How the club came to be haunted goes back almost a century and a half to when the building was the home of Dr. James H. Baker. When the house was built in 1840, it was located in the middle of rich farmland on the western edge of Knox County. Dr. Baker had a successful medical practice and was a well-respected member of the community until the Civil War broke out. East Tennessee was largely pro-Union in its sympathies, but Dr. Baker and his family were staunch supporters of the Confederacy.

At first, all went well for Dr. Baker, as the Rebels remained in control of East Tennessee until late in the war. In the waning days of the Late Unpleasantness, however, the Federals made a determined effort to liberate the area from the secessionists. Not surprisingly, being both a doctor and a man sympathetic to the cause, Baker opened his home to the retreating Confederates and turned it into a makeshift field hospital.

The local postmaster, William Hall, informed the Yankees that the Baker home was being used as a safe house for Rebels. In areas of divided loyalties such as Tennessee, the Civil War was anything but civil. Unionists and secessionists often gave no quarter when they fought. Descending on the Baker home in force, Yankee troops broke down the front door and demanded that the doctor turn over any Rebels he was harboring. He refused. Retreating upstairs, he barricaded himself in his bedroom. The Federals shot through the door, killing Dr. Baker.

His death was not the end of the story, however. His son, Abner, was serving with the Confederate army at the time the murder occurred. When young Abner returned home soon after the end of hostilities and learned of his father's betrayal by a neighbor, he vowed revenge. The details of what happened next are murky. What is known is that Abner killed the postmaster and then was killed in turn by a mob made up of Hall's friends.

Ever since that terrible vendetta played out to its bloody end, the restless ghosts of Abner Baker and his father have resided in the old family home. Father and son refuse to give up the place where they lived and died.

One regular patron described being inside Baker-Peters as feeling like he was trespassing—as if he was in someone else's home uninvited. Of course, when the music is playing and drinks are flowing and restaurant customers are dining on fine food, the convivial atmosphere overcomes any discomfort patrons or staff may otherwise feel. Rather, it is during the quiet hours of late night and early morning when visitors are likely to pick up on the strangely dolorous mood.

Neither Dr. Baker nor Abner has actually materialized before employees or customers, save for that eerie face in the window. But their presence is felt nonetheless. Aside from occasional mischievous pranks, neither ghost has ever done any harm to the jazz club or those visiting.

It is a subject for speculation as to what the ghosts' attitude is toward modern-day visitors to their home. Despite their turbulent lives and the violent ends that caused them to remain tied to the earthly plane, father and son may at times appreciate the festive atmosphere that the nightclub and restaurant bring to a place so otherwise full of painful memories.

So, those who go to the Baker-Peters Jazz Club and see the phantom photo or inspect the door with the bullet hole still in evidence might raise a toast to the unseen hosts still dwelling in the shadows. Perhaps in so honoring them, visitors may lighten their burden.

At least one thing is sure: the Baker-Peters Jazz Club is Dr. Baker's and Abner's favorite haunt, just as it is for many living members of Knoxville's citizenry.

> **Baker-Peters Jazz Club**
> **9000 Kingston Pike**
> **Knoxville, TN 37923**
> **(865) 690-8110**
> **www.bakerpetersjazzclub.com**

CHAPTER 4

The Read House Haunting

The elegant, ten-story Read House Hotel has been described as "Chattanooga's only first-class historic hotel." While other local hoteliers might dispute that claim, no one doubts the Read House's fame as the city's premier *haunted* hotel.

Soaring up in the heart of downtown Chattanooga, the Read House stands in elegant distinction thanks to its brick and terra-cotta finish. In this richly appointed Georgian-style hotel, the luxury of yesteryear merges with all the conveniences of modern life. Presently owned by the Sheraton Hotel chain, the hotel features every amenity guests could want. A few rooms even come with resident spooks at no additional charge.

The present building at 827 Broad Street dates to 1926, but its roots—and likely most of its spectral guests—go back to before the Civil War. The Crutchfield House, the first hostelry on the site, was constructed in 1847. The Crutchfield family built it on the promise that the new railroad coming through Chattanooga would construct a train station nearby. In those days, trains were the fastest mode of transportation known to man. But it still could take travelers several days to reach their destinations, so hotels were needed near rail lines to provide food and lodging for weary passengers.

By all accounts, the Crutchfield House provided first-rate accommodations for its time. Travelers enjoyed the luxury of sleeping only two to a bed. Bedbugs and lice were minor inconveniences. And the rats and mice roaming the halls at night were hardly a problem. All in all, the Crutchfield was as swanky a place as rail travelers could find in those days.

Just before the Civil War, Jefferson Davis was returning home to Mississippi after resigning from the United States Senate when he made an impromptu speech to fellow secessionists in the lobby of the Crutchfield House. The owner's brother, William Crutchfield, was a staunch Unionist. Learning of Davis's treasonous meeting, he and his friends determined to break it up. Tempers flared in the lobby of the Crutchfield. Harsh words passed between William Crutchfield and Jeff Davis. Not only was a duel between the two imminent, a full-scale battle among their followers threatened to erupt. Fortunately, William's brother Thomas, a secessionist, separated the two men and whisked his brother out of the hotel, barely preventing a gunfight.

As it turned out, the bloodletting was only postponed, not prevented, and not just between the North and the South but also within Tennessee. Folks all across the Volunteer State began choosing sides. William Crutchfield wore the blue, eventually serving as a major in Wilder's Brigade with the Army of the Cumberland. Other members of the Crutchfield clan opted to wear the gray.

After being under Confederate control in the early days of the war, Chattanooga fell into Federal hands by the spring of 1863. The Crutchfield House was one of the first buildings occupied by the bluecoats. Initially used to billet officers, the hotel was converted into a hospital as battle casualties mounted. Within its brick walls, men's limbs were amputated by the hundreds, often without anything to kill the pain. Wounded men suffered and died there in large numbers.

The Crutchfield House survived the siege of Chattanooga and the war, only to burn down in an accidental fire in 1867. The location remained an excellent spot for a hotel, however. In 1871, Dr. John T. Read and his son Samuel decided to build a bigger and better hostelry where the Crutchfield once stood. The Read House quickly acquired a reputation for luxury and excellence. In the ensuing decades, not only Chattanooga's elite but the rich and famous from across the nation—President McKinley among them—chose to stay there.

By the Roaring Twenties, the original Read House was showing its age. In 1926, it was rebuilt from the ground up. A year later, a new and even grander Read House opened to the public. Over the course of the twentieth century, the hotel played host to presidents, foreign dignitaries, movie stars, and even a notorious gangster or two.

In 2004, during the latest renovations, modern amenities were added while all the elegance of the old hotel was preserved. In the Silver Ballroom, for example, contractors were about to tear out what looked like old iron sconces when one of the veterans of the staff, a bellman named Howard Johnson, told them to simply polish them. Those heavy old candleholders turned out to be solid silver.

Another thing the Read House has preserved is its haunted heritage. While local legend swirls around one particular room, the venerable hotel abounds with the spirits of the dead, if accounts of employees and guests are correct. Throughout the hotel, televisions have been known to go on and off in vacant rooms in the middle of the night. From time to time, employees hear the sound of luggage racks rolling down the hallways, only to turn around and find no one there.

Far and away the greatest number of supernatural encounters has come from the third floor and from one room in particular—Room 311. Unless someone requests a specific room, lodgings are normally assigned at random, so many guests given Room 311 over the years were totally unaware of its spooky reputation.

As a longtime employee, Howard Johnson has seen it all during his years at the Read House. For example, a female guest once came down to the lobby in the middle of the night dressed only in her robe. She had been in Room 311 and vacated it abruptly, terrified out of her mind. The guest demanded Johnson go upstairs, pack her bags, and bring them down. She told him she refused to return to her room while "that lady is sitting in the corner." Apparently, she awakened in the night to see a female ghost staring at her.

Another employee related a similar experience in 1995. A wealthy patron came to Chattanooga on his private jet one night. After being picked up by one of the Read House staff, he checked into Room 311. Later that same night, the man came off the elevator dressed only in boxer shorts and a T-shirt, a panicked look on his face. He had the staff gather his belongings and chauffer him to another hotel. As he was checking into the new accommodations, he related how he had been chased out of the room by a female phantom. The lady ghost apparently took offense at his cigar smoke.

Howard Johnson has never actually seen the ghost in 311, but other employees have. The ghost is invariably described as a female wearing a long, white, wispy gown. Some room-service workers flat out refuse to deliver to the third floor because of her. On occasion, guests riding the elevator find that it makes an unexpected stop at the third floor. As the doors open, a chill floods the elevator. Although no one gets on, the lady in white is occasionally visible in the hallway.

Not everyone staying in Room 311 has been spooked out of their wits. It may even be that the ghost was once intimidated by an occupant of the room. Legendary gangster Al Capone was kept there during his criminal trial in the 1930s. Although the ghost reputedly dislikes men who smoke, no serious disturbances were reported during his stay in Room 311, despite Capone's well-known love of cigars. Up until the renovations in 2004, the room retained the iron bars on the windows installed during Capone's stay.

Such is its reputation that, in recent years, some guests at the Read House have sought out Room 311 to stay in—or at least to visit. On a number of occasions, these amateur ghost hunters have had interesting encounters. A few even claim to have captured paranormal phenomena on film.

In one case, a guest staying on an upper floor prevailed on the bartender in the lounge to let him visit the room. Room 311 was vacant at the time, so the hotel, always willing to accommodate its guests, gave him a key.

At the stroke of midnight, he entered. To his surprise, he found the room disheveled. The furniture was disturbed. Some pieces were even knocked over. The bedsheets were tied in a knot. To top it all off, the lights wouldn't work. The visitor saw no lady in white but did get an overwhelming sense of something angry and evil lurking in a dark corner of the room. Not waiting for the entity to act, the man hightailed it out of there.

When returning the key to the front desk, the guest told how some-one had already been in 311 and torn the place up—that it was not his doing. The front-desk and lobby personnel greeted his declaration with stunned silence. Only a short while before the man went up to 311, a cleaning crew had made sure the room was in good order for the visitor. When the crew left, it was neat and tidy for the guest's midnight tour.

Guests staying in this psychic ground zero have heard weird noises in Room 311. Some have described them as sounding like a woman moaning. One guest felt a hot spot in the room even though the air conditioning was turned on full blast. When witnesses catch sight of the ghost in the hallways, she is always described as wearing a white gown or dress.

On rare occasions, guests staying in 311 have been awakened by the sound of the shower. Venturing into the bathroom, they see the silhouette of a young woman behind the curtain. As they watch, the figure disappears into thin air.

Pinning down the exact cause of the haunting of Room 311 has proven difficult. One persistent legend says that the female ghost was a prostitute murdered by a soldier during the Late Unpleasantness. Some versions have him as a Rebel soldier, while others claim he was a Yankee.

Some debunkers have tried to discredit the haunting on the grounds that the hotel did not exist in the 1860s. While it is true that the current structure dates to the 1920s, there are numerous docu-mented cases of ghosts continuing to occupy the same physical space long after the original building they haunted was demolished and re-placed. The property where the Read House stands has been the site of hotels since the Crutchfield House in 1847, so a Civil War–era haunting is not impossible.

In fact, staff members have on occasion spotted the specter of a Confederate soldier. He has been seen pacing back and forth on the mezzanine level just above the main lobby. During the siege of Chattanooga, wounded soldiers certainly suffered within the walls of the Crutchfield. That the spirit of one of those who died here may linger remains a possibility. At least a few guests have spied a lady in white sitting in a chair on the mezzanine as well. How these two ghosts relate to the haunting in 311 is unknown, however.

An alternate explanation exists as to who the lady haunting 311 may be. On the face of it, this seems more based in fact than the Civil War story. Those versed in Chattanooga lore can put not only a name to the ghost but a year to her demise as well. According to this version, the ghost in white in Room 311 is a young woman by the name of Annalisa Netherly, who lost her head over love in 1932.

One version of Annalisa's tale has it that she was spurned by her married lover. Having been seduced and abandoned, she committed suicide in the room. Another version relates how Annalisa's jealous husband—a chain smoker fond of big, stinky cigars—suspected her of infidelity and cut off her head while she was taking a bath. A maid found her naked, headless corpse in the bloody tub. This latter version at least explains why the lady in white has a dislike for both men and cigars.

The story of Annalisa's death in 311 is often cited as documented fact. For that reason, many prefer it over the Civil War story as an explanation for the haunting. However, in recent years, researchers have combed the local archives and failed to locate any record of poor Annalisa, alive or dead, with or without her head.

Those attracted to haunted hotels will find far more in store for them at the Read House than just the stories connected to Room 311. For example, some visitors to the hotel in April 2009 caught a glimpse of two dark, humanlike figures in the mirrors in the opulent Silver Ballroom. Other than the witnesses themselves, no other persons were in the room at the time. At other times, people going down darkened hallways late at night have seen pairs of tiny crimson-colored eyes staring back at them from the depths of the darkness. On the fourth floor, guests have occasionally spotted a woman in 1800s costume roaming the hallways.

Prior to the last major renovation, a pair of ladies on a business trip booked rooms on the fifth floor. Shortly after four o'clock in the morning, one of them was awakened by what she thought was a door slamming. Startled, she sat up but could see nothing.

Just as she was falling back to sleep, she felt her mattress deepen on one side, as if a large person had sat on the edge. Initially, she thought it was just her imagination working overtime in the dark room. The she felt, but could not see, a large, heavy arm pressing against her shoulders. Terrified, she jumped out of bed and went to wake her associate. But even with the lights on, they could see no one else in the room. Badly rattled by the unexpected encounter, the two hurriedly dressed, packed, and went downstairs to check out of their rooms.

While awaiting transportation, they had breakfast in the restaurant and decided to wash it down with alcohol. When the waitress asked why they wanted vodka at six in the morning, they told her their tale of terror on the fifth floor. The waitress was only mildly surprised. "Usually, it's Room 311," she said. "All the construction has probably got them on the move again." It was then that the ladies learned of the Read House's haunted heritage.

Ghost hunters have captured some unusual photographs in and around the Read House in recent years. Other electronic devices have also documented paranormal phenomena, leading many to conclude that there is indeed a high degree of psychic activity in the hotel.

Even without such evidence, however, the abundance of eyewitness testimony over the years makes it clear that, at no additional cost, those who book a stay at the Read House may well get a room with a boo!

CHAPTER 5

East Tennessee Supernatural University

Nestled deep in the heart of Appalachia, East Tennessee State University may not enjoy quite the fame of its sister school in Knoxville. But in one respect, ETSU exceeds the University of Tennessee—in the sheer number of hauntings per square yard. Why this should be is a mystery—one of many that abound at the school's scenic campus.

Since 1911, ETSU has been educating Appalachia's sons and daughters, spreading learning and culture throughout ruggedly beautiful East Tennessee. Founded as a normal school to train teachers, it has grown in size even as its mission has expanded to encompass other vocations. One institution unique to ETSU, for example, is the Center for Appalachian Studies and Services, a repository and research facility devoted to the study of the cultural heritage of the Southern mountains. So not only does the university educate the people of the region, it learns from them as well.

Over the years, both professors and students have researched and documented the "haint" lore peculiar to East Tennessee. Truth be told, they don't even have to leave campus to hear about ghosts and hauntings. So thick is its supernatural atmosphere that East Tennessee State has earned the epithet of "the South's most haunted college campus."

Although many buildings on campus have resident spooks that have received more press, the most psychically active structure may be Lucille Clement Hall. Clement Hall—known to many at ETSU simply as "Luci"—is one of the largest dormitories on campus. Luci's many paranormal events have generally been attributed to two entities. However, at least one previous resident claimed that "many different ghosts and spirits live in the dorm."

Opened in 1967 as a women's dorm, the five-story residence has undergone renovations in recent years and is now coed. One thing hasn't changed, though: the spectral antics of Marble Boy and Sink Girl. While the ghosts' nicknames make them sound like campy comic-book heroes, the two are real enough. They have been familiar presences in Luci for generations.

Some years back, the story goes, a janitor's son was playing on the roof with his marbles. Left alone, the boy came too close to the edge and plunged to his death. Alternately, some say the boy fell down the elevator shaft or stairwell while playing with his marbles.

Ever since, students have heard what sounds like marbles rolling above their rooms. Male residents on the second floor frequently hear Marble Boy losing his marbles through the ceiling above them and assume it is coming from the third floor. "Marble Boy is real," one freshman said. "It sounded like hell." The girls on the third floor, however, have heard the same strange sounds emanating from the ceiling above them.

Not everyone who has dwelt in Clement is in agreement that Marble Boy is real. One female who lived there for three years asserted that the "marble noises" were simply people walking around the upper floors, and that "the building is falling apart."

While it is true that at one point Clement Hall showed its age, Luci's physique has undergone reconstructive surgery in recent years. Nevertheless, residents continue to report spooky goings-on. For one thing, even residents of the top floor—the fifth—report hearing the sound of falling marbles coming from above their heads, where there are neither rooms nor hallways. Other denizens of the dorm have reported what looked like a small child's handprints on the walls of the stairwell. If Marble Boy isn't real, then quite a number of present and former students have apparently lost their marbles.

Another common phenomenon in Clement is that of bathroom faucets turning themselves on. While some dismiss this as faulty plumbing, more than a few students who have returned to their rooms to find them flooded have inspected their sinks and discovered no burst pipes, faulty valves, or other such failures. Faucets have been turned on full blast in locked rooms, with no access other than by the residents whose personal property has just been ruined by the flooding. When students confront such incidents in Clement, they know Sink Girl has paid them a spectral visit.

Despite such campus traditions, it is far from certain that Marble Boy and Sink Girl are in fact distinct entities. One student referred to the ghostly presence in Clement simply as "Lucy." Another reported waking up and seeing a specter standing over her slumbering roommate's bed. The girl was certain the door was locked. In a panic, she woke her roommate. The coed looked up sleepily and said, "Go back to sleep. It's just Lucy, you know that."

Other paranormal phenomena abound in Clement Hall as well. Elevators stop at floors whose buttons no one has pushed. When the doors open, passengers feel a gust of frigid air, even in summertime. A student staying in Clement for band camp one summer found the stairwell ice-cold, despite temperatures in the high nineties. During the same summer session, students walking down the stairs at times felt something brush against them, as if an invisible presence were passing them. A girl at band camp awoke one night to see a woman in a dress standing between her bed and her roommate's. The only other person with access to the room was their chaperon.

During the regular school year, students throughout the dorm hear doors slamming when no one is present. Furniture rearranges itself. Many students complain that their rooms are chronically cold no matter how many times the maintenance staff works on the furnace. In 2007, one student reported that her lighted cosmetic mirror kept being turned off and on by a ghost. She also heard weird rapping sounds that she attributed to spectral activity. On another occasion, a coed had a plate of lasagna on her bed, ready to eat, when it suddenly flipped upside down and crashed to the floor. Still other residents report objects in their room moving about on their own.

Although some may question the dorm legends regarding Marble Boy, Sink Girl, and Lucy, there is no doubt about Lucille Clement Hall's intense paranormal presence.

Of all the resident spooks known to inhabit ETSU, one of the most famous is certainly Alice. According to campus tradition, Alice was the beautiful daughter of George L. Carter, a wealthy local businessman. Carter was an influential force behind establishing the college in Johnson City in the early 1900s, donating the original 120 acres for the campus to the state. According to legend, he doted on his only daughter, who as a result grew up to be a headstrong young girl.

As she matured from a child into a woman, Alice caught the eye of a young man. They fell deeply in love and made plans to marry. When they approached Alice's father, however, they met with a sharp rebuff. George Carter deemed Alice's beau an unsuitable match for his daughter. He vowed he would never allow her to marry a poor boy. George Carter had greater plans for his only daughter.

Not used to being denied, and desperately in love with her penniless fiancé, Alice became deeply depressed. If she could not live with her one true love, then she did not wish to live at all. One dark night, Alice ended it all by taking a dose of rat poison.

George Carter was grief stricken over his daughter's death. That is believed to be why he had a stained-glass portrait of her made. The twelve-by-eighteen-inch portrait, showing Alice with long golden hair, was installed in the tile-roofed white stucco mansion where he and his wife lived until his death in 1936. On his passing, ETSU purchased the Carter home and property, which lay adjacent to the campus. The university administration renamed the mansion Cooper Hall and turned it into a women's dormitory.

Soon after the first female students moved in, reports began to surface that the building was haunted. Senior-class members quickly dubbed their resident revenant "the Screaming Ghost." A disembodied female voice could be heard singing in the halls. That singing often turned into an unearthly screaming that reverberated through the night. Many of the girls complained of a feeling of being watched by unseen eyes. Students' personal effects mysteriously disappeared, only to reappear elsewhere in the building.

Both students and staff noticed that the strange goings-on most often occurred near the stained-glass portrait of the long-haired child. That was perhaps how the story of Alice first became current on campus. For years, the legend of Alice was accepted without question to explain Cooper Hall's hauntings. However, Ray Stahl, a local historian and the director of public relations for ETSU from 1968 until 1977, investigated the history of both Cooper Hall and the Carter family. He found out that the Carters did indeed have a child, but its name was not Alice. It was James!

Whether out of concern over paranormal infestation or simply a desire to upgrade the senior women's housing, the old mansion ceased to be a dormitory. Cooper Hall was converted into administrative office space and renamed Cooper Annex. The college's FM radio station was wedged into the attic. The ghost—whether James or Alice or someone else—remained active and in fact became something of a mascot for the station.

In 1984, Cooper Annex was torn down. The reason given was that the old building needed such extensive repairs that the cost simply couldn't be justified. However, many on campus at the time believed the real reason was that both students and staff were reluctant to live or work in the old spook house. The stained-glass portrait believed to be the focus of all the haunting mysteriously disappeared shortly before Cooper Annex was bulldozed.

The destruction of the old Carter mansion ought to have been the end of the Screaming Ghost, but it wasn't. Apparently, Alice—fond of singing (and screaming) at odd hours—moved with the radio station, taking up residence in Warf-Pickel Hall. Unlike the maintenance crews that used to clean Cooper Hall at night, the station's staff proved tolerant of Alice's pranks and welcomed the ghost to their new abode. At the threshold of the broadcasting suite, staff members posted this notice: "You can be our ghost anytime."

Some ghosts howl, scream, or sing. But the ghosts that haunt old libraries are of a more mellow sort. The phantom that inhabits Roy S. Nicks Hall—sometimes known as "the Old Sherrod Library"—is of the latter kind.

The Old Sherrod Library was built in 1931. Its neoclassical lines formed a suitably serious sanctuary for aspiring scholars for generations. The structure served as ETSU's main library until 1999, when a new and greatly enlarged Charles E. Sherrod Library was built elsewhere on campus.

In most universities, the bulk of the main library's collection is housed in the stacks. As a rule, they are dimly lit affairs, their old metal bookshelves crammed close together. The stacks are kept chilly summer and winter; some have described the atmosphere as deathly cold. Windowless and with rows of books that seem to go on in the dark labyrinth forever, the stacks are a place where it is easy to lose track of time, where one's senses are strangely altered. The stacks of the Old Sherrod Library were no exception.

Over the years, more than one earnest young scholar became creeped out while doing research in the stacks. Most often, they experienced an uneasy feeling that invisible eyes were watching them. On occasion, students would be alone in the lower levels and hear the sound of footsteps padding behind them. Turning suddenly, they would find no one there.

On a number of occasions, researchers pulled dusty old tomes from the shelves, intending to check them out once they found all the books they needed, only to return to where they had laid the books to find them gone. On searching, the scholars would find their books already reshelved in their proper places, even though no one else was down there with them.

One alum who did a stint of work-study in the Old Sherrod Library claimed to have seen the phantom that haunted the old structure. At that time, a spiral staircase connected the different levels of the stacks. During a period when most students were on break for the holidays, the alum witnessed an apparition descending the rickety staircase. Only the upper portion of the ghost was materialized, but it was distinct enough for the witness to see its prune-faced scowl, granny glasses, and hair done up in an old-fashioned bun. The antique clothing and severe look gave the alum the distinct impression that the ghost had once been a college librarian—the type fond of shushing students and giving them dirty looks if they appeared to be enjoying themselves.

The consensus on campus was that the spirit haunting the Old Sherrod Library was indeed the ghost of a former librarian who toiled too long among the tomes of quaint and curious lore. Even when the woman retired, she volunteered to help out a few days a week. Her particular concern, it was said, was that "her" books be reshelved in their proper order. One day a score or more years back, she had a massive coronary and died in a lower level of the stacks. Her spirit apparently never left.

Another alum, reading an account of Nicks Hall's haunting, expressed surprise that it was ever a library. He knew it as "the Old College of Medicine" building. The alum asserted that the building's lower levels were haunted because that was where the medical school's cadavers were once kept. It was his understanding that the spirits of the restless dead remained long after the medical school moved. If this is true, then Nicks Hall may indeed house more than one ghost within its walls.

After the Old Sherrod Library closed in 1999, the building lay vacant for several years. Then, in 2005, after extensive renovation, it reopened as Roy S. Nicks Hall. The building now houses the nursing school, the Center for Appalachian Studies and Services, the university's IT department, and various administrative functionaries. It is unknown if the resident ghost of the Old Sherrod Library—be it a former librarian or a former cadaver—roams the remodeled facility. If the past is any gauge, however, witnesses will again hear from the phantom, if only to be reminded to keep the noise down.

It would be doing a disservice to school staff and alumni to leave the impression that the above hauntings were the only ones at ETSU. Burleson, Gilbreath, Yoakly, Mathes, and many more halls on campus are known to host their own resident ghosts.

Why so many ETSU buildings should be spook filled remains an enigma. Perhaps, being located high in the Appalachians, a region rich in supernatural lore, the campus has simply absorbed some of the many haunts and provided a convenient home. One graduate has expressed the belief that the university sits on an area that contains "extra-dimensional gates"—portals to otherworldly dominions and powers. If so, then perhaps Tennessee's Board of Regents should change ETSU's acronym to ETS-Boo!

CHAPTER 6

Things That Go Bump
Creatures Weird, Wild, and Wonderful

"From ghoulies and ghosties
And long-leggedy beasties
and things that go bump in the night,
Good Lord, deliver us."
Ancient Scots prayer

Whether or not the Volunteer State possesses any ghoulies such as the old Scots prayer warns against is a matter of speculation. But Tennessee certainly has plenty of ghosts. As for "long-leggedy beasties" and other fey creatures that roam the night—and sometimes the day—they, too, occur in abundance. Some of these beasties that go bumping about may be beyond belief to many, but that doesn't mean they aren't real.

Perhaps the best known of the long-leggedy creatures roaming the mountains is a big, hairy gent who people elsewhere call Bigfoot. In Tennessee, he has been given various nicknames over the years: "Skunk Ape," "Ole Woolly," "Whistling Jack," "Woolly Booger," and even "Whirling

Whimpus." All these names seem to refer to a seven- or eight-foot-tall, hairy, two-footed, apelike creature haunting the woodlands who occasionally comes down from his high lair to terrify his human neighbors.

Traditionally, the remote, rugged highlands along the Tennessee–North Carolina border are the stomping grounds of these size 19 EEE unshod beasties. Although written reports were rare before the mid-twentieth century, some researchers believe an oral tradition about a big, hairy biped stretches back to the early nineteenth century. The few early written accounts are tantalizing.

From Jack Neely, the master of all things weird and wonderful in Knoxville and environs, comes a report from the frontier era of a close encounter with something that sounds like a Bigfoot. In 1784, among the routine accounts of scalpings, raids, and trade in the *Knoxville Gazette* appeared a run-in with what Neely refers to as "Goosefoot." Some militia scouts were out in the woods on patrol when they stumbled upon a being the like of which they'd never seen. The creature was large and two-legged and had a tall, white tuft of hair on top of its head and huge red eyes. Instead of fur, the creature was covered in scales. Stranger still, its tracks resembled those of a giant goose, rather than a human or an ape!

In the 1870s, a creature of similar description was captured in Tennessee, placed on public exhibition in Louisville, and billed as "the Wild Man of the Woods." It had huge eyes, two feet, and fish scales. Whether it was the product of Bigfoot inbreeding or an uncanny creature of a different sort is unknown.

Judging by modern accounts, these hairy beasts don't always hide deep in the mountains. In the modern era, some encounters have been reported in Knox County on the outskirts of Knoxville proper. The most famous case was an incident in September 1959. Over several nights, somebody or something terrorized the local gentry along Clapps Chapel Road. Reported as eight to ten feet tall, yet able to move rapidly and quietly, it stomped about one resident's front porch and scratched up his car. As the disturbances continued, police were summoned but proved unable to nab the big, hairy perp. While some ex-girlfriends have been known to cause more damage than this Bigfoot did, neither the residents of Clapps Chapel Road nor the local constabulary were amused by the ape-man's antics.

Around Tracy City, people have long known of a giant beast that finds great sport in teasing and terrorizing the local farmers' hounds. Whenever he is chased by hunting dogs, he "whistles like a groundhog," according to one witness. Try as they might, the hounds can never catch him. In fact, whenever the dogs lose track of the beast, he stands up and whistles to let them know where he is. Once the hounds are duly notified, he takes off again, bounding through the woods. The locals refer to him as "Whistling Jack."

In the late nineteenth century and into the early twentieth, quite a bit of logging was carried out in the Cumberland Mountains and along the upper Cumberland River. Lumberjacks cut down so much old-growth forest that they apparently roused the ire of another Bigfoot variant, "the Whirling Whimpus."

Sometimes, lumberjacks failed to return to camp at the end of day. As often as not, their badly mangled bodies were found deep in the forest, yet more victims of the Whirling Whimpus. Shorter in stature than a Bigfoot, it had a gorilla-shaped head and body and enormous arms equipped with powerful claws. It would lie in wait along woodland trails for some despoiler of its habitat, then ambush the unsuspecting lumberman.

The apelike creature would whirl round and round on its short but powerful legs, its giant paws and claws extended. Like a spinning top, it went faster and faster until it became invisible. The only warning lumbermen had of their impending doom was the loud whirring sound it made as it spun. No ax could save the intended victims, for they couldn't hit what they couldn't see. Days later, search parties might find what was left: decaying shreds of flesh and a gooey red mess along the trail.

If early artists' imaginative drawings of the beast seem to resemble a more famous imaginary creature from Warner Brothers cartoons, bear in mind the Whirling Whimpus predated that Hollywood creation by several decades. Devil he may have been, but the Whirling Whimpus was homegrown in Tennessee and definitely not from Tasmania.

Just about every county in East Tennessee has had its Bigfoot sighting over the decades. More reports come in every year. However, Ole Woolly does not dwell just east of the Cumberland River. Abundant sighting have come from Middle and West Tennessee as well.

Even affluent Williamson County has had its share. Back before little old Leipers Fork became the abode of country-music executives and New York literary types, Bigfoot was stomping about the woodlands where South Lick Creek Road crosses Lick Creek. The creature was not overly big—perhaps in the six-foot range—but it was powerfully built and had a head and arms much like a gorilla's.

If the adolescent-sized man-ape of Williamson County was relatively well behaved, the same could not be said for one of his relatives who visited Flintville in 1976. In April of that year, a foul-smelling eight-foot apelike creature terrorized the small West Tennessee community. It climbed onto the roof of one woman's auto and proceeded to jump up and down on it till it was scrap metal. It nearly kidnapped a small child, made unwelcome sexual advances to area housewives, and generally made a horrific nuisance of itself. Finally, a posse of good ole boys drove it off with shotguns.

While some remain skeptical, enough folks ranging from East Memphis and Reelfoot Lake to the North Carolina border have seen Bigfoot to convince many a doubting Thomas.

Other creatures are weirder still. Surely, the most curious of the lot is the Wampus Cat. As it has rarely been seen and never caught, disagreement exists as to what the creature actually is. One definition says it is "a cryptid cougar-like feline that is said to live in the Appalachian Mountains." While that is as good a working definition as any, the cat's range extends well beyond East Tennessee and the Appalachians. Moreover, the Wampus Cat's most distinguishing characteristic is that it walks on two legs like a human.

Once upon a time, the Wampus Cat's main stomping ground was the thickly forested backwoods of East Tennessee. In recent decades, however, sightings have become more frequent in urban and suburban settings. In Johnson City in the 1950s, for example, a local carpenter was walking the city streets one night when he spotted a large feline. He reckoned the cat was about four feet in length. Apart from its size, nothing seemed preternatural about the beast as it prowled on all fours. Then the carpenter saw it stop in front of a glass-fronted store and put its front paws on the window sill. It then pulled itself upright onto two legs and gazed into the store. After staring intently for a moment or two, it continued walking down the street, still on two legs.

From Knoxville near the sprawling University of Tennessee campus comes a more recent report. A female student spied a human-sized cat with glowing eyes walking on its hind legs outside Strong Hall one night. Located on busy Cumberland Avenue, Strong Hall is hardly the backwoods. One observer of such things has suggested that perhaps the Knoxville Wampus Cat hides in the many caves that dot the hilly city and thereby avoids human detection.

In the late 1980s, a two-footed humanlike cat was sighted near Shelbyville. In fact, sightings of the Wampus Cat go back to the 1930s and 1940s in southwestern Virginia and North Carolina, from the legendary (and haunted) Barter Theatre in Abingdon to North Carolina's Dismal Swamp. Recent sightings have extended the Wampus Cat's range to Kentucky and West Virginia as well.

In Southern lore going back at least a century, the Wampus Cat has been associated with unruly human behavior and activities on the wrong side of the law. In the old days, "cat" or "wildcat" was a Tennessee euphemism for a moonshiner.

Up around Cades Cove before the government took over the land in the 1930s, menfolk regularly went in search of the Wampus Cat at night. Sometimes, a shot would ring out in the hollow. Then the men would gather up their shot bags, guns, and dogs and head out on the run. Usually, they didn't return until near dawn, red-eyed and worse for wear and with no dead Wampus Cat to show for their efforts.

In truth, the initial gun blast was the signal that a fresh batch of white lightning was ready. The good ole boys would then gather round the still, occasionally firing a round in the air to let the womenfolk know they were hot on the trail of the cat. Likely, a real Wampus Cat could have walked into their midst after a few rounds of passing the jug and they wouldn't have noticed at all.

The Wampus Cat has inspired country-music groups and served as a mascot for various sports teams. All this indicates that, despite its physical rarity, it is deeply ingrained in Southern culture. How far back tales of the cat go is hard to say. Some would trace it to Native American legends about catlike creatures such as the *Ewah*, or "Underground Panther." Others might trace tales of two-footed humanoid cats as far back as ancient Egypt and Mesopotamia. So perhaps the Wampus Cat is not so rare as imagined, just better than other animals at outwitting humans.

Both the Wampus Cat and Bigfoot at least resemble known animals. Some Tennessee creatures, however, positively defy all known categories of nature.

Up around White Bluff, folks tell tales of a creature they call "the White Screamer" or sometimes "the White Thing." It has been known to attack not only small game and dogs but even full-sized deer and humans on occasion.

One person who saw it and survived to tell the tale described it as having long white hair and being "nearly as tall as a basketball goal." It stood upright on two legs like a Bigfoot but had cloven hooves on its hind legs. Its front paws resembled human hands—with the exception of its razor-sharp claws. It had blood-red eyes and let out an unearthly sound that started off like a baby's cry and grew in intensity until it became a horrific high-pitched screech—hence the creature's name.

If the White Screamer is not enough to worry about, there is also a distinct possibility that the creature called "Mothman" that terrorized West Virginia several decades back may have relocated to Tennessee.

In July 2005, an experienced paranormal investigator encountered a tall humanoid late one night in a remote part of Williamson County. The creature was standing in plain sight on a country road in the area of Thompson Station. The witness noticed that it had webbing that ran from its outstretched arms all the way down its sides to about its knees. The head seemed similar to a human's but had an odd rounded triangular shape to it. The witness could discern no facial features.

No sooner had the driver passed the creature than she doubled back to take a second look, doubting her eyes. But by the time she reached the same spot, the creature was gone. Although she knew what she had seen, the rational side of her brain resisted accepting it.

Three years later, the same or a similar creature was spotted in broad daylight, again in Williamson County. This time, it was seen flying, its webbed appendages outstretched. Moreover, instead of a dark and lonely country back road, it was airborne over I-65, soaring in plain sight. It flew right where Route 840 crosses the interstate. Although the creature was viewed from farther away than in the first sighting, the clear sky and bright light made identification more certain. The eyewitness could clearly tell it was a Mothman type of creature and not simply a large vulture. What it was doing in broad daylight in Williamson County, however, remains a deep, deep mystery.

The name "Mothman" was coined by a reporter decades ago during the original rash of sightings near Point Pleasant, West Virginia. Perhaps the name reflects a fear of copyright infringement, for eyewitness descriptions of this bizarre humanoid creature—then as now—suggests its wings more closely resemble those of a bat than a moth. Regardless, any mainstream biologist worth his salt (and worried about his academic reputation) will insist that no such creature exists or could exist. But then, they've never met Mothman up close, have they?

Many other beasties out there also defy the experts' categories. For example, this account hasn't even touched on the "freshwater sharks" (giant man-eating catfish) that inhabit Old Hickory Lake and the Cumberland River or the Beast of Bray Road, which once terrified Knoxville.

Perhaps one of these weird, wondrous beasties may yet be captured alive. Until that day, if you're alone in the woods at night and hear an unfamiliar noise, you may wish to remember the words of that old Scottish admonition and start praying.

Chapter 7

The Curse of the White Mule

Every year, the town of Columbia throws a big bash to honor its equine heritage. The "Mule Day" celebration includes parades, live music, contests, and all manner of merrymaking to celebrate the lowly mule. Knoxville also has a tradition involving a mule, but it's not exactly something the folks there like to celebrate. It's called "the Curse of the White Mule."

Although nowadays most Knoxvillians don't take the curse seriously, the good folks of the 'ville for many years believed themselves to be "hoodooed." As with most things supernatural in the South, the origin of that belief goes back a long time—in this case, to around 1867.

It was a sunny, cheery day in Knoxville when the Gypsy Circus came to town. While a few locals may have watched their change purses more closely with the Gypsies in town, people young and old were for the most part elated at the prospect of seeing a circus. In the days before television, movies, and even vaudeville, a traveling circus was a rare and marvelous diversion from the humdrum workaday world.

Jugglers, clowns, sword swallowers, fire-breathers—all things weird and wonderful were to be seen at the Gypsy Circus. Things freakish and unusual were also on display, the Midway being a particular draw for those whose tastes ran to the bizarre. The menagerie included the usual exotic animals—lions and tigers and bears (Oh, my!)—but also something no one in Knoxville had ever gazed upon before: a snow-white mule.

To jaded modern Americans, a white mule may not seem so special. And the citizens of Knoxville and the surrounding farm country had seen many a mule in their day. But a white mule? Why, that was something rare indeed—magical, even.

The Gypsy Circus pitched its tents on a baseball field located in what is now the 400 block of Gay Street in downtown Knoxville. The circus people could barely contain the crowds. Business was good. The Romany owners were only too glad to take the rubes' hard-earned money.

All went smoothly until just before the end of their stay. At this remove in time, it is hard to say what went awry. Perhaps the white mule caught the bots, perhaps a child fed it something he oughtn't have, or perhaps it was just the white mule's time to go. Anyhow, the Gypsy Circus's prize attraction sickened and died.

Angry words were exchanged between the Gypsies and the city fathers. While no one bothered to write down what was said, the language was no doubt quite colorful. The upshot was that the Gypsies uttered a series of imprecations against the town that later came to be collectively called "the Curse of the White Mule."

Since time before counting, albino animals have been looked upon as sacred. This has held true not only for the mountain folks of East Tennessee but the Scots-Irish, the Cherokee Indians, and many other cultures. The white wolf is sacred to the Cherokees and is considered a messenger from the Great Spirit. Likewise the white buffalo. Gypsies or no Gypsies, old-timers in East Tennessee foretold that no good would come of the white mule's death.

For a time, nothing happened that could be laid at the foot of the

Gypsy curse. In time, therefore, folks around Knoxville forgot about it and went about their business.

Then came 1897. That year, a fire broke out in the 400 block of Gay Street. In the thirty years since the mule's death, all manner of businesses had popped up along the busy thoroughfare. Where before men played ball, hotels, hardware stores, dry-goods establishments, pharmacies, and the like now flourished. All this went up in flames in what was billed in the newspapers as "the Million-Dollar Fire." On April 8, a small fire broke out in the back of a hotel and quickly spread to other establishments on the block. Before the flames were quenched, the fire took five lives and at least a million dollars' worth of property. It was the worst fire in Knoxville up to that time.

The 1897 inferno was the first and perhaps the worst of the Gay Street fires, but it was by no means the last. A few years later, another conflagration erupted on the same block. It was not as bad as the first, to be sure, but a second fire in the same area set tongues wagging. Was there something, after all, to that old Gypsy curse?

For many in Knoxville, the answer was not long in coming. Sometime after two in the morning on Saturday, November 12, 1904, a passerby in front of Woodruff Hardware on Gay Street noticed fire erupting from the store. He hurriedly notified a passing constable, Dan Leahy. They called the Knoxville Fire Department.

As Officer Leahy ran toward the building, angry flames burst through the front. Firemen arrived in short order and had streams of water playing on the crackling fire. But in front of the store stood a powder magazine filled with high explosives. Flames were licking at the storage bin.

A bystander saw the danger and gave a shout for all to get back. In an instant, the explosives went up with a loud report, knocking dozens of men off their feet. Those nearby felt as though they had been kicked by a mule.

The scene the next day on Gay Street was one of utter devastation. Some facades had been blown down. Fire had gutted other buildings. Water had ruined any stock not damaged by the flames. The heart of the downtown business district was in shambles. Had the white mule's curse struck again?

It certainly seemed so. In the aftermath of the massive fire and explosion, some blamed the curse. One town elder voiced his opinion that it was indeed the white mule working its hoodoo spell: "Don't you know that anywhere a white mule dies is forever cursed?"

Captain Woodruff, owner of the building where the fire broke out, would have none of it, however. "Curse be damned!" he responded to talk of the white mule's jinx on the block. In fact, Woodruff ignored all the naysayers and boldly rebuilt his business once again.

Third time's the charm, the saying goes. The Woodruff Building managed to survive the incendiary inclinations of the white mule through the remainder of the twentieth century.

In the 1990s, the old brick building was sold and converted into a restaurant and brewpub, the Downtown Grill and Brewery. Perhaps to mollify any lingering resentment by the spirit of the white mule, the pub crafted a special potion. Patrons are encouraged to quaff as much of that special brew—White Mule Ale—as they desire. While it is not known if the white mule has indeed been mollified by this special potion brewed in its honor, it is a fact that no fires have broken out in the building since White Mule Ale began being consumed there.

To be sure, many modern denizens of Knoxville remain skeptical of the whole affair. Still, whenever a bad fire breaks out in the city, the Million-Dollar Fire and the Curse of the White Mule invariably come up in conversation. For example, when a fire started in the old Philco Building in February 2007, one observer claimed he saw "a white mule running from the area with a book of matches."

More recently, a group of street performers called "the White Mule Players" has begun giving readings from literary works relating to the city all over the downtown area. The white mule may be gone, but it is not forgotten.

Downtown Grill and Brewery
424 South Gay Street
Knoxville, TN 37902
(865) 633-8111
www.downtownbrewery.com

This establishment is located on the spot where the white mule died. Its special brew may or may not deserve credit for quenching the incendiary inclinations of the occult equine, but it is guaranteed to quench patrons' thirst on hot summer nights in downtown Knoxville.

CHAPTER 8

Phantoms of the Bijou

Theater people are a superstitious lot. One tradition is for a lone stagehand to plant a pole topped by a bare bulb on the empty stage. Theater folk call this a "ghost light." The light's purpose is not to aid the cleanup crew but rather to ward off spirits.

In the case of Knoxville's Bijou Theatre, the ghost light is a much-needed piece of equipment. The Bijou has been described by one local expert as "the most haunted building in Knoxville." By all accounts, that label has been amply earned. Some buildings may have one or two ghosts. But the venerable Bijou plays host to a gaggle of them.

The building in which the Bijou resides has had a long—and at times violent—history. The theater dates to 1908, but the structure itself goes all the way back to 1817, making it the fourth-oldest building in Knoxville. It was opened to the public as Archie Ray's Tavern. In the ensuing years, the building operated mainly as a hotel, going through a variety of names and more than doubling in size.

Just before the Civil War, it was renamed the Lamar House. It was from the balcony of the Lamar House that Senator John C. Breckenridge gave a speech to a crowd of supporters in 1861. He told them he was swapping his seat in the United States Senate for a musket in the

Confederate army. Some historians have noted that Breckenridge was more competent as a politician than as a general—and he was a mediocre politician.

When the Yankee army occupied Knoxville, the Lamar House's owner—a Confederate sympathizer—found it wise to flee the city. Part of the building was converted into a military hospital, while the remainder was used to billet Union officers. Besides the many ordinary soldiers who died of wounds or disease in the hospital, Union general William P. Sanders was brought there after being wounded in a skirmish in 1863. He later died in what had once been the bridal suite.

After the war, the Lamar House returned to civilian hands and soon became the place to stay for visiting dignitaries and the region's social elite. In 1877, President Rutherford B. Hayes gave a speech from its balcony. Nor was Hayes the first or the only president to stay at the hotel. Andrew Jackson had lodged there decades earlier. Theodore Roosevelt and William Howard Taft were also guests.

Despite its prestigious reputation, the hotel changed hands—and names—several times. Finally, a development company bought it and, after extensive renovations, converted part of the building into an up-to-date theater that opened in 1909. The first performance in Jake Wells' Bijou Theatre was a musical featuring the legendary George M. Cohan. In the ensuing years, the theater hosted a succession of vaudeville acts, many of whom later became famous, among them the Marx Brothers and Al Jolson.

By the 1930s, vaudeville was on the wane. The Bijou switched over to showing motion pictures exclusively and for many years continued providing entertainment for generations of Knoxvillians.

By the 1960s, however, Gay Street was in decline as people moved to the suburbs and downtown was no longer the social core of the city. The nature of the movies shown at the Bijou also underwent a change. The now-aging theater began airing X-rated adult "art" movies. Meanwhile, the hotel located behind the theater, with a separate entrance on Cumberland Street, catered to winos, drug addicts, and prostitutes. Long gone were the upscale customers of the old Lamar. Finally, civic leaders resolved to turn things around on Gay Street. They shut down the seedy hotel. The "art" theater followed soon afterward.

For a long time, the theater was left to its ghosts. Finally, in the late 1970s, the Bijou was rescued from the wrecking ball by preservationists. It was restored and reopened as "Knoxville's Gem of the South," a venue for modern musical groups and other contemporary acts, a function it continues today.

Exactly when people realized the Bijou was haunted is difficult to say, but it seems certain that staff and visiting actors were the first to realize the old theater had its resident repertory company of spooks. Based on various eyewitness accounts, the paranormal activity was most in evidence after hours. In recent years, the theater's revival has meant that more folks are visiting and working there, so reported sightings have become more common.

One of the ghosts is the spirit of a young girl who has been heard singing on the stage when workers are present. On one occasion, a box-office employee was locking up for the night and saw a girl in the lobby. Thinking some child had been left behind by accident, the worker told the girl to come over. Instead, the child disappeared into thin air.

Voices without any apparent source are frequently reported from various parts of the old theater. The sound of footsteps is heard on staircases. Actors and actresses occasionally catch sight of figures in the balconies, usually out of the corners of their eyes. One apparition is seen standing toward the front rows of the first balcony; others seem to haunt the center rows. Yet another spirit prefers a seat in the left rear of the second balcony.

Perhaps the best known of the Bijou's ghosts is "the General"— commonly assumed to be the shade of General Sanders. The general died in the hotel part of the building, but his ghost wanders the theater as well, even though it did not exist during the Civil War. The room where he died is not accessible to the general public. Experts who have investigated the room claim it exhibits a high level of supernatural activity.

In July 2006, an East Tennessee ghost-hunting group paid a visit to the Bijou. Although the investigators did not actually witness any physical manifestations with the naked eye, they did document quite a bit of psychic evidence that cannot be easily explained away.

Throughout the theater, they recorded extensive electric voice phenomena (or EVP) that were clearly the sounds of people talking where nobody was to be seen. The voices were recorded throughout the building but were particularly prevalent on the fourth floor.

A number of photos taken during the investigation proved interesting. What are referred to as "shadow ghosts"—amorphous misty shapes—were caught on camera in the second-level ladies' room and the balconies. One photo seemed to be the apparition of a small child. Infrared videos taken under the stage recorded a cluster of faces, some seemingly of actors in costume. What are commonly called "orbs" were captured on camera as well, many in the same locations as the shadow ghosts.

The evidence gathered by the paranormal researchers seems to support the popularly held belief that, in addition to the General, the ghosts of many past performers and theatergoers haunt the auditorium. The Bijou also seems to hold the shades of several former hotel guests.

Modern audiences don't seem to be unduly disturbed by the spectral residents. By all accounts, the ghosts haunting the Bijou are mostly of the happy sort. So visitors to Knoxville who catch a performance should fear not. The friendly phantoms of the Bijou don't mind sharing their home with guests.

Bijou Theatre
803 South Gay Street
Knoxville, TN 37902
(865) 522-0832
www.knoxbijou.com

CHAPTER 9

Mountain Witches

For as long as anyone can recall, Appalachia has been home to witches of one sort or another—good witches, bad witches, water witches, weather witches, and the like. The curious thing is that, while everyone admits that wicked witches exist, nobody has ever owned up to being one—leastways not if they're the real deal. Among the other varieties, some may admit to casting a spell or two, but many do not think of themselves as witches at all.

Of course, a lot of folks these days have seen too many Hollywood movies or perhaps taken too many illicit substances and fancy themselves New Age witches or promoters of "the old religion." While everyone is entitled to their beliefs, such pop fads have no connection to the ways that have been around since the first settlers came over the mountains.

Witch is derived from an ancient Celtic word that did not necessarily mean someone who cast magic spells. Rather, it had the more general meaning of "wise." In Ireland, ladies with such a store of knowledge were commonly referred to as "wise women." It is this much older meaning of the word—one that also encompassed the ability to see hidden things and cast spells—that the traditions of Appalachia preserved more or less intact up until recently.

Such folks were pretty much eliminated in the English parts of Britain by the Puritans during the seventeenth century. In the Celtic parts of the British Isles, however, they continued to hold a place of honor in many rural communities. As the South was largely settled by folks from those Celtic lands, it is not surprising they brought the tradition with them to the New World.

Just because people were held to be "wise" or practiced specialties with the word *witch* attached at the end didn't necessarily mean they were practitioners of the dark arts. Up around Cookeville, for example, one lady was popularly acclaimed as a "weather witch." She was uncommonly skilled at reading "the signs" and thereby divining what the weather would be.

Water witching—also known as "dowsing" or "water divining"—is another traditional skill that is still widely practiced in many parts. At one time, it was the nearly universal method of finding water where no springs were visible on the surface. A forked stick—preferably from a hazel tree, although different diviners have their own favorite types of wood—is the standard "divining rod."

Two bent metal rods held loosely in the hands may be used for finding iron ore or hidden treasure. Sometimes, a surveyor's plumb is suspended by a string over a map. Ivor Noel Hume, chief archaeologist at Colonial Williamsburg, used geomancy to locate artifacts and the hidden foundations of lost buildings. One modern diviner in the employ of oil companies uses nothing but his mind when flying over likely areas in search of petroleum deposits. The fact is, almost any substance hidden beneath the earth can be found by divining. For folks in the mountains, it is a form of witchery.

Where the old-fashioned mountain witches of East Tennessee excelled was in the healing arts. Today, few associate medicine with magic. The antiseptic world of modern medicine has allied itself solidly with science. Yet in olden days, that was not so. Nor were doctors the only practitioners of the healing arts.

In frontier days, any number of folks wandered about calling themselves doctors. Generally, they sold bottles of "root medicine," which could contain just about anything. Usually, it had a high alcohol content and included painkillers such as tincture of opium. Such medicines might not have cured anybody, but they at least dulled the pain. When it came to things such as treating victims of scalping, backwoods doctors were handy. The standard treatment for scalping was called "pegging." The doctor would take a wood augur and drill a series of holes in the top of the skull where the skin had been taken by the Indians. A thick goo would ooze out, then scab over and eventually heal. It didn't look pretty, but at least the victim survived.

Many wanting to be cured of ailments turned to one or another of the mountain "grannies." Such women were not necessarily grandmothers or even particularly old. Rather, it was a term of deference. In Ireland or Scotland, they would have been called "wise women." What these women had was a store of wisdom handed down from their mothers and grandmothers across the sea. They also had knowledge of healing herbs borrowed from the Indians, as well as touches of Negro folk medicine and magic.

A granny's ways of treating disease did not exactly square with modern notions of medicine, but they generally worked. For example, a small bag of asafetida tied around the neck was thought to ward off childhood diseases. To prevent chickenpox, a granny might prescribe bathing the child in the blood of a freshly killed chicken. For adults, a pinch of graveyard dust, or "goofer dust," carried somewhere on the person was usually enough to ward off ills. A short length of slightly used hangman's rope also prevented ailments. A buckeye carried in the pocket would ward off bone diseases. If folks had bedbugs, a granny might advise them to touch all the corners of the house on a certain night in the spring (*Walpurgisnacht?*).

While many a granny had an accumulated store of knowledge about potions, poultices, and plasters to treat one or another disease, some cures were a mix of medicine and magic, with bits of religion thrown in. For example, the recommended regimen for treating a burn was to apply spring water and blackberry leaves to the wound while reciting this incantation:

> There came three angels out of the East.
> One brought fire and two brought frost.
> Out fire and in frost!
> In the name of the Father, Son, and Holy Ghost!

Often, pieces of scripture that applied to certain situations were copied by hand in the belief that they could cure disease. In southwestern Virginia, some healers employed the "magic square," which was basically a scrambled version of the Our Father in Latin. In East Tennessee, however, King James mostly held sway.

More than a half-century ago, a Nashville lawyer by the name of Kennedy had a prize horse that took sick. It was so ill that the man was afraid he would need to have it put down. The man finally resorted to mountain medicine. In this case, the "granny" was a male. But like his female counterparts, he was steeped in the lore and wisdom of East Tennessee healers.

First, he took a handful of gravel and rubbed it against the horse's mouth. Then he put the gravel back exactly where he found it. Next, he removed the tail from a peafowl and touched the horse from head to tail with it, reciting this spell:

> An old woman came over a hill with a bag of bots.
> Some were black, some were brown, and some were blue.
> They are gone!

The mountain healer repeated the charm three times, then declared the horse cured. The city lawyer was dubious about the whole affair but had nothing to lose except his horse. To his amazement, it soon began consuming fodder again. Within a short time, all signs of colic were gone.

Perhaps the most famous of East Tennessee witches was a granny whose exploits were still the stuff of legend in the 1930s, many years after her time. One WPA researcher disguised her name as "Mammy Wise," but in fact her Christian name was Weiss (sometimes spelled Weice). She lived close to the North Carolina border. Over the course of many years, she earned respect—and fear—for her reputation as soothsayer, healer, and caster of spells.

Whether or not Granny Weiss was a seventh daughter is uncertain. But it is known that her father died before she came into the world. Children born after their fathers' deaths were commonly believed to have the power to cure thrush, among other abilities. This fact of birth may also account for her prodigious talent as a seer, which was said to exceed that of all other mountain grannies of her day.

Granny Weiss was a tall, heavyset, large-boned woman with a coarse, thick mane more like braided hemp than human hair. Her dark eyes were like a pair of small black pearls. In complexion, she was said to be "dark as an Injun." Truth be known, she may well have had some Indian blood in her. Many mountain folk did, but up until recently few would own up to it, attitudes being what they were. Of course, a life spent working in the hot Southern sun may have turned most anyone's skin dark.

Granny Weiss performed the usual healing functions, such as blowing into newborns' mouths to cure thrush (or rush). Where she excelled, however, was in her second sight and her uncanny ability to soothsay the true causes of disease.

Around the second decade of the nineteenth century, a family named Johnson settled along the Davidson River on a piece of land later known as "the old Deaver place." It happened that the man of the family got "the gravel" (kidney stones) and sent for Granny Weiss to cure his urinary problem. As it turned out, the Johnsons had hosted a traveler by the name of Carson a short time earlier. Carson was a successful cattle merchant and was carrying several hundred dollars on him. The next morning, the merchant realized his money was missing. Granny Weiss divined that Mr. Johnson was the culprit, and that his thievery was the cause of the ailment. Johnson's wife wanted to throw the tainted money into the river, but Granny Weiss wouldn't hear of it. Johnson was compelled to summon the cattle merchant back and return his money. Granny Weiss persuaded Carson not to prosecute the thief. But word got out, and the Johnsons had to leave the area anyhow. However, Johnson was at least cured of the gravel.

Another time, a farmer was missing some money he'd stashed under his mattress. Granny Weiss divined that his wife had taken the cash to give to her grown son by a previous man, who was now on the run from the law.

Like most women with the gift, Granny Weiss excelled at cures for those suffering from love sickness. One tale collected in the 1930s related how she found a husband for the community's "old maid"—which by the standards of her day could have been just about any unmarried female over the age of sixteen.

Far and away Granny Weiss's greatest fame centers around the claim that she predicted the Civil War. She allegedly had a vision in which she saw a star from points north travel across the sky and collide with a star at the southern end of the heavens. Granny Weiss divined that it foretold war between the North and the South. This legend is quite likely true, after a fashion. Just before the outbreak of the war, an omen did appear in the heavens. That portent was "the War Comet," a "hairy star" that appeared early in 1861 and was clearly seen by a great many. It was widely interpreted as an ill omen. While Granny Weiss was not the only person to interpret it as a harbinger of war, her prediction cemented her already prodigious reputation in the Tennessee Valley.

While Granny Weiss and others of her kind generally sought to use their knowledge and powers for good—often without compensation—folks certainly didn't want to get on their bad side. Although no one in the mountains ever owned up to practicing malicious witchcraft, any number of people openly presented themselves as witch doctors—individuals skilled in defense against the dark arts. As a rule, it always seemed to be someone in the neighboring community or the next county who was the witch. Suspicions of malicious witchcraft often fell on people who lived across the state line. One lady interviewed in the 1950s was quite blunt about it: "The witches over there in North Carolina would witch everything you had."

Most commonly, attacks took the form of bewitching livestock, especially cows. A cow's milk might also be bewitched to keep the cream from being churned into butter. Witch doctors employed a multitude of remedies to cure bewitchments and to prevent witch attacks. Pity the poor witch who ran afoul of them.

"Iron lays the devil," according to an old saying. Indeed, iron and steel were used in various witchcraft remedies. In Big Creek, which today lies just outside the Great Smoky Mountains National Park, there once lived a family whose cow was giving bloody milk, a clear sign of bewitchment. The wife consulted Sam Evans, a self-anointed witch doctor, who advised her to put the lid of a Dutch oven in the hearth fire until red-hot, then peck at it with an iron reaping hook. The operation was performed as directed, and the milk indeed cleared up. It was so successful, in fact, that the suspected witch tracked Sam down and raised a ruckus about his meddling. The two got into a heated argument that turned physical. During the fight, Evans pulled up her dress to reveal scars on her body—scars that looked like the sort a reaping hook might peck into her flesh.

Another farmer's wife had trouble making butter no matter how hard and long she churned. However, by putting an iron bridle on top of the churn, the bewitchment was cured. Another cure for a troublesome churn was to stir the cream with a switch cut from the hazel tree.

For more serious cases of bewitchment, a witch doctor might take an iron nail and hammer it seven times into a drawing of the witch hung on a beech tree. Whatever part of the sketch was penetrated by the nail, the corresponding portion of the witch's body would be affected.

Silver was an equally effective, if more costly, substance in combating witches and their malicious spells. For example, a dime placed at the bottom of a butter churn would draw out the spell. Likewise, a drawing of a witch affixed to a tree might be shot by a silver bullet. As with an iron nail, whatever part of the sketch was shot, that part of the real witch would be injured.

Witch doctors did not consider themselves to be witches. Rather, they seemed to regard themselves as backwoods physicians whose specialty happened to be diseases of the supernatural sort. In truth, however, their techniques were clearly magical in nature. They sometimes even employed the same tools as evil witches.

For example, a "witch ball" was frequently used as a means of casting a spell on a person. The witch ball consisted of wax mixed with human hair and a few less savory ingredients. It was thrown at the intended victim to conjure up an enchantment, or it was buried on a path the victim was known to use; merely by walking over it, the victim came under the witch ball's spell. But witch balls were also used by witch doctors to break witches' power. Moreover, blacks employed them in the practice of hoodoo. Mark Twain, whose father once defended accused witches in Jamestown, Tennessee, referred to Jim's belief in the power of witch balls in *The Adventures of Huckleberry Finn*. In the 1820s, Dean, the Bell family's trusted farmhand, threw a witch ball at the Bell Witch upon encountering her in the shape of a devil dog. Mountain witches around Cades Cove were also accused of using witch balls in the olden days. In the war of light versus dark, they were clearly weapons used by both sides.

Of course, it was best if a person never fell under a witch's spell to start with. Any number of charms were believed to ward off bewitchment. Putting a silver dime in one's shoe was effective protection against enchantment. For folks too poor for that, an iron nail carried in the pocket was almost as good.

Laying a broom across the threshold of the home was guaranteed to keep all witches out. Newlyweds in particular made sure to place a broom across the entrance to their cabin, lest a jealous ex-lover try to hex their wedding night. It was so common a charm that "jumping the broom" became synonymous with marriage in the mountains.

Spreading salt around the outside of a cabin worked wonders to keep witches out as well. Every fool knew that salt prevented corruption and decay, so using it against the corruption and decay of servants of the Lord of the Flies made perfect sense.

Nowadays, people may still hang an iron horseshoe over the door for good luck. The tradition began as a means of keeping witches out.

Real mountain witches, for good or ill, are mostly just a memory. A few folk here and there still have a store of old-time wisdom in their heads. But the grannies who would birth babies, cure the newborn of diseases, and work up spells to help girls get husbands are long gone.

Still, given that so many people have been influenced by the false glamour of Hollywood-inspired witchcraft, it is an open question whether or not some of the newer sort might by accident hit upon an effective spell or two and do someone harm. So it can't hurt to lay in a store of salt, to carry a piece of silver in your shoe, and to keep a twig broom stowed under the front porch beneath the threshold. And oh, yes, hang your grandfather's old horseshoe over the entrance to your home for luck. You never know, it just may come in handy.

CHAPTER 10

Caves of Wonder
Tennessee's Mysterious Underworld

Aladdin's adventures in the Cave of Wonders are justly renowned for their magic, mystery, treasures, and supernatural beings. While the wonders to be found underground in Tennessee are mostly of the natural sort, some of the state's many caverns boast supernatural wonders as well.

Supernatural encounters beneath the earth in Tennessee stretch into the distant mist of prehistory. Native American medicine men took to the caves that honeycomb the mountains to conjure up magic spells and get in touch with the spirit world. In fact, so renowned were the Cherokees for this that their northern neighbors the Iroquois referred to them as Ayada Onnon—"the Cave People."

The Cherokees had numerous encounters with the supernatural beings that dwelt beneath the earth. One tale tells of a tribe of "underground panthers" that an Indian brave encountered by accident. The panthers—who could walk on their hind legs like humans—invited the brave to sing and dance with them in their town underground. The entrance to the cave was guarded by a door normally invisible to mortal eyes but that, like the lair of Ali Baba and the Forty Thieves, would magically open upon the proper incantation.

Another supernatural creature that lived underground was Tsulkulu—"the Slant-Eyed Giant." Native American lore relates how he married a Cherokee maiden. Even giants are not immune from in-law troubles, however, and Tsulkulu eventually resolved to remove his bride from her native village to live in his home. The giant's domicile was a cave whose entrance was on the side of a sheer cliff. The only thing to distinguish it was a wooden door like that on any log cabin. Tsulkulu and his bride lived contentedly there. The bride's relatives journeyed to the giant's lair and pleaded with her to return to the sunlit land of her ancestors, but she preferred to remain with her husband's subterranean kinfolk.

A race of fey folks called the Nunnehi, or "the Immortals," figures large in Cherokee tradition. Similar in size and shape to humans but possessed of magical powers and able to make themselves invisible at will, the Nunnehi lived in large towns inside the mountains and under the water. John Ax, or Itagunehi, a venerable Cherokee tradition keeper, told of a time before the Removal when the Nunnehi came to the Cherokee villages along the Hiwassee and Tennessee rivers and warned of coming misfortune. They offered to let the Cherokees come and live with them in their homes beneath the Great Smoky Mountains. Some of the villages heeded the warning and went with the Nunnehi. But the majority of the tribe did not. When they were driven from their homeland in 1838, the Cherokees were forced to leave their underground relatives behind.

Up near Johnson City is the Tipton-Haynes farm, which happens to lie along an old Indian trail called "the Warriors' Path." It was the traditional route the Southern tribes used both to hunt game and to raid their neighbors to the north—first the Iroquois and later the whites. Long hunters and other pioneers used it for travel as well. On the Tipton-Haynes farm was a cave used for shelter by all these folk at various times.

More recently, a father and son traveled the old trail while they were out hunting. Since it was getting late, they, too, sought shelter at the mouth of the cave. They lit a campfire to keep warm, had their supper, and turned in to sleep. Sometime in the early hours of the morning, they were awakened by sounds from deeper within the cave. Peering toward the source, they saw Native Americans gathered about what seemed a blazing fire. That was odd, for the Indians had long since been moved across the Mississippi, and none were known to be left in those parts. Looking closer, father and son realized the figures were transparent! The two hunters beat a hasty retreat from the haunted cave.

Once a remote mountain community, Cades Cove is now a popular destination for visitors to the Great Smoky Mountains National Park. In Cades Cove is a notorious spot known as Haunted Cave. Generally off-limits to visitors, it is not just a simple shelter but a labyrinth of caverns—and a dangerous one at that. In the days before the park, local children would go adventuring in the cave, despite their parents' prohibitions. On one occasion, two boys—Will and Jack—entered the cave on a dare and became lost. Although Will eventually found his way out, Jack never did. It is believed that his spirit remains trapped in Haunted Cave. From time to time, explorers hear Jack plaintively calling for help—especially when the modern lighting system is turned off.

Midway between Knoxville and Chattanooga sits the town of Sweetwater. Above the ground spread verdant valleys and scenic slopes. But beneath it lies a truly spectacular attraction—Lost Sea Cave.

As the name implies, this cave's claim to fame is a large, sunless sea. It encompasses over four acres in one large chamber but extends deeper into numerous other chambers whose full extent is unknown. Long billed as the world's largest underground lake, the Lost Sea has been demoted in recent years to number two by the discovery of another such lake in Africa. It remains the largest underground lake in the Western Hemisphere and a perennial favorite of tourists.

Although the lake was not discovered by whites until 1905—when a local boy exploring deep underground came upon it—the cave has been known by humans since the Stone Age. Indian medicine men visited parts of it over the course of centuries. During the Civil War, it was used to mine saltpeter for making gunpowder. Back in the 1930s, the remains of a prehistoric jaguar were found in the cave, and the bones were packed off to a museum in New York. Lost Sea Cave even served at one time as a nightclub. Today, however, its only inhabitants are ghosts.

From time to time, visitors have felt something akin to the tail of a large animal brush against them. Locals swear that a phantom jaguar haunts the cave. While it has never been known to cause harm, the jaguar has led more than one visitor to beat a hasty retreat back to the light.

Of more recent origin is a human ghost believed to be the shade of a Yankee soldier killed in the cave during the Civil War. In those days, soldiers who slipped behind enemy lines were called "scouts." They frequently dressed in civilian garb or even in enemy uniforms. If caught, such scouts, or spies, were subject to summary execution. The Yankee in question was apparently spying on the Rebels' gunpowder manufacturing operation in the cave when he was caught and killed. Ever since, his ghost has remained trapped in Lost Sea Cave, doomed to roam the vast passageways forever.

Cannon County and its environs are best known for hand-made rockers and baskets. One of the area's main attractions for tourists is Cumberland Caverns. Although the caverns have been open to the public since the 1950s, parts of the labyrinth have been known since frontier days. When explorers realized that the different segments were part of a single cave system, they gave the caverns their present name and fame.

Legends about Cumberland Caverns abound. Particularly credible are the reported encounters with Ball's Ghost. During the 1960s, a party of experienced spelunkers from Chicago visited the caverns. In the course of their explorations, they penetrated an area not visited by tourists. Taking a break after a long hike, one of their number suddenly felt something wet splatter onto his hand in the dark. Shining a light on his hand, he saw a large red splotch. The group scanned the walls and ceiling of the chamber with their lights for the source of the bloodlike stain, but their search was in vain.

Five years later, another group of explorers—this time from northern Alabama—ventured deep inside the caverns. Taking a break at a point called Ball's Pit, one of them felt a liquid substance dripping onto his glove. Looking down, he thought he may have cut himself on a jagged rock. But once again, a thorough search revealed no injury or any place the blood could have come from.

Ultimately, a local caver with knowledge of the caverns' history and lore concluded that the bloody show was caused by Ball's Ghost—the shade of the man for whom the deep pit was named. Ball's Ghost is said to mark with blood those persons he fails to lure over the precipice.

Another cavern in the area bears the cheery name of "Devil's Cave" and has an even more sinister reputation. Several years back, a pair of explorers attempted a vertical descent into its dark depths. As one man stayed up top to let out rope, the other was slowly lowered into the cave in a harness. After the man had descended some distance, his partner suddenly heard an ungodly scream from out of the darkness. The rope man hurriedly pulled his friend up, fearing he had somehow been injured. When the caver emerged from the pit, he was barely recognizable. His hair was snow white and his skin pale and clammy. Most shocking of all was the expression on his face—a look of inexpressible terror. His friend quickly undid the rope and tried to get the caver to tell what had frightened him so. But his partner was in a total state of shock and was unable to utter anything coherent. He never told anyone what unspeakable horror he had seen, taking the secret of Devil's Cave to his grave.

The famous Bell Witch Cave is widely reputed to be demon haunted. Located on the northern end of the Highland Rim in Adams, Tennessee, close to Kentucky's own cave country, it is modest in size, its entrance just a little opening in a cliff overlooking the Red River. Although small as far as Tennessee caverns are concerned, the Bell Witch Cave makes up in supernatural infestation what it lacks in size.

The tale of the Bell Witch has been told in full elsewhere. Suffice it to say that the mysterious spirit that bedeviled the Bell family farm in the 1820s was alleged to have departed the area a few years after the death—some say the murder—of the family patriarch, John Bell. But strange occurrences have continued to haunt the cave and its surroundings to this day—proof, some say, that the witch never really left at all.

On a number of occasions, visitors have claimed to see an apparition in the cave. One pilgrim even photographed a diaphanous shade floating just outside the entrance. Others who have seen no spirits have nonetheless felt the Bell Witch's wrath, for it is said that removing so much as a pebble from the cave will bring down her curse. Misfortune will follow until the object is returned.

Some say these uncanny happenings are not the doings of the Bell Witch at all, but rather those of the restless spirit of an Indian medicine man. This much is true: within the cave lies the grave of some nameless prehistoric Indian. The skeleton in the stone-lined grave was likely a shaman, someone who regarded the cave as a place of power. He may have been a source of strife ever since his resting place was disturbed long ago.

Not every cave in Tennessee boasts a resident ghost or the grave of an Indian shaman. For example, underground Knoxville has been described as a "Swiss cheese of cavey limestone." According to local lore, one cave leads from near the University of Tennessee Hospital all the way beneath the Tennessee River to the other bank, finding egress in Chilhowee Park. But how haunted Knoxville's caves are is a subject of debate. The same goes for Nashville, where old Fort Nashborough was said to be built over a legendary treasure cave, where the State Capitol sits on a rocky knob known to have subterranean chambers beneath it, and where a stout oaken door in the basement of Belmont Mansion marks the entrance to Adelicia's Tunnel.

But given Tennessee's eight thousand caves—more than in any other state—quite a few are indeed haunted. Whether Native American spirits, lost souls, or inexplicable entities, the caves of Tennessee have wonders—and dangers—in abundance.

II
Cumberlands

Strange Tales of the
Cumberland Valley,
the Cumberland Mountains,
and Nashville

CHAPTER 11

Opryland Apparitions
The Haunting of
Music Valley

For generations, the Grand Ole Opry was a mainstay of uptown Nashville's entertainment district. Year after year, the Opry's weekend performances attracted the country-music faithful to the city's Lower Broadway to watch aspiring singers try to trade their blue jeans for rhinestones. In 1973, all that changed when the Grand Ole Opry moved from "the Mother Church of Country Music" (Ryman Auditorium) to new digs where cows still grazed lazily in the fields. Christened Opryland, the site included not just a new Opry house but a whole complex.

Fans of the paranormal may be familiar with Ryman Auditorium's haunting. But few are aware that the Opry's new home is also host to a unique set of ghosts.

Scenically situated in an outlying area of Nashville, Opryland has attracted millions of visitors from the world over. The music has always been the main attraction, of course, but over the years the sprawling complex along a bend of the Cumberland River has grown to include many other attractions. Originally, Opryland's main feature was a theme park where the whole family could take in performances of live music all day long in the summer. Several years back, however, the beloved amusement park was replaced by an outlet mall, Opry Mills. A large sternwheeler showboat, the *General Jackson*, was added. Moreover, the Opryland Hotel, originally just an adjunct to the theme park and the Opry house, has grown into a virtual indoor city that is a destination in its own right. Today, it is one of the largest hotels in the world, catering to business meetings and conventions year-round and transforming into a winter wonderland with millions of lights, decorations, and a wide assortment of holiday activities from November through January.

Despite all the changes, Opryland and the Grand Ole Opry remain Music City's premier destinations, attractions that few who come to Nashville can resist seeing. Millions have enjoyed Opryland over the years. For a few, however, their visits have proven a frightening—sometimes even a deadly—experience.

Major landmarks such as Opryland seem to attract a small minority of people intent on doing something extreme—whether to themselves or others. The Golden Gate Bridge and the Empire State Building, for example, are notorious as locations for committing suicide. Although normally a safe and secure place to visit, Opryland has also sometimes attracted an element intent on dark deeds.

One morning, fire erupted in the Opryland Hotel's back parking lot. Hotel security was alerted that a car had burst into flames and exploded. At first, it was thought that someone had been the victim of foul play or even a terrorist attack. When police sorted things out, however, it turned out that a man whose life had taken a tragic turn had chosen Opryland as the site to end his life in spectacular fashion.

Then there was the murder-suicide that occurred inside the hotel several years back. A couple from Hopkinsville, Kentucky, had been having marital problems and apparently decided that a weekend getaway would be just the tonic to heal their relationship. It wasn't.

The details of the incident remain sketchy. According to reports, the husband had been drinking heavily and was being verbally abusive to his wife in one of the hotel's restaurants. Embarrassed by his boorish behavior, she finally became so disgusted that she got up from the table and headed for the door.

His wife's reaction enraged the husband. He grabbed her and flung her over the balcony railing, sending her to her death. Realizing with horror what he'd done, he followed his wife over the railing, plunging to his death.

Ever since that day, the long-suffering wife has haunted the balcony where the crime occurred. Her ghost has been witnessed mainly by hotel staff. Workers in the Cascades restaurant say she is most often seen on the anniversary of her death.

Of course, the focus of the massive complex remains the performances in the Grand Ole Opry. While the new Opry house does not boast the level of spectral activity of Ryman Auditorium, it, too, has apparitions frequenting its hallowed halls.

Normally, after the late show at the Opry is over, the crew cleans up, stores the stage gear in its proper place, and finally draws the curtain and turns off the lights just prior to leaving. On occasion, however, Opry workers find that on double-checking the theater before locking up, the stage lights are back on and the curtain pulled open. This has happened to more than one befuddled stagehand.

No one has ever been seen pulling such pranks, nor have any crew members admitted to leaving their work undone. On the contrary, everyone knows the late-night routine and doesn't wish to linger in the cavernous theater any longer than necessary.

From long experience, many Opry workers ascribe these antics to a ghost inhabiting the theater. Who the ghost may be is a matter of dispute. A few feel it is the spirit of a stagehand who once worked there and who died of natural causes but so loved his job that he decided to take up ghostly residence.

Another candidate for the haint is none other than Roy Acuff, the legendary country fiddle player and longtime member of the Opry troupe. Certainly, there is no question of Acuff's devotion to the Grand

Ole Opry. Not only was he a regular performer for many years, he even lived in a small house adjacent to the theater so he had easy access both to the Opry and his loyal fans.

Today, Roy Acuff's mortal remains lie a short drive away, across the Cumberland River in Springhill Cemetery. His tombstone is easy to spot—it's the large marble marker with a fiddle and bow carved on it. But his spirit will always remain in the Grand Ole Opry. That Roy should be so devoted that he continues to haunt the theater is entirely credible. However, no one is entirely sure he is in fact the Phantom of the Opry.

The Lady in Black is the complex's best-attested spirit. Several things stand out about her. For one, she doesn't seem limited to any one place in Opryland. She has been reported at various times in both the Opryland Hotel and Opry Mills Mall. She also isn't identified with any known incident in either the hotel or the mall. Some reports say she was even spotted at the amusement park before it was torn down.

The ghost's presence is generally detected late at night, mostly by hotel or mall personnel. In 2003, a cleaning crew was waxing the floors in one part of the complex when workers spotted her. She was seen hovering over a place they had just cleaned. A crew member called security, but she disappeared by the time officers arrived. One cleaning lady allegedly quit on the spot after sighting the Lady in Black. Mall employees have witnessed a shadowy figure passing through walls and locked storefronts. Others have heard footsteps following them when no one was to be seen.

The ghost wears a long black gown that is generally said to have an antique look. Judging from details gleaned from reports, it seems to be an antebellum-style costume. She is described as a young woman. Some witnesses have characterized her as "Hispanic looking." It may be that they mistook her black veil or "widow's weeds" for an old-fashioned Spanish mantilla. Some hotel staff members have heard her dress making a gentle rustling sound as she walks.

The Lady in Black's resemblance to a portrait hanging in the lobby

of the Magnolia wing has led many in the hotel to label her "Mrs. McGavock." Just down the road from Music Valley sits Two Rivers Mansion,
the centerpiece of a luxurious antebellum plantation that once encompassed what is now Opryland, as well as the current Two Rivers Park
and Golf Course. Two Rivers initially belonged to the Harding family,
the builders of Belle Meade. It passed to the McGavocks through the
marriage of Elizabeth Harding to David McGavock in 1850. The mansion that now stands in Two Rivers Park was built in 1859, replacing
a smaller, earlier brick building. It remained in the family for over a
hundred years, until the widow of the last McGavock willed that the
remainder of her estate be sold to fund an endowment for Vanderbilt
University's medical school. The city purchased the mansion and most
of the remaining property, preserving the house and turning the surrounding turf into a golf course and park.

During my stint as guide, living-history interpreter, and curato-
rial functionary with the Nashville museums, I visited the old mansion
on a few occasions. I can't say that I had any spectral encounters, but
other Metro Parks staff who worked there on a daily basis certainly
did. Since then, reports by visitors have confirmed that the mansion is
indeed haunted. Some have heard the sound of footsteps echoing in the
empty halls. Others have reported the sensation of being watched by
unseen eyes. On occasion, objects have disappeared when left in plain
view. Lights turn themselves on and off inside the mansion.

Some have ascribed these creepy goings-on to the presence of the
graves of Native Americans or Civil War soldiers. However, given the
abundance of sightings of the Lady in Black roaming the land that was
once part of Two Rivers, it is not hard to focus on the McGavock clan
as the origin for the spectral activity. While no specific tragedy is associated with Mrs. McGavock's continued presence on the property, it
may simply be that she is unaware she is deceased. Perhaps her spectral
visits to the mansion and what are now the hotel and mall simply reflect
her daily routine in life, when she made the rounds of the plantation to
see that all was running smoothly.

Given the many folks who have made Opryland one of their preferred places to visit, it is not surprising that more than one postmortem resident has found it a favorite haunt as well. Should you stay in the grand hotel, visit the mall, take in a show, or simply play a round of golf here, you may find yourself sharing space with the elegantly dressed Lady in Black or another specter. Perhaps a tip of the hat or a polite, knowing nod is in order. It wouldn't hurt, after all, to pay your respects to those who were here before you.

**Gaylord Opryland Resort
and Convention Center
2800 Opryland Drive
Nashville, TN 37214
(615) 889-1000
www.gaylordhotels.com/gaylord-opryland/**

CHAPTER 12

Williamson Wonders

Not so long ago, Williamson County was a pastoral paradise of horse farms and green pastures where cows grazed and the occasional antebellum home dotted the countryside. In recent years, however, that rustic scene has been replaced by rambling suburban subdivisions and bustling office parks. Williamson is the most affluent county in the state, and no one seems to be complaining about the change.

But some things remain from the old days. Williamson County is still a place where strange wonders abound and close encounters with the supernatural are not uncommon.

For example, neighbors along Concord Road in Brentwood woke one morning in July 1999 to find a large, elaborate crop circle impressed on a wheat field. The formation consisted of three large circles linked by bars and assorted odd shapes. The hub of all this was a Celtic cross measuring twenty-four feet. The largest circle was nearly ninety feet in diameter.

At the time, the usual explanations were put forward. One neighbor said the crop markings were the result of "deer lying around" in the field. A member of the local constabulary speculated that "someone could have gotten in there with a Bush Hog, I guess." A bearded stranger claimed he knew who did it. "God has blessed that property," he said. That the field belonged to a local church may have added some weight to the stranger's theory.

Truth be known, genuine crop circles defy easy explanation. After a rash of crop-circle reports in the late 1980s and early 1990s, two Brits came forward and said they had made *all* those crop circles with only a rope, a plank, and a baseball cap. However, researchers found serious flaws with the two men's claim. No doubt they created a number of fake circles in Britain, but they could hardly have made them all worldwide.

Crop circles are nothing new. Up north, the Pennsylvania Dutch referred to them as "Hexen Danz" and blamed them on dancing witches. They claimed such circles were particularly prevalent on *Walpurgisnacht*—the night of April 30, the spring equivalent of Halloween. More recently, UFOs have been suggested as the source.

People have occasionally witnessed the creation of crop circles. Eyewitnesses have reported glowing lights and what seemed like a vortex of energy flattening the crops. But in the case of the Brentwood crop circle, the only witnesses were the cows in the pasture across the road. "And they aren't uddering a word," one wit observed. The phenomenon will likely remain a mystery.

The Brentwood crop circle was a singular event, but Williamson County is also home to wonders that recur on a regular basis—some would say with alarming frequency.

Along the Franklin Pike in the heart of Brentwood is Mooreland Mansion. Where once it stood in magnificent isolation, it is today surrounded by a cluster of office buildings known as Synergy Business Park. Unlike many of its sister antebellum homes, majestic Mooreland has survived modernization relatively intact. Of course, instead of an old Southern family being served drinks on the veranda, the contemporary scene at Mooreland is one of high-powered lawyers accepting retainers from corporate clients. What has not changed, however, is Mooreland's haunted reputation.

I heard of Mooreland's ghost through John Mitchell, the indefatigable editor of my first book. The resident spirit here is what the

Romans called a *lars familiaris*, or family ghost. Such ghosts are never malicious and rarely scary, save for those with nervous dispositions.

Mooreland was built in 1846 by the Moore family, who had migrated from North Carolina some years earlier. The family also gave its name to nearby Moore's Lane. The house had twenty-eight rooms, a full basement, finely wrought woodwork, and a metal roof imported from England. In its heyday and well afterward, it was a grand place to live.

The spook haunting Mooreland is a lady named Ruth whose story dates to the 1850s. Ruth Moore was the daughter of Robert Irwin Moore. Not long after she came of age, she became engaged to a young man. Strangely, on the eve of her wedding, she was found dead in her upstairs bedroom. No explanation was ever forthcoming.

Ruth's presence was a familiar sight to twentieth-century residents of the home. One longtime occupant of Mooreland, Susa Belle Thompson, regarded her as a sort of houseguest and always welcomed her company.

When the mansion and grounds were converted into offices, it was reported that the ghost went with the last resident family to its new digs at the old Cauldwell place. However, according to at least one attorney whose offices are in Mooreland, Ruth is still inside the mansion. Indeed, she has apparently gained skills in working office machines. The attorney and his staff have arrived at Mooreland many mornings to discover that the copy machine has been turned on overnight, though the office was securely locked.

Ruth may or may not have moved to Cauldwell Mansion, also located just off the Franklin Pike. But if she isn't there, *something* spooky definitely is. Years ago, when the aforementioned editor was still a college student, he had the opportunity to attend a party in Cauldwell Mansion. In the attic space, he and his friends witnessed what seemed to be a cloudlike entity without definition or shape that slowly expanded and contracted, as if breathing. When he approached the entity, it vanished. Only heaven—or hell—knows what it truly was.

A little farther down the pike heading toward Franklin is Aspen

Grove, another old mansion that has been adapted to modern purposes. Today, Aspen Grove serves as headquarters for the Tennessee Golf Foundation. After purchasing the old home in 1987, the foundation began a complete modernization, including the addition of a new wing in the rear. During the renovations, the contractor had at least one employee walk off the job site in fright. The work evidently stirred up the resident ghost. Several workers sighted an apparition in the hallway, and more than a few were unnerved by the experience.

Since then, those who work at Aspen Grove—now called "the Golf House"—have experienced a variety of spooky and kooky phenomena. Commonplace objects disappear from where they were laid, only to reappear days or weeks later elsewhere. Employees hear footsteps or catch sight of someone with their peripheral vision. But when they turn to see who it may be, nothing is visible.

An apartment was set up for a resident custodian in the rear ell of the house. One worker who dwelt there for several years had the most run-ins with the ghost. He would be awakened by the sound of vacuuming coming from the older front part of the house. Rushing to see who was there, he would discover all the lights on but nobody present. Aspen Grove's resident spirit is apparently quite fastidious.

Aspen Grove was built in the 1830s by Christopher McEwen, but its resident ghost is not believed to be that old. As with the other Brentwood mansions, it is thought to be haunted by a family spirit. In this case, the ghost is a female relative of the last residents of the mansion. When the family still lived here, her ghost would occasionally walk to the old kitchen fireplace or even stride right out of the chimney on the outside of the house, as if it were a doorway instead of solid brick. Both the mother and son of the family saw this ghost frequently, as did a farmhand who helped out about the place and was reputed to be gifted with second sight. The mother had no doubt about who was haunting her house, as she recognized the ghost as her own mother. For Golf Foundation employees and their affiliates today, she is simply "the Lady."

While Brentwood is possessed of its fair share of haunted houses, next-door Franklin, the county seat, is positively overflowing with them. This may be due in no small way to the fact that one of the blood-iest—and most senseless—battles of the Civil War was fought there.

A select few places in Franklin have become famous for their Civil War ghosts. Carter House and Carnton Mansion in particular have earned renown for their well-documented paranormal phenomena.

Carter House, although modest in size, loomed large during the Battle of Franklin in the late fall of 1864. It lay smack in the center of the line, in the one weak point of the Union defenses, where the Columbia Pike passed north toward Nashville. It was against that point that the full brunt of General John Bell Hood's Army of Tennessee fell upon the entrenched Yankee rear guard.

Starting late in the afternoon on November 30 and continuing into the dark of the night, vicious hand-to-hand fighting swirled around Carter House. Blood flowed on the ground like a spring flood. Corpses piled up in heaps where they fell from Yankee shot and shell. Still, the Rebels pressed their attack. By dawn of the next day, the stench of death hung heavy around Carter House. The moans of the dying were a low and terrible dirge.

One of those dying Rebels was Captain Tod Carter. A quartermaster, Captain Carter was not assigned to the front lines, yet he rode to the sound of the guns anyhow. That chill December morn, his family found his riddled body only a short distance from the family house. Young Tod was barely clinging to life. It was a tragic homecoming repeated many times in Franklin and Middle Tennessee that December. After lingering for several days, Captain Carter died.

After his wake was held in the front parlor, Tod Carter was buried in Resthaven Cemetery. But his spirit has lingered in Carter House ever since. In the rear of the home off a long, narrow porch is the small bedroom where Tod lay mortally wounded. On occasion, visitors have seen—or thought they saw—a young man abed, wrapped in bandages. Not even knowing the fate of Tod Carter, tourists have described him accurately to docents and staff in the house.

Other family members apparently haunt the house as well. A female ghost has been sighted running about the second floor and scampering down the front stairs. Poltergeist pranks are not uncommon throughout the house. Some believe these phenomena may all be attributed to the ghost of Annie Vick Carter, a sister of the young Rebel captain. But given the number of soldiers who died on the grounds, it is likely that other spirits also haunt the place.

On the Columbia Pike just across the street from Carter House sits Lotz House. The Lotzes were a family of hardworking German immigrants. The patriarch, Johann Albert Lotz, was not only a master carpenter but a highly skilled maker of musical instruments. During the battle, the family took refuge in the cellar of Carter House. A good thing, too, as at least one cannonball came through the roof of Lotz House, penetrating three stories and ultimately rolling about the first floor. The scar the cannonball made on the floor is still visible.

Although Lotz House was in the middle of the battle, the main ghosts haunting it seem to be of civilian origin. The most common paranormal phenomena here seem to be of the poltergeist sort. Small objects vanish, only to reappear later. Strange sounds including disembodied voices are heard as well. More rarely, apparitions have been seen—those of a woman in an old-fashioned nightgown and a small girl staring out the window.

If the spirits of the dead cluster close to the Columbia Pike, they abound in even greater numbers around the grounds of Carnton Mansion on the far eastern end of the Franklin battlefield. It was here that most of the Confederate wounded—and many of the dead—were brought after the battle. Carnton Mansion—which means "Place of the Dead" in Gaelic—served as the main field hospital and became the repository for most of the wounded and dying. Beyond the mansion stands one of the largest Confederate cemeteries in the South. Both house and grounds have numerous ghosts.

In the aftermath of the battle, the dead were piled like so much cordwood behind the house. On the rear porch of Carnton, five Confederate generals were laid out. Dozens of regimental commanders were also slain that day. Little wonder, then, that Carnton's reputation for ghostly sightings is so great.

The most famous of Carnton's ghosts is referred to as "the General." It has been seen mostly on the second floor's rear porch, as if looking out over the grounds. It is thought to be one of the generals killed in the battle, still watching over his soldiers. Alternately, it may be Colonel McGavock, the master of the house at the time and a veteran of the Confederate army.

Inside the house, visitors have spied a Rebel spirit wearing a military hat and playing a fiddle. The serenade, by all accounts, is a sad one. Nor is he the only spirit reported to dwell within. "The Weeping Maiden" has been seen on the second story as well, peering out a front bedroom window or on occasion moving from room to room. Witnesses have reported her to be sobbing. She is thought to be a member of the McGavock family still distraught over seeing so much suffering and death. Then there is "the Kitchen Ghost," which haunts the ground floor and areas adjacent to the house. She has even been captured on film by surprised tourists. This spirit is believed to be a black slave who cooked for the family.

Around the grounds and in the cemetery, visitors occasionally come across what they take to be uniformed reenactors. While Carnton does occasionally host Civil War reenactments, such sightings have often occurred when no participants were on the property.

After the battle, not just Carnton Mansion but the whole city of Franklin became a charnel house. The armies moved on to Nashville, but the wounded and dying did not. What little medical care was available in Franklin was swamped by the enormity of the bloodletting. Local citizens did what they could, but many men endured slow and agonizing deaths for want of proper care. Premature deaths, suffering, trauma—all led to restless spirits remaining bound to the ground they fought over. Throughout the old parts of town, phantoms and poltergeist activity are commonplace, although many property owners choose not to publicize the fact.

For example, at 118 Third Avenue North in the heart of downtown Franklin is Shuff's Music, the abode of at least one Civil War ghost. On occasion, an old woman is seen in a rocking chair in one of the loft studios upstairs. Thanks to a bit of historical detective work, local ghost hunters have come to believe that this apparition is an older version of a beautiful young lady who was a Confederate spy. Her nom de guerre was Sallie Carter, but she was born Sara Ewing. Using her charms on Yankee soldiers stationed in Franklin, she would pump them for information and pass it along to the Rebel army.

The old section of Franklin is home to so many haunts, in fact, that the town now hosts a ghost tour. Truth be known, however, neither Brentwood nor Franklin exhausts the spookiness to be found throughout Williamson County. For example, a "shadow ghost" inhabits the now-disused underpass along old Liberty Pike, while the ghost of frontier highwayman John A. Murrell haunts a remote spot in Farmington. Even little Leipers Fork has its resident spook light.

So, be they rural, suburban, or urban ghosts, Williamson County holds wonders in abundance and offers enough strange tales and supernatural sights to please even the most jaded of haunt hunters.

Brentwood

Mooreland Mansion (Synergy Business Park)
278 Franklin Pike (Highway 31)
Brentwood, TN 37027

Although the mansion now houses professional offices and is not open to the general public, the grounds are accessible.

Franklin

This town has so many haunted locations that I can list only a few. Call Franklin on Foot at (615) 400-3803 for more information. It offers several ghost tours of the town.

Aspen Grove (Golf House Tennessee)
400 Franklin Pike
Franklin, TN 37069
For those addicted to golf, the old mansion is a home away from home. While not generally available for tours, it does house a small museum dedicated to golf. Call before barging in.

Carter House
1140 Columbia Pike
Franklin, TN 37064
(615) 791-1861
www.carterhouse1864.com
I didn't see any ghosts when I visited, but I did get creeped out by putting my hands on the bullet-riddled south end of the house. The room where young Tod Carter died is in the rear ell.

Lotz House
1111 Columbia Pike
Franklin, TN 37064
(615) 790-7190
www.lotzhouse.com/
This house now offers a special ghost tour on request.

Carnton Mansion (Historic Carnton Plantation)
1345 Carnton Lane
Franklin, TN 37064
(615) 794-0903
www.carnton.org
This is spook central insofar as Franklin's ghosts are concerned. At one time, administrators tried to downplay the museum's haunted heritage, but that did not diminish the number of sightings. In recent years, the museum has become more open about the ghostly reputation of the

house and grounds. Check as to hours and accessibility; it is not okay to trespass after closing time.

CHAPTER 13

Hauntings of the Hills

Tourists visiting Music City for even a brief time generally take in the downtown entertainment and shopping area—"the District"—filled as it is with famous honky-tonks, glitzy gift shops, and Western clothing emporiums. However, well-heeled locals—and those who wish they were—more often head to another area to get their fix of shopping, food, and music. Green Hills is a popular destination for those in the know in Nashville. It features the best the city has to offer. The atmosphere is less hillbilly heaven and more Athens of the South. Green Hills and the adjacent neighborhoods of Forest Hills, Oak Hill, and Hillsboro are sometimes collectively called "the Seven Hills" or more commonly just "the Hills." And the Hills are also home to a number of the city's haunts.

Although the Hills are now the abode of shopaholics, workaholics, and blue-haired society matrons, this slice of Nashville was once a verdant, thickly forested wilderness. Later, the woods gave way to stone-lined fields and pastures. Running through the heart of the area today is the busy Hillsboro Pike—originally a prehistoric buffalo trail, then a pioneer trace used to traverse the untamed wilderness.

The Hills' cosmopolitan look is thus deceiving, for it disguises the area's oft-troubled history. In frontier days and during the Civil War, these rolling hills were the scene of much bloodshed. Little wonder that the Hills have haunts galore.

Ground zero of this modern shoppers' paradise is Green Hills Mall, around which cluster any number of satellite boutiques, bistros, and specialty stores. In addition to buying the latest fashions, patrons can listen to cool jazz or acoustic country and perhaps see the next top songwriter. Inside the mall are the usual trendy department stores. No surprises here—except for those who happen to shop alongside the ghost haunting the mall's hallways.

If the Music City media is to be trusted, the shoe department at Dillard's may be a popular hangout for spooks. Several years back, the men's shoes section—normally not the most interesting place in the store—had a rash of incidents that defied rational explanation. A shoe clerk was in the stockroom checking inventory one day when an apparition suddenly appeared. Experiencing any paranormal event is surprising, but when a ghost materializes in pioneer garb complete with tricorn hat and flintlock rifle, it can be very disconcerting.

It is easy to explain away a one-time affair. A person can always rationalize that it was just his imagination, or maybe something he ate. He might even chalk it up to a waking dream. But the encounter with the man in the tricorn hat that day was just the beginning. Over a period stretching at least five months, salesman Paul Meyer witnessed this same apparition repeatedly in the men's shoes section. The incident was sufficiently unusual for a local television station, WKRN, to run a segment on the haunting on its nightly news show.

Who the pioneer spirit may have been and why it chose an upscale department store to haunt remain mysteries. Given the history of the area, however, a guess may be hazarded as to the ghost's origin.

From the city's founding in 1780 until statehood in 1796, the area saw almost continuous clashes between white settlers and one or another of the Southern tribes. Farmers tilling fields, travelers traversing the old buffalo trail, hunters out seeking to put meat on the table—all were liable to sudden ambush. No accurate accounting was ever made of the deaths, scalpings, and raids during that era. Certainly, the loss of life numbered in the hundreds, if not the thousands. The oddly dressed Dillard's ghost may well have been one of those unlucky souls. And what better place for a lost soul than a shoe store?

Closer to the classic image of a Southern Gothic haunting is that at Glen Oak Mansion. Located off the Hillsboro Pike just north of the mall neighborhood, this aging antebellum home is nestled along one of those odd little avenues that stops and starts, then doglegs back and forth, as if the city planners were drunk when they laid it out. While Glen Oak was not built in the opulent style of the King Cotton palaces of the Deep South, the delicately carved and pointed arches of its front door, foyer, and hall and the ornate Victorian-era additions point to a tasteful sensibility.

Glen Oak was built around 1854 by the Reverend Charles Tomes, the English-born rector of beautiful Christ Church Episcopal in Nashville and the guiding light behind the construction of Holy Trinity Episcopal Church. Another family took up residence in Glen Oak after the Civil War and remained there until the 1920s. In those days, a double line of magnolia trees led up the path from the estate's entrance all the way to the broad porch.

That graceful colonnade of magnolias is long gone, and what had been the front yard is now thickly built with more recent homes. However, one thing that has remained despite all the changes is the Reverend Tomes himself. At odd hours of the day or night, his footsteps are heard in the house when not a soul is present who might have made such sounds. Stranger still are the reports of old coins falling to the floor from out of thin air, like manna from heaven. The appearance or disappearance of objects is a phenomenon that psychic researchers refer to as *apportation*. Usually, the objects disappear from a house, only to mysteriously reappear a few days or weeks later. Cases like Glen Oak, where antique objects materialize out of nowhere, are much rarer. Such objects might be old watches, small keepsakes, or, as here, coins. No doubt, more people would welcome living in a haunted house if they knew the ghosts would pay them hard cash!

Sometimes, the best person to ask about haunted houses is someone who buys and sells homes for a living. Richard Courtney is one of Nashville's most experienced and respected real-estate agents, as well as past president of the area's realtors' association. Not surprisingly, Courtney has over the years come across more than one home that was haunted. He provided information about yet another haunting in the Hills.

A decade or so ago, a prominent developer bought a piece of prime real estate in Green Hills with the notion of tearing down an old home and replacing it with a bigger, better, and more expensive one. As the developer was inspecting the property, a neighbor approached and asked if he intended to have the old home exorcised.

At first, the real-estate mogul didn't understand what the neighbor was talking about. She then explained that the house was haunted. Although the developer was a no-nonsense businessman and something of a skeptic, he decided to take no chances and summoned a local psychic with a reputation for "cleansing" houses. In the meantime, he also hired a contractor to begin demolition of the house and to salvage any usable fixtures.

As the teardown proceeded apace, workers came across a large chandelier in the basement. It was built in the shape of a wagon wheel. Considering all the country-music folks in Nashville, the developer thought for sure he could find a market for the unique piece.

The electricity had been shut off preliminary to beginning the demolition, so the crew thought nothing about taking down the chandelier. As the workers started to dismantle it, however, all the lights on the wagon wheel suddenly lit up. Assuming the electricians had been negligent, the contractor angrily went to the breaker box to shut off the hot circuits. When he opened the box, however, he found that all the breakers and attachments had been completely removed. Nothing was connected! The crew made a second attempt to remove the reluctant chandelier. Again, the bulbs lit up. The contractor gave up on the haunted wagon wheel and left it to the ghosts.

The psychic subsequently came in and cleansed the house of no fewer than four ghosts. The fifth, a former caretaker, refused to leave, citing his duty to look after the land. After the house on Hampton Place was torn down, the caretaker's ghost finally did depart the property, only to take up residence in the house across the street.

A short drive—and an even shorter walk—from the Hillsboro Pike stands Longview Mansion. Like Glen Oak, this Italianate-style home dates to before the Civil War. Also like Glen Oak, it is haunted.

Longview began in the 1840s as a modest four-room cottage on a two-thousand-acre plot. The land was given to Henry and Laura Norvell as a bridal gift by Laura's grandfather John Sevier, frontier hero and the first governor of Tennessee. Because of the lush vegetation, the couple nicknamed the place "Leafy Lot."

As with most of the Hills, the land around Longview was caught in the middle of the Battle of Nashville in December 1864. The Confederates commandeered the home and turned it briefly into a field hospital, so it was the scene of much suffering. During the siege and subsequent battle, Rebel troops cut down most of the large trees on the property to provide warmth from the bitter cold. By the end of the battle, it was no longer "Leafy Lot" but rather "Hood's Waste."

It was not until after the war that the home took on its present form. Financier James Caldwell bought it in 1878, enlarged it into a two-story villa, and renamed it Longview. In 1906, the house went through further renovations, including the addition of a third story, to bring it to its current ten thousand square feet. Today, Longview Mansion is part of David Lipscomb University's scenic campus, where it serves as the Center for Spiritual Renewal, a sort of ministry for ministers.

Church authorities who oversee the property are understandably reluctant to weigh in as to whether or not the building is haunted. However, over the years, students, staff, and security officers at David Lipscomb have all had unusual experiences in and around Longview, so much so that many have been convinced that the old place is inhabited by ghosts.

Visitors often experience lights switching on and off by themselves.

More commonly, people going inside for the first time get an overall sense of creepiness. During patrols at night, campus security guards regularly see windows open on the second and third stories where earlier they were shut. On going inside to secure the property, the guards find every door securely locked and no signs of forced entry.

The grounds outside Longview are a popular spot for young couples to "get comfortable." They regularly park near the glass-enclosed fountain room, especially on moonlit nights. In one case, a pair of lovers saw what looked like a large man staring at them from inside the house. After they called campus security, the man vanished from sight. A security guard went inside Longview to check on the possible trespasser, only to find the place vacant and everything locked up tight.

Some years earlier, when the school first took over the old mansion, workers were renovating the third floor when they felt waves of heat suddenly coming over them. The heat was so intense that they had to flee. When they finally returned to the third floor with their foreman, the temperature was normal again. Such hot spots as the workmen encountered, while rarer than cold spots, are yet another symptom of a supernatural presence in a building.

Another haunted mansion connected to the Battle of Nashville is Sunnyside, which lies along Granny White Pike. Now the center of a small city park and headquarters for the Metropolitan Historical Commission, it was in the middle of some of the heaviest fighting in 1864. In fact, bullet holes are still visible on the front porch and elsewhere in the house. Like Longview, Sunnyside was used as a field hospital, although by the Yankees instead of the Rebs. Its paranormal phenomena seem clearly connected to the battle. As for Granny White, her grave lies several miles down her namesake pike. During frontier days, she ran a "stand." Her hospitality to travelers was legendary, as were the pumpkins she used to sell them. According to local lore, those who stand on Granny White's grave can still hear her heartbeat today.

The Seven Hills were the focal point of the Battle of Nashville. The Confederate Army of Tennessee under Lieutenant General John Bell Hood was completely defeated by the Union men of Major General

George H. "Pap" Thomas, who was himself a Southerner—a Virginian, in fact. In the aftermath of the battle, many of the dead were buried where they lay, some in shallow single graves but many in mass graves, where they were unceremoniously tossed by the Yankee victors.

Some years back, when I worked for the city's museums conducting living-history programs, a lady who lived in Green Hills visited Fort Nashborough with her children. In talking about Nashville history, she mentioned that a developer building a subdivision in Green Hills had uncovered a mass grave containing hundreds of skeletons. He could have called in authorities to have archaeologists come and remove the war dead for a decent burial. But he feared that would delay his building schedule, so he simply ordered his crew to run their bulldozers and bury the soldiers again.

How many homes in that tract have since experienced unexplained phenomena as a result of the developer's desire to turn a quick profit? If the hauntings are subtle enough, many folks may find it easy to ignore them, perhaps dismissing their kids' comments about seeing people as just childhood imagination. Most are probably unaware that their homes were built on a bloody battlefield.

The known hauntings of the Hills likely just scratch the surface of the area's paranormal phenomena. However, lest it be concluded that the Seven Hills are unduly burdened with the spirits of the dead, it bears noting that the entire city has a surfeit of spirits. "Nashville," as realtor Richard Courtney observed, "is a hub of paranormal activity." Nashville's haints will for the foreseeable future continue to amaze, bewilder—and occasionally frighten—the living.

Sunnyside Mansion in Sevier Park
3000 Granny White Pike
Nashville, TN 37204
(615) 862-7970 (Metropolitan
Historical Commission)

CHAPTER 14

Holy Ghosts

Hollywood tends to portray hauntings as the product of malevolent or demonic forces, but the truth is that real ghosts are for the most part benign. Some are even benevolent and protective. Hauntings are often the result of spirits that have become lost in space and time or have grown so attached to particular places that they are unwilling to move on. While witnesses may well become scared at encountering such supernatural entities, that usually is not the spirits' intent—if indeed they are even aware they're dead.

Although most Christian sects are reluctant to discuss ghosts, it is not uncommon to come across churches and church-related buildings that are haunted. Great Britain is chock-full of them. In fact, the founder of Methodism, John Wesley, had a famous encounter with a ghost in the Borley Rectory. So it should not be shocking to learn that Nashville has several such places that are haunted.

In the heart of uptown Nashville (downtown to Yankee transplants) stands the oldest church in Nashville, St. Mary's of the Seven Sorrows. Consecrated in 1847, St. Mary's has survived war, pestilence, and the passage of time.

Walking up the stone steps worn by the passage of the faithful for more than a century and a half and passing over the threshold into the sanctuary, visitors are transported back in time. The lingering aroma of incense fills the air. The spare decorations on the walls reflect the simple piety of an earlier era.

A place of solace and refuge, St. Mary's has seen its share of suffering and woe. The Yankees commandeered all the merchant buildings when they occupied the city in 1862. To gall the secessionist citizenry, they also seized churches and turned them to profane uses. Holy Trinity Episcopal Church became an ammo dump, while both St. Mary's and Assumption Catholic churches were made military hospitals.

Even in the best of times, hospitals are places of pain and suffering. During the Civil War, many wounded soldiers lying on cots at St. Mary's experienced agony. During the war, some three hundred soldiers died here. Nor was war the only cause of death here. During the church's construction, one priest is alleged to have fallen to his death from a scaffold while making an inspection. Another died from a fall out a rectory window after the war.

Given its long history, St. Mary's has seen far more than seven sorrows over the years. Still, the general feeling inside the church today is one of peace and serenity. And perhaps that is why at least one ghost is believed to have resided here.

How long St. Mary's spirit was active is not known. Judging by eyewitness accounts, it began haunting the premises before the 1930s.

During the Depression, an Irish housekeeper, Nell Hines, worked here. One day, Nell was cleaning the kitchen when she noticed a new priest walking up the stairs at the rectory. Wondering if he might want a bite to eat, she called up the stairs after him. Curious as to who the new cleric might be, she went up to the office of the parish secretary, a gentleman named Richard Quick, and inquired after the visitor. Quick had seen no visitor. They both tried to rationalize the incident by telling themselves the new priest had somehow slipped out of the building without their noticing. However, Nell had similar experiences several more times.

She finally went to the parish priest, Father Duffy, to ask how long the visiting clergyman might be staying and whether or not she should set an extra place for breakfast. This caught Father Duffy by surprise, for he knew of no visitor. A thorough search of the rectory and church discovered no one. Nell continued to see the mysterious visitor climbing the same stairs. But she never caught sight of the phantom cleric in the sanctuary.

During this same period, however, the church's custodian had repeated encounters with a phantom priest in the church proper. John Walker cleaned St. Mary's during the daytime and then closed up in the evening when all the churchgoers were gone. At night, he would lock the doors and turn off all the lights in the sanctuary. The only illumination came through the stained-glass windows. In their dim glow, he saw on more than one occasion the figure of a priest walking down the center aisle and approaching the altar in a slow, measured gait. He witnessed the apparition often enough to gain a clear idea of how it looked. The ghost was upwards of six feet in height, wore a tall hat, and held a long walking stick or staff that touched the floor as he strode forward. The mysterious apparition did not resemble any of the priests at St. Mary's.

The parish priests themselves never saw the phantom cleric, but over the years each one had his own anecdote about St. Mary's hauntings.

At times, Father Duffy would be sitting in the rectory library when the heavy wooden door suddenly swung open on its own, then closed. Then, in quick succession, the door to his bedroom on the opposite side of the room would also open and close. It was as if someone had walked through the room while he was sitting there.

Another priest who served at St. Mary's often heard footsteps in the church during the night. At other times, he was awakened in the rectory by someone knocking loudly on his door. On rare occasions during his twelve years at the church, the bells of St. Mary's would start ringing of their own accord. The bell rope was in the choir loft at the rear of the church. The bells were large, heavy, old-fashioned affairs. While one did not need to be a hunchback to work them, a good bit of elbow grease was required to get them ringing. Certainly, no mere gust of wind could have done it. Each time the incident occurred, the priest investigated. Each time, he found no sign of anyone in the loft.

In 1937, the chief priest at St. Mary's of the Seven Sorrows was Monsignor John Morgan. One evening, he was soundly sleeping when he was awakened by a pounding on his bedroom door. Getting up to investigate, he found the door to the hallway still shut. He was just drifting back off when there came a rapping not on his chamber door but on the headboard of his bed. Again, no one was there. A few days later, the monsignor was attending to his duties as director of Calvary Cemetery. The Catholic burial ground was located not far from town along the Lebanon Pike. It sat adjacent to the more prestigious Mount Olivet Cemetery, where the city's elite lay. Father Morgan had not been long at his duties when, without warning, he had a massive coronary and died. Was it coincidence that his death followed close on the heels of his uncanny encounter, or was the nighttime rapping a summons home?

Several theories seek to identify St. Mary's resident haunt. The deaths of two priests on the grounds put them in the running. The church's service as a hospital during the Civil War allows other possibilities. The most likely candidate, however, dates back to the origin of the church. He was Richard Pius Miles, the founding bishop of Nashville's Catholic diocese. The apparition sighted by the janitor in the 1930s was reported to be wearing a tall hat very much like a bishop's miter. Moreover, the staff in the ghost's hand may well have been a crosier, the symbol of a bishop's office, patterned after a shepherd's crook.

Also weighing in favor of the bishop as the ghost is the fact that in 1969, Bishop Miles was discovered to have been entombed in the foundation of the church, in a chamber at the rear of the building. He was buried in a large cast-iron coffin with a glass panel, clothed in his ceremonial robes. The bishop's body was found to be in a remarkable state of preservation for someone so long dead.

Rather than being reinterred where he was discovered, the bishop was moved upstairs to a small side chapel at the rear of the church, where visitors still may say a prayer or two over his remains. Since his relocation upstairs, the ghost's nightly visitations have reportedly ceased. Apparently, the change of scenery suited the bishop's spirit. It may be assumed that the prayers of the faithful and the heavenly scent of incense in the sanctuary proved more congenial to his soul than the cold, lonely, musty crypt.

Bishop Miles is not the only religious spirit roaming Nashville. Other church-related buildings in Music City also have a reputation for present or former hauntings.

For many years, the old St. Thomas Hospital on Church Street was home to a ghost that medical staff referred to simply as "Mary." The hospital began in 1898, when the Daughters of Charity of St. Vincent de Paul took over the old Dickinson home. The property included about eight acres stretching between Twentieth and Twenty-first avenues on Church. In 1900, the old house was razed and construction began on a hundred-bed hospital. Over the years, new wings were added until the facility occupied the entire block.

However, by the 1960s, St. Thomas Hospital was in need of modernization and expansion. It was judged best to move the entire facility to a new campus several miles down the road, where Harding and White Bridge roads met. Moreover, next-door neighbor Baptist Hospital needed additional bed and office space, so the old St. Thomas building was sold to that Christian medical institution. It was a perfect win-win situation—for everyone save Mary.

Before the old hospital was turned over to the new authorities, its former chapel had all its furniture removed, including a statue of the Virgin Mary. A fresh coat of paint was then applied to the room. When the new staff took over, however, observers noticed a curious thing. Where the statue of Mary had been, a shadow remained on the wall, like a silhouette of the figure. The room was windowless, so no shadow was possible. Even after the wall was sanded and repainted, the image of Mary kept coming back, as though she did not wish to vacate the premises. Nor was there any doubt as to the image's identity. No one who saw it could mistake it for anyone other than Mary.

The silhouette was not the only curious thing about the old St. Thomas facility. Sometimes late at night, nurses on duty in that section of the hospital heard vague whispering and the rattle of wooden beads, as if someone were saying the rosary. Staff referred to this invisible apparition as "the Bishop," although the spirit's actual identity remained unknown. In addition, nurses in the old hospital wing sometimes heard babies crying at night when all was otherwise quiet. This would not have seemed unusual except that the maternity ward was in a newer wing nowhere nearby. Uncanny happenings continued in the old St. Thomas wing until the early 1980s. At that time, the aging facility was torn down to make way for state-of-the-art medical buildings, and that was the last of Mary.

Only a few blocks up from where St. Thomas formerly stood was another old building with a religious affiliation also alleged to be haunted. Built in the 1920s on what is now Elliston Place, Father Ryan High School was founded to provide a Christian atmosphere for educating young men. Over the years, an apparition was occasionally spotted roaming its hallways. Described as being clothed in the dress of a priest, the ghost was commonly referred to as "Father Ryan."

There is reason to doubt that the ghost was actually that of Father Ryan. The school was named in honor of the cleric who earned the title "poet-priest of the Confederacy" for his support of the Lost Cause. The school's name was chosen mainly due to the high esteem in which Father Ryan was held in the South. However, his actual connection to Nashville was minimal. He is believed to have visited a few times but had no strong attachment to the city or its populace.

At this late date, it is impossible to identify the ghostly presence that roamed the halls of the old Father Ryan, but a vague reference to its being headless may provide a hint. Unlike the more famous Father Ryan, one priest during the Civil War was closely associated with the town's Catholic young men. The Tenth Tennessee Volunteer Infantry, CSA, was part of the Army of the Tennessee. The unit was commonly referred to as "the Fighting Irish," as it was comprised in large part of Irish Catholics who had immigrated to Nashville in the 1850s to help build the State Capitol. In truth, the regiment had a number of German Catholics as well, stone masons who had likewise settled in the city to ply their trade. The home parish to both groups was the Church of the Assumption, located in Germantown, a neighborhood within sight of the State Capitol and also not far from the later location of Father Ryan High. When the Civil War broke out, many young men of these two ethnic communities volunteered for service in the Confederate army. The men of the Tenth fought—and died—bravely in some of the bloodiest battles of the war.

Upon being sent to the front, the young men—mostly teenagers—felt their regiment needed a chaplain to minister to their spiritual needs. They elected their parish priest, Father Emmeran Blemiel. A Benedictine priest born in Bavaria, Blemiel likely had little understanding of the political issues at stake in the war. What he did understand was that the young men of his parish desired his spiritual guidance. After some resistance from church authorities, Father Blemiel was appointed regimental chaplain for the Fighting Irish of the Tenth.

He joined up with the regiment in Georgia, where it was involved in a series of bloody battles defending Atlanta from the Yankees. During one particularly deadly encounter against Sherman's bluecoats, the regimental commander, Colonel Grace, was mortally wounded. Chaplain Blemiel, ignoring the gunfire, rushed to the dying man's side to administer last rites. As he knelt over Colonel Grace performing the sacrament, a Yankee cannonball came whistling by and blew off his head. Father Blemiel was the first priest in America to die in combat. So if the priestly ghost was indeed of the headless sort, likely it was Father Blemiel.

Father Ryan relocated to the suburbs. The site of the old school at the corner of Twenty-third and Elliston Place is an empty lot today. Only a stone wall remains. The ghost is mainly a memory in the minds of former students.

At 1400 Eighteenth Avenue South, deep in the heart of Music Row, stands a curious-looking office building with a curious history and a curious nickname. Today, it is home to the Sony Records Nashville group of music labels. Its current mission has nothing in common with prayer and fasting and nuns begging for a living. Nonetheless, the place is commonly referred to as "the Convent."

Every day, high-powered music executives, recording artists, and other glamorous folks come and go from the building, all in a rush. No doubt, few who visit take notice of anything unusual about the place, other than the fact that it looks more like a Renaissance Italian villa than a modern office building. However, a few people who work in the old building can probably recite a litany of odd and curious things that have happened there since it became office space.

The Little Sisters of the Poor was founded in the 1830s in France as a mendicant order of nuns. As part of their religious discipline, the nuns went about begging for a living. Unlike the beggars in downtown Nashville today, they weren't trying to amass enough money to buy booze. Rather, they were begging for money to help the city's elderly sick, who lacked both shelter and medical care.

The nuns came to Nashville in 1903 with the mission of ministering to the city's indigent seniors. Within a few years, by begging door to door, they managed to build a facility in Edgefield housing two score or more of the poor. However, the East Nashville fire of 1916 destroyed the building, and they had to start all over again elsewhere. But luck—or divine grace—was on their side. By 1917, they opened a new and larger home on a plot of land between Seventeenth Avenue South and Eighteenth Avenue South.

Although its nickname suggests otherwise, the new building was not a convent at all. Its actual title was the Little Sisters of the Poor Home for the Aged. Back in the days before Social Security, Medicare, and universal health care, the old, poor, and sick who had no families to take care of them were literally better off dead. Fortunately, Nashvillians have always been generous folks. By going door to door downtown, the sisters were able to provide care and shelter for the poorest and sickest of the city's elderly.

Times changed, however. By 1969, the home was closed and the nuns—by now themselves mostly elderly—had moved out of the building. For several years, it remained empty. Then it had a brief life as a private nursing home, after which it again fell vacant. The pastor of St. Mary's referred to the structure as "a big tomb—100,000 square feet of tomb."

Finally, in 1999, BMG Music bought the old brick building with a view to renovating and restoring it as executive office space. The news was welcomed by all. BMG's move meant a historic site would be preserved. And the company would have elegant offices for its growing enterprises.

In due course, a contractor was hired and construction crews began their work. Whether the demolition crew stirred something up or the "big tomb" had always been spiritually active is not known. But during the renovation, workmen began to notice unusual things inside the building. The uncanny incidents became so frequent and bothersome that a number of them walked off the job.

Despite the troubles with spooked crews, the contractors finished the renovations, and the new building became the headquarters of BMG Nashville. In the process, its main entrance was moved from the Horton Street side to 1400 Eighteenth Avenue South. The nuns' old chapel was converted into "Chet Atkins Place," a twenty-five-hundred-square-foot showplace complete with wet bar, sound baffles around the windows, and memorabilia preserved from the old building. Also preserved were the nuns' ghosts.

As with most Music Row businesses, the building on Eighteenth Avenue keeps changing with the times. BMG has been absorbed into Sony Music, so the Convent is now ground zero for that corporation's many music enterprises in the city.

From what can be gathered through offhand remarks by people who have worked or visited there, the haunting is not intense by any means. Small objects occasionally move themselves around, but no one has ever seen them levitate. During the hustle and bustle of a routine office day, little is likely noticed. At night when all is quiet, however, odd noises become noticeable—subtle sounds like the quiet mumbling people make when deep in prayer. Rarely, small, hooded figures in black have been sighted. Are the Little Sisters still making their ghostly rounds?

The haunting of the Convent has not seemed to pose serious problems for the high-octane offices of the major recording-industry labels housed there. Doubtless, dealing with musicians and other entertainers on a daily basis has given industry folks a higher tolerance for the unusual than that possessed by construction workers.

Even should the businesses that occupy offices at the Convent wish to be shed of their spectral tenants, an exorcism would likely do no good. Exorcisms are designed to expel evil spirits from a person or place. But what could be done with spirits that are holy ghosts?

St. Mary's of the Seven Sorrows
460 Fifth Avenue North
Nashville, TN 37219
(615) 256-1784
bellsouthpwp.net/j/c/jcoonce/stmary/index.html

The phantom bishop's resting place is in a small chapel at the rear of the church, to the left as you come in. In the parking lot on the backside of the church, you can see where the brickwork was disturbed when his sepulcher was discovered.

CHAPTER 15

Phantoms of the New Morgue

In recent years, the once-sedate city of Nashville has experienced rapid growth. People from all over are dying to move to Music City.

Much like the ever-widening interstates with their growing traffic jams, Nashville's city morgue experienced a logjam as well. Most who pass peacefully (and prosperously) have their neighborhood funeral home prepare them for the great voyage. But the poor, the dispossessed, and the disreputable must resort to the municipal morgue. Luckless losers with no home, petty hoodlums iced in deals gone bad, winos sleeping under piers when the river rises—all end up under the medical examiner's scalpel in the morgue.

For decades, a rambling complex of stone and brick buildings on a bluff overlooking a bend of the Cumberland was home to Metro General Hospital. Part of that complex housed the morgue. Although the morgue warehoused the less fortunate only briefly, the spirits of the dead often stayed long after their bodies moved on.

A popular theory as to what causes ghosts holds that when someone dies a violent or premature death or dies with important business unfulfilled, the spirit fails to move on, instead staying bound to the earthly plane. Since the city morgue housed the bodies of many such individuals, it is perhaps not surprising that it collected spirits as a matter of course.

Originally, the morgue was housed on the top floor of the oldest wing of the hospital. Nurses and aides frequently referred to that floor as "the Haunted House." The aging Victorian brick structure looked eerie enough to give the House of Usher a run for its money.

Over the years, many on the hospital staff had weird experiences in the old morgue. So common were spooky encounters that attendants became reluctant to go to the top floor, to the point that, when compelled to bring a corpse up there, they would hastily leave the gurney bearing the body sticking halfway out the swinging doors, then make a quick retreat. Often as not, a nurse with more grit would end up going upstairs to store the body properly.

Finally, as the need for storage space increased and the need for forensic exams grew apace, the city morgue was moved to a larger facility, a gray stone outbuilding at 84 Hermitage Avenue. No doubt, many in the hospital breathed a sigh of relief.

But the transition to more spacious quarters in no way brought a halt to the morgue's spectral visitations. The squarish brick-and-stone two-story building's basement became the morgue's new home. Soon, it began experiencing uncanny phenomena much as the old morgue had. Medical investigators working there witnessed strange sights. A shadow without any accompanying object was seen levitating across a room and disappearing inside the opposite wall. Notations written on a message board in the lab vanished without cause or explanation.

As time went on, the incidents became even harder to explain. On one occasion, a staffer caught a glimpse of a man in a striped coat reflected in a window. When he turned around, no one was there. Another time, a large metal tray was heard loudly clattering to the floor in the M.E.'s office in the dark of night. When someone went to investigate the commotion, nothing was out of place. More commonly, staff members working in the new morgue admitted to the eerie sensation of being watched or of feeling they were not alone when no one living was there besides themselves.

Over the years, employees of the city morgue became convinced that the facility was genuinely haunted, although few were willing to discuss such things on the record. An exception to this was medical investigator Gary Biggs. On at least one occasion, Biggs gave journalists a long history of encounters he had in the new morgue.

For example, he told of the instance when he spied a lady in a vivid yellow dress, only to see her disappear before his eyes. Then there was the time he saw a man out of the corner of his eye coming down the hallway. The man seemed to be looking over his shoulder at something. When Biggs turned to look directly at the mysterious gent, the spectral visitor was not there. While Biggs seems to have been more sensitive than most to paranormal phenomena, his experiences in the new morgue were far from unique. Even staff members who had no such dramatic encounters did not question the morgue's haunted reputation.

By its very nature, the morgue was prone to being a favorite haunt of restless spirits. However, the paranormal activity on Hermitage Avenue may owe its origin to events farther in the past than the old general hospital and city morgue.

Only a few blocks from Metro General lies the site of an Indian massacre dating to the city's early days. On the western shoulder of Rutledge Hill, a violent clash took place between settlers and Indians. Afterward, the bodies of the slain were hastily tossed in a shallow grave somewhere in the vicinity. Later, in the Civil War, a Union fort stood where the hospital later went up. During the Battle of Nashville, men fought and died on the same turf where the morgues, old and new, were located. Then, too, a "contraband camp" sprouted just downhill from the fort during the war. Fugitive slaves camped there in their bid for freedom. Lacking food, money, and decent shelter, many of them died from exposure and starvation in that place and were unceremoniously buried in unmarked graves.

And if all this was not sufficient to attract the spirits of the restless dead, the old University of Nashville's medical department once stood a block from the city morgue. Cadavers were stored there in days gone by. After the Civil War, the university went out of existence, but its medical school was grafted onto the new Vanderbilt University. A staid Victorian building still proudly bears the name of the department in the arch over its entrance. Not surprisingly, spectral goings-on have been reported at the former medical school on Second Avenue South as well.

If old Metro General witnessed pain and suffering, it also helped many folks in need and saved untold lives over the decades. But as Nashville grew, so, too, did the demand for a newer facility to better serve the city. The new millennium witnessed the move of Nashville General Hospital to a more up-to-date facility in another part of town. Not long after that, the medical examiner's department also departed Hermitage Avenue. In July 2001, in an arrangement involving the state, the city, and a private forensic medical group, the examiner's operations were moved to a state-of-the-art facility adjacent to the Tennessee Bureau of Investigation's new headquarters—one stop chopping, as it were. The medical buildings on Rolling Mill Hill were left vacant—except, of course, for the spirits of the dead.

Today, the grounds of the old city hospital are undergoing yet another transformation. Once a frontier trail, then a Civil War fort, then an inner-city hospital, they are now being converted into a complex of upscale townhouses, condominiums, and shops. The "new" morgue at 84 Hermitage Avenue is gone completely, the building razed along with most of the rambling hospital complex. But the oldest section of Metro General—the Victorian wing known as "the Haunted House"—has been preserved and renovated for residential use.

Amid all these changes, one question remains unanswered: will the new, young urban pioneers who move to the old hospital grounds be able to reach an accommodation with their spectral neighbors? Only time will tell.

CHAPTER 16

Honky-Tonk Highway
The Ghosts of Lower Broad

Nowadays, people call it "the District." It has also been known as "Honky-Tonk Highway" and even "Hillbilly Heaven" by some. Situated at the foot of downtown Nashville, it consists of the first five blocks of Lower Broadway (or Lower Broad) and the side streets branching off it. For good or ill, it remains the heart and soul of Nashville. It is a must-see for visitors to Music City. Day or night, this stretch of Lower Broad and the nearby blocks are filled with live music, free-flowing beer, gift shops, good eats—and ghosts.

The District is in fact the oldest part of town. Behind the neon and the good times stretches a long and at times violent history. Frontier fights, Civil War occupation, feuds, and monster floods—this part of town has weathered them all and somehow survived.

The District is also the place where aspiring performers come with empty pockets and old guitars on their backs in hopes of stardom.

Some have managed to succeed; many have not. Good times and bad have left their mark on the spirit of the District. And if this part of Nashville has one thing, it is spirit—quite a number of spirits, in fact.

Of course, the best-known haunt in the District is the old Ryman Auditorium, for decades the home of the Grand Ole Opry. Built in the 1890s to house religious revivals, "the Mother Church of Country Music" later became the Opry's theater. Its existence stretching back over a century, the theater has managed to accumulate several ghosts. Although I have chronicled the many haunts of the Ryman before, one curious fact has not been previously noted by me or others—that is, many of the spirits seem to wander back and forth between the theater and nearby Tootsie's Orchid Lounge. For anyone who has hung out at either landmark, the reason for this is not hard to see.

Tootsie's Orchid Lounge—which modestly bills itself as "world famous"—is located at 422 Broadway, just around the corner from Ryman Auditorium. In fact, Tootsie's back door opens into an alley directly in line with the old stage door to the Ryman. In the Opry's glory days, old-time performers would walk across the alley to Tootsie's to kill time—and several beers—until they had to go back on the stage for the late show. In death, several of the ghosts of the District still meander between the two old haunts.

Some country stars got so relaxed at the bar at Tootsie's that they never quite made it back to the Ryman stage. Moreover, as often as not, they would start jamming at Tootsie's. From what old-timers have told me, the free shows in the honky-tonk were far better than the ones on the stage of the Opry.

Tootsie's was first known as Mom's. The mom who originally ran the place was a lady named Louise Hackler. Then, in 1960, another Louise—Hattie Louise Besse, better known as Tootsie Besse—took over the place. Tootsie presided for many years. It was her odd choice of paint during remodeling that is responsible for the honky-tonk's distinctive look today. Apparently, she wrote down the wrong code, so it came out a plum orchid color instead of a red hue. Rather than throw a fit, Tootsie took a what-the-hell attitude, and the plum orchid color remained. Ever since then, the bar has been known as Tootsie's Orchid Lounge.

Many's the tale told of Tootsie. Over time, some of the stories of her predecessor have merged with hers to create a legend of one great honky-tonk woman. During the 1950s and 1960s, the two Louises gave breaks to many down-and-out musicians. It was well known that Tootsie would often allow performers to write IOUs to her for drinks, knowing full well they would never redeem them. She would put them in a big jar that sat on the bar.

At one time, Roger Miller was one of those penniless musicians with high hopes whom Tootsie befriended. According to legend, once he found success, he would buy up Tootsie's worthless IOUs whenever he came to town so she would not go out of business.

Tootsie also allowed musicians to crash in the apartments upstairs in exchange for cleaning up the bar. Willie Nelson was one of those hopefuls. In his off hours, he wrote songs upstairs. One of the tunes he penned in this manner was Patsy Cline's "Crazy."

When the Opry moved to the suburbs in 1974, not only Tootsie's but the whole downtown entertainment scene went downhill. Tootsie died in 1978, which only accelerated the bar's decline. The music stopped. The place became just one more wino bar.

Still, there remained a special aura about Tootsie's. Perhaps it was that the owner's spirit refused to give up on the place. Some believe she still presides there today.

In the early 1990s, new owners took over the bar with a view to restoring it to its old glory. Perhaps the honky-tonk's renewed atmosphere accounts for the greatly increased reports of ghost sightings in recent years. The revived spirit of the place may have inspired the old country ghosts to show up more often.

The most-sighted ghost in Tootsie's is that of Hank Williams. He has been reported haunting the bar and ordering drinks. A photo taken of Tootsie's stage shows a grayish mist that some say looks for all the world like Hank Sr. His ghost has also been sighted in the alley behind the bar—the one that leads to the old stage door of the Opry.

Other legendary country performers have also been reported haunting the club. Among them are Roger Miller, Ernest Tubb, and a female apparition dressed in calico whom many think may be Patsy Cline. How far back Tootsie's hauntings go is uncertain. But it is known that in the late 1800s, the upstairs served as a brothel, so some of the ghosts may date to the era before Tootsie's became a country bar. Willie Nelson routinely heard odd noises when he was rooming upstairs.

Tootsie's may be the best-known haunt of the District, but is by no means the only one. Across the street at 401 Broadway is Merchants restaurant, another building with a long history and well-documented spectral activity. The three-story structure dates to around 1870, when it replaced an earlier building. Originally, the ground level was a pharmacy, the second floor housed a hardware manufacturing company, and the third floor held a wholesale drug company.

It was not until 1892 that the Merchants Hotel opened in the building. There was a thriving steamboat trade in those days, and the hotel aimed to snag some of the business that came with merchants in town for commerce. Although each room had a bed and a fireplace, single occupancy was not guaranteed. Guests often had to share a bed with a stranger. Then, when the Grand Ole Opry began its performances across the street at the Ryman in 1925, the hotel became the favorite place to stay for performers. During the 1920s, it also held a speakeasy. In World War II, a brothel operated upstairs to cater to the large number of GIs in town on leave.

Despite all the changes over the years, Merchants always retained its connection to the Grand Ole Opry. Truth is, despite the glamour attached to performing there, the Opry never did pay performers much, and Merchants was a cheap place close to the theater for musicians to hang their hats. Hank Williams, Dolly Parton, Porter Wagoner, Little Jimmy Dickens, and others were all patrons.

When the Opry moved out, the hotel fell on hard times. By the 1980s, it was ready for the wrecking ball. Fortunately, a local restaurateur saw it as a diamond in the rough rather than a sleazy old hole and bought it. Following extensive renovations to the interior, the old hotel reopened as a classy upscale restaurant with a piano bar. Today, Merchants is a jewel of a place that retains much of its old charm and all of its old ghosts.

The main spirit haunting Merchants is believed to be a ghost named Charlie. Employees and guests have seen a male apparition walking the halls. Visitors entering the restaurant have looked up at the third floor and witnessed a man hanging inside a window there. Employees have also reported intense paranormal activity. Supposedly, some workers are so spooked by the ghost on the third floor that they have resigned rather than go up there.

On the bottom floor, a supernatural presence haunts a storage area called "Charlie's Room." Staff members commonly report getting the creeps just going in there. The room is chilly no matter what the weather and has a cold spot at its center.

One explanation has it that the ghost is the son of the pharmacist who ran his operation there in the 1870s. By this account, the pharmacist's young son, despondent for reasons unknown, committed suicide upstairs.

Another story says the ghost is that of Charlie Keenan, a former Confederate soldier, a cad, and the sometime lover of a girl named Georgia Edmundson. The restaurant in fact has some of the original correspondence between the two. Despite professing his undying love for her, Charlie cheated on Georgia with another woman, so she broke off the relationship. The dejected Charlie committed suicide by hanging himself in his hotel room.

Some eyewitnesses have seen a ghost that looks like a soldier roaming the hallways. Yet Charlie died much later than the Civil War, so such reports do not square with the above account. It may well be that more than one apparition haunts the old hotel. Although the building was constructed after the War Between the States, some of its ghosts may have lingered from the previous structure. Perhaps future investigations of Merchants' haunted history will clarify the situation.

Down at Ernest Tubb Record Shop at 417 Broadway, there is no doubt that the old place is haunted by more than one ghost. In fact, the adjacent business, the Nashville Crossroads honky-tonk at 419 Broadway, shares the same gaggle of ghosts.

A mainstay of the Broadway scene since 1947, Ernest Tubb Record Shop is a legend among country fans, much as the man himself is. Diehard fans come from far away on their quests to locate hard-to-find country classics. Rarely do they go away disappointed. The downtown store was also the home for many years of the Midnite Jamboree, a show held after the Opry performance on Saturday nights. Although the show now broadcasts from out near Opryland, this old building was its home for decades.

Longtime workers at Ernest Tubb's are accustomed to odd happenings. The stairs in the store have both hot and cold spots, a sign of strong spectral presence. The stairs to the basement are particularly active. The store's CD player is programmed to play its songs in random order, yet on more than a few occasions, customers talking to the staff will mention a vintage country artist's name, only to have the CD player start a song by the artist in question.

Like so many old buildings in the District, the one housing Ernest Tubb's and Nashville Crossroads was taken over by the Yankees for military uses during the Civil War. According to some, the basement was used as a morgue for soldiers who died in the hospital upstairs. However, the paranormal experiences with the CD player argue for more recent ghosts as well. Since so many legendary country stars came through the doors to sing and play, it may be that some of them also came to stay.

A few doors down, Lawrence Record Shop at 409 Broadway has a few haunts of its own. While not so famous as Ernest Tubb's, it, too, is a mecca for those in search of rare country recordings. Employees often smell cigar smoke, even though no smoking is allowed in the building. The former owner was a big cigar smoker. Workers believe that their former boss, while dead, is not entirely gone.

Many more haunted honky-tonks are located on Broadway and nearby Market Street (Second Avenue). At Layla's Bluegrass Inn, for example, a mischievous spirit likes to hide patrons' packs of cigarettes.

Past Perfect on Third Avenue South, a trendy restaurant that occasionally offers live music, has multiple ghost stories to tell, including one about a Black Aggie. Many of the buildings on Second Avenue date to before the Civil War; most served as hospitals during the conflict, and almost all are haunted. The Melting Pot fondue restaurant offers up a pair of ghostly lovers along with its melted cheese. At Buffalo Billiards, the ghost of at least one old warehouse worker still hangs around past closing time. Mulligan's Pub and Restaurant is allegedly haunted by an unhappily married pair of spooks. B. B. King's Blues Club supposedly has a patron left over from a previous nightclub who likes to play pranks. The relatively new McFadden's Restaurant and Saloon at 134 Second Avenue has evidently inherited a poltergeist or two from the previous tenant.

Regardless of which store or honky-tonk visitors may enter, odds are it is haunted in some manner. For those with a taste for spirits as well as live music with their beer, the District rarely disappoints. So should you have a sudden chill on a hot summer night or feel an unexpected fright you can't explain, just chalk it up to the ghosts of the District welcoming you.

Ryman Auditorium
116 Fifth Avenue North
Nashville, TN 37219
(615) 458-8700
www.ryman.com

Filled with more than a century of memories, this legendary concert hall has hosted everyone from Caruso and Toscanini to Hank and Dolly, so it is no surprise it rates as the most spooktacular of all the downtown haunts.

Tootsie's Orchid Lounge
422 Broadway
Nashville, TN 37203
(615) 726-0463
www.tootsies.net

"World famous" to country-music fans, this venerable venue is fun even for those who don't know Hank Snow from Hank Williams. Its many ghosts are renowned as well.

Merchants
401 Broadway
Nashville, TN 37203
(615) 254-1892
www.merchantsrestaurant.com

This is a neat place to eat. The ghosts come at no additional cost.

Earnest Tubb Record Shop #1
417 Broadway
Nashville, TN 37203
(615) 255-7503
www.etrecordshop.com

Civil War ghosts and perhaps an old-time country singer or two all crowd this small building and its next-door neighbor, Nashville Crossroads.

Nashville Crossroads
419 Broadway
Nashville, TN 37203
(615) 313-8012
www.nashvillecrossroadsbar.com

Lawrence Record Shop
409 Broadway
Nashville, TN 37203
(615) 256-9240
http://lawrencerecordshop.com

Boasting four floors of music in every format since 1954, Lawrence Records likely has that long-lost oldie you crave, as well as a resident phantom or two.

Layla's Bluegrass Inn
418 Broadway
Nashville, TN 37203
(615) 726-2799
www.laylasbluegrassinn.com

Not an inn but an authentic haunted honky-tonk, this place sits catawampus from the downtown arena and elbow to elbow with other music venues.

Past Perfect
122 Third Avenue South
Nashville, TN 37201
(615) 736-7727
www.pastperfectnashville.com

This trendy watering hole is located in a historic two-story brick building filled with local memorabilia and ghosts.

If you've made it this far in the District and haven't yet seen a ghost, leave your empty mug at the last bar and stagger up Market Street (Second Avenue), where still more haunts await:

Melting Pot
166 Second Avenue North
Nashville, TN 37201
(615) 742-4970
www.meltingpot.com

This restaurant is supposedly haunted
by two former employees who wish to
remain together in death. Sounds cheesy
to me.

Buffalo Billiards
154 Second Avenue North
Nashville, TN 37201
(615) 313-7665
www.buffalobilliards.com

This combination pool hall and nightclub is located above an even raunchier
nightclub. The gray ghost that haunts it
is either a Civil War spook or a deceased
warehouse worker.

Mulligan's Pub and Restaurant
117 Second Avenue North
Nashville, TN 37201
(615) 242-8010
www.mulliganspubandrestaurant.com

Here, visitors can get pub grub and a few
boos to go with the booze.

B. B. King's Blues Club
152 Second Avenue North
Nashville, TN 37201
(615) 256-2727
www.bbkingclubs.com

Save for the resident specter, this place is twenty-five thousand square feet of nothin' but the blues.

McFadden's Restaurant and Saloon
134 Second Avenue North
Nashville, TN 37201
(615) 823-7072
www.mcfaddensnashville.com

This is a popular place to get your Irish up. The resident spook is much older than even McFadden's best aged whisky.

CHAPTER 17

The Case of the Psychic Cabbie
The Skull Murder Case

For as long as anyone can remember, Printer's Alley has been a place where the elite meet the street, where high life mingles with low life—a place where good times and good music can always be found. For many years, it was the Nashville equivalent to Beale Street in Memphis, only with a country twang.

When I first saw the alley years ago, the nightclubs ran from Union Street at the top of the hill all the way down to Lower Broad. As the entertainment district along Broadway has grown, however, the alley has shrunk. Nowadays, Printer's Alley is just a block long, the rest of it having been replaced by high-rise office towers and condos. However, what remains is still filled with hot music and colorful characters.

One of the denizens of the alley was David "Skull" Schulman. He was a mainstay for decades, so much so that he was dubbed "the Mayor of Printer's Alley." Originally, Skull ran a "gentlemen's club" featuring "exotic dancers" that went by the name of the Rainbow Room. It was set apart from other such clubs downtown by the fact that a live band played for the dancers. In the 1990s, Skull kept the live music and dropped the dancers, and the place became a country bar. Skull's Rainbow Room was a favorite destination in the alley, playing host to many of the greats of country music. Skull himself made cameo appearances on the old *Hee Haw* TV series.

Everyone loved Skull Schulman, whose kindness and generosity were well known. Often, Skull would give people down on their luck some part-time work cleaning up the bar. Most any night, he could be seen sitting at the end of the bar in his bib overalls—the mayor presiding over his domain. For forty years, Skull Schulman was virtually synonymous with Printer's Alley. Then, one fateful night, everything changed.

Around four-thirty in the afternoon on January 21, 1998, a cab dropped Skull off at the Rainbow Room to open up for the evening. He was sitting at the end of the bar when Joe from the establishment next door stopped by to say hello. After chatting a few minutes, Joe left. That was about five o'clock. The next known visitor was a man named Bill, who regularly sold supplies to the bars in the alley. It was about six when Bill walked into the bar. Normally, Skull would have been at the bar reading the daily paper. This time, however, he was nowhere in sight. Walking to the end of the bar, the salesman finally saw him. He was lying on the floor in a pool of blood, his hands at his throat. Skull was alive—but just barely.

Bill told Skull to hang on and rushed into the alley to find a police officer. A detective just happened to be standing at the end of the block. Alerted, the officer hurried in to witness the bloody scene.

It was obvious that a violent struggle had taken place in the bar. A barstool was knocked over, Skull had several stab wounds to the throat, his dentures lay broken next to him, and he had been severely beaten. The paramedics arrived within minutes, and the ambulance whisked Skull away to the hospital. He died in the early hours of the following morning.

At first, police detectives didn't have a clue as to who did it or why the murder occurred. In trying to save Skull's life, the paramedics had disturbed the crime scene before investigators could inspect it. And the police themselves never bothered to dust the cash register or the bottles behind the bar for fingerprints. Samples of blood were taken from the ladies' restroom, where someone had tried to clean up after the crime. But the blood, when analyzed, turned out to be Skull's.

Bit by bit, however, by interviewing witnesses and gathering leads, detectives pieced together what happened. Finally, arrests were made and convictions obtained. James Charles Cavaye was convicted of first-degree murder and especially aggravated robbery. His crony, Jason Pence—whom Skull had befriended by giving him odd jobs—was convicted of being an accomplice to the crime. The two criminal masterminds had robbed and murdered old Skull for the princely fortune of forty-five dollars. All of which goes to show that crime *does* pay—just not very well.

As far as police were concerned, the deadly duo's convictions were the end of the story—case closed. For anyone interested in the paranormal aspects of the case, however, authorities had scarcely scratched the surface.

With no witnesses to the crime, no fingerprints, and a disturbed crime scene, readers may well wonder how detectives ever managed to wrap up the case, much less obtain a conviction. Was it dumb luck or John Bull's dogged persistence? Or did the police have a little outside help?

I knew "Barbara" for some years before she told me about her involvement with the Skull murder case. A lady cabbie, she eked out a living hauling drunks, carrying tourists, and transporting suit types to and from the airport. A mature woman with grown sons, she nonetheless retained a certain innocence despite in many ways having had a hard life. Weird things had a knack of happening to her. Her family home up north was haunted. One time, she had a tarot reading done for her, and the death card turned up; soon thereafter, her boyfriend passed away. Moreover, Barbara often had premonitions of events that uncannily seemed to come true.

I ran into her one day sitting in her car at a cab stand, waiting her turn for a fare. To kill time, she was engrossed in a book on ESP and parapsychology. I gently kidded her about it. That was when she told me about her firsthand experiences with the paranormal.

Back in 1998, she had been driving the night shift for another Nashville cab company—one sporting distinctive red, white, and blue colors. Printer's Alley at night was one of the best spots for cabbies to work. Drunks came out of the alley in need of rides home all evening long. Often, the fares were good and the tips generous.

On the night of January 21, business was slow. As Barbara was sitting idly at the stand, hoping to snare a fare, a young drifter came up to her and engaged her in conversation. This was the other side of downtown nightlife; an assortment of vagrants, drifters, and panhandlers was always hanging out on the street, trying to bum money from revelers for their next drink. Barbara recognized the young man, Jimmy Cavaye, as one of the regulars who hung out downtown at night.

As Jimmy came within chatting distance, a weird sensation overwhelmed Barbara. She had a flash of insight so startling and sudden that it made her gasp for air. As she described it later, it was like a series of pictures flashing in rapid succession in her mind's eye. She saw Jimmy grappling with Skull, a knife plunging into Skull's throat over and over, Jimmy pounding Skull over the head with a liquor bottle and then grabbing money from his overalls and the cash register. All of these images flooded into her mind in a torrent.

When he approached closer and started chatting her up, she saw he was a mess. He had blood on his clothes and was walking with a limp. Jimmy claimed he'd been in a fight with another street person—a not uncommon occurrence—and never admitted to the crime to her. But he didn't need to. Barbara already had a complete vision of what really happened at Skull's that night.

As the sergeant of detectives went around questioning people about the murder, he heard mention of a lady cabbie. No one knew her name, only that she drove a red, white, and blue cab. The sergeant tracked her down and interviewed her as a material witness, since she was able to place the suspect in the vicinity of Printer's Alley soon after the murder. She testified to that fact at the trial.

What Barbara did not testify to on the witness stand, however, was what she knew about the murder from her flash of intuition. When she was being interviewed, she told the detective what she had seen in her vision in all its horrific detail. None of this, of course, made it into the official record. But Barbara's description confirmed what detectives had already begun to piece together from analyzing the crime scene.

When detectives interrogated the two suspects and were able to give them a detailed and graphic description of what they had done and how they had done it—thanks to Barbara—the duo felt the police had them nailed. They stopped protesting their innocence and confessed. In truth, lacking fingerprint evidence and eyewitness testimony—psychic eyewitness testimony doesn't count—a conviction would have been hard to obtain without the two thugs' confessions.

Television would have viewers think that science and high-tech gadgets are what solve crimes. The truth is that, more often than not, police go by gut instinct and then gather evidence accordingly. Intuition—even of the everyday sort—is not far removed from the dramatic flash of insight that Barbara experienced in the Skull murder case. It is not something people can go to school to learn, but it is something everyone is born with—some more than others.

After Skull Schulman's death, the Rainbow Room was never the same. No one wanted to step into old Skull's shoes. A kind of dread fell over the place. The nearby Bourbon Street Blues Bar rented out the old club for a while to use as storage space. However, employees from the blues club had weird experiences when they went inside the Rainbow Room. Some claimed they heard Skull's voice crying out, while others saw a dark shape moving about the space. They said the shape closely resembled Skull. It got to the point where some of the blues bar's employees flat out refused to go inside the place at night.

Nowadays, even tourists who stand outside the old club's entrance get an eerie feeling. Visitors have described having a sensation that someone is standing behind them and staring at them. Others have described suddenly feeling very cold standing in the doorway of the shuttered club, even on hot summer nights. A few even claim to have taken photos of what looked like the head of a ghost visible in the entranceway.

Printer's Alley lies between Third Avenue North and Fourth Avenue North just off Church Street. While Skull's Rainbow Room is now defunct, the other nightclubs in the alley are still going strong. The entertainment runs the gamut from naughty to nice—mostly naughty, though. The majority of the clubs sit in the basements of old buildings that front on Fourth in the block formerly referred to as "the Gentlemen's Quarter." Establishments such as The Turf Club used to serve as "sportin' houses"—that is to say, houses of ill repute, where the patrons' behavior was anything but gentlemanly. Nowadays, the buildings mostly house law offices and financial businesses—places only slightly less disreputable than in days gone by.

Given Printer's Alley's long history, it may be home to ghosts of even older vintage than Skull Schulman. But this much is sure: the Mayor of Printer's Ally still presides over his domain.

CHAPTER 18

Sumner Spirits

As elsewhere in the Cumberland Valley today, Sumner County is a mix of old and new. Prehistoric Indian mounds and pioneer graveyards jostle uncomfortably with modern suburban tracts, shaded frontier-era homes sit hidden behind gleaming new shopping centers, and herds of deer roam where new office parks soon will be. Despite all the changes, the communities of Sumner retain a strong sense of local pride. They also retain an abundance of hauntings.

Coming into Sumner County from Nashville, right after crossing Mansker's Creek, visitors see an antebellum mansion on a hill with newer apartments clustered all around. This is the old Fite House, now called Monthaven. When I first toured the place some years back, the grand old home was a spacious bed-and-breakfast run by the scion of the family that had dwelt in it for many decades. Located at the gateway to the county in Hendersonville, Monthaven sits astride the junction of two old buffalo trails. Over the years, many folks have passed by its doors. The ghost of Monthaven is one such wayfarer who came and stayed.

The best estimate is that the spirit haunting Monthaven dates to the Civil War, during which the house was used as a temporary medical aid station. The notorious Confederate cavalry raider John Hunt Morgan and his boys clashed with the Yankees nearby where the old Gallatin Pike crossed the creek. By all accounts, the Yankees got the worst of the fight. Casualties from both sides were carried to an upper room with a fireplace, where a spare door laid sideways across sawhorses served as a less-than-sanitary operating table. As the Rebel surgeon performed his gruesome task, blood spilled from the table onto the floorboards. Buckets more blood were thrown out the back door.

Afterward, the homeowners cleaned the scene as best they were able, but the bloodstains would not come out. No amount of scrubbing, bleaching, and scraping could remove them from the floor. Finally, the floorboards were taken out and new ones installed. Today, visitors can see the difference in size and shape between the old boards and the new. It is in this upstairs parlor where the ghost is most active.

Since Monthaven served as a private home for generations, few knew about its resident ghost. When it became a bed-and-breakfast, however, lodgers unaware of the house's history and haunted reputation would tell of weird sounds and odd encounters while staying upstairs.

On one occasion, a medium visited Monthaven. She went to the room where the surgery had been done during the war and without any prompting was able to give a physical description of the ghost in the room. The medium described a young Confederate trooper, lost in time and space, who died on the operating table. Given the practices of the era, the Rebel was probably buried in a hastily dug grave somewhere on the property in unmarked, unhallowed ground. His spirit now roams the mansion.

Monthaven is far from unique in Hendersonville. One psychic who has "cleared" many homes and businesses described the city as a hotbed of paranormal activity. A few miles up from Monthaven, just north of the town's modern parkway, is a whole subdivision that is believed to be haunted. Not many years ago, it was open pasture and orchard. Now, large suburban homes fill the fields. However, as in the film *Poltergeist*, the developers chose to erect them over an Indian burial ground—and with similar results.

As a rule, builders like to fit as many houses into a tract as the law allows—and the law is very friendly to developers. However, one street in the subdivision has a large plot that was left empty. It was pointed out to me by a longtime resident who said that the contractor had indeed begun to build there but had so many accidents, malfunctions, and other weird happenings that he stopped construction. It is believed that the plot contains the remains of an Indian medicine man, whose less than restful spirit still guards the land.

To varying degrees, many homeowners have had paranormal encounters. In one house, a family had particularly intense experiences. Some seemed ordinary enough at first: the toilet would flush by itself; the bedroom closet doors would open and close by themselves. Then the family's youngest child began to experience night terrors in the crib. After one such episode, the mother removed the toddler to her room. Through the nursery video monitor, she saw what appeared to be a small figure still in the crib. The ghost of an Indian boy was occupying her son's space.

Elsewhere in the subdivision, homeowners have reported seeing the apparition of a large, dark man with glowing red eyes. While it has not caused anyone physical harm, its random appearances at night have frightened more than a few. One homeowner was so spooked that he claimed a "gateway to hell" was in his kitchen and vacated his house.

A short distance south of the parkway, at 157 Old Shackle Island Drive, stands an old house converted into a store. A number of merchants have come and gone there in the last few years. At one time, the structure housed a gift shop called One Man's Treasure; the last tenant was a New Age–style center featuring a smorgasbord of services from psychic healing to tattoos. One feature was not advertised by any of the merchants: the ghosts inhabiting the place.

According to a business owner who lived upstairs, the place was quite haunted. The owner's family often heard loud knocking in the middle of the night. Sometimes, scratching or rushing sounds came from within the walls of the upper story. Orbs and what looked like a woman's face were photographed in one of the mirrors there. In another incident at the former One Man's Treasure, a wooden door known to be difficult to close suddenly opened and shut all by itself. Downstairs, similar poltergeist activity was observed. In one case, a row of paintings in a hallway all fell at exactly the same time.

Elsewhere in Hendersonville, ghosts continue to reside in local schools. The haunting of Ellis Middle School (the old Hendersonville High building) has been well known for some time. The circular building resembling a large flying saucer was built on land originally belonging to the Berry family. On a hill overlooking the school stands Hazel Path, the Berrys' ancestral home. Colonel Horatio "Harry" S. Berry was a prominent local citizen who served as an officer in World War I. Berry Field—now Nashville International Airport—was named after him. In fact, Colonel Berry put the *B* in the *BNA* on air travelers' luggage tags. The old gentleman died in 1967, a year after the high school opened. That was when the first reports of hauntings in both the school and Hazel Path came to light.

Back then, the caretaker of Hazel Path was also the custodian for the school. Being on duty in both buildings late at night made him doubly exposed to the eerie goings-on. Link Wingo grew used to hearing invisible feet walking the halls of Hazel Path. When he began to notice similar sounds inside the school, he concluded that the ghosts of both buildings were members of the Berry family.

The footsteps are the most common phenomenon heard inside the school. Custodial staff, coaches, and teachers working late have all heard them. Every time someone goes to investigate, however, nothing can be seen. Occasionally, someone spots a silhouette or shadow out of the corner of the eye, but the ghost remains elusive to adults.

Over the years, however, students have occasionally reported seeing an old man in the boys' room. They commonly refer to him as "Colonel Harry" or simply "the Colonel." The Colonel has also received credit for occasional pranks by unseen hands, such as gym lockers opening by themselves and trash cans in the boys' room being moved when no one is present. For nearly half a century, scarcely a student at the old high or the current Ellis Middle School hasn't had some uncanny experience or at least known someone who encountered the Colonel.

Farther along the Gallatin Pike, the number of paranormal hot spots increases in number, if anything. Just a few miles up the road from Hendersonville lies a once-famous estate that has been turned into an exclusive subdivision called The Last Plantation. The former Fairvue was not a plantation in the same sense as the large estates of the Deep South. Its main product was not cotton or other crops but prize horse-flesh. The plantation's claim to fame was its thoroughbred racehorses.

Built in 1832 by Isaac Franklin, a wealthy businessman and planter, Fairvue Mansion sits on a hill overlooking what were once rolling pastures filled with grazing horses. Franklin's beautiful young wife was Adelicia, better known by her second husband's surname, Acklen. Despite Adelicia's privileged life at Fairvue, all four of her children by Isaac Franklin died by the age of seven. After Franklin, too, died, Adelicia remarried and moved to Nashville, where she built the even more opulent Belmont Mansion.

Fairvue continued through varying fortunes and owners into the twentieth century. It came into the possession of the Wemyss family in 1934. Will and Ellen Wemyss were not only wealthy but active in community affairs. Ellen, generally referred to as "Miss Ellen," was particularly interested in historic preservation. The Wemyss family restored Fairvue to its former glory. Thoroughbred horses were brought back. A herd of prize Angus cattle was introduced as well. Every horse had its own small individual stable of solid brick with an upstairs apartment for its personal groom. Some of those stables still line the driveway leading to the old mansion.

I remember meeting Miss Ellen some years back, when she was a spry young lady of ninety-four. Neither time nor changes to the estate had diminished her love of culture or the community's respect for all she had done for Sumner County over the years. Since Miss Ellen resided in Fairvue longer than any of its previous owners, it is not surprising that she was more aware of the spectral goings-on at Fairvue than anyone else.

The fact that the mansion was used as a temporary field hospital during the Civil War may have something to do with reports of phantoms from that era on the grounds. For example, on the landing between the second and third floors is a bloodstain that has been cleaned repeatedly but keeps reappearing. Visitors to Miss Ellen's have seen Civil War soldiers trooping up and down the stairs. The basement, being cooler that the rest of the house, is believed to have been used as a temporary morgue. Several people have reported it as especially active spectrally.

One guest who had several drinks while playing cards one night claimed to have encountered a ghost in the servants' quarters in the rear of the house. Not only that, he allegedly held a conversation with the ghost until the sun came up! Of course, some may question exactly the *nature* of the spirits he encountered. But other visitors have also spied specters on Fairvue's grounds. Former tenants who dwelt in the "dependencies," or slave quarters, reported paranormal encounters there as well.

In all Miss Ellen's years at Fairvue, only one ghost bothered her. This was an apparition of a young girl. The child ghost would ride a tricycle up and down the hallways of the mansion at night. It disturbed the mistress of Fairvue that someone so young should have died there. While the identity of the tricycle ghost remains a mystery, the fact remains that Adelicia Franklin Acklen lost four young children to disease in the mansion. The presence of at least one child spirit, therefore, does not seem terribly unusual.

Years ago, the scenery around Gallatin proper was filled with greenery and dotted with grazing cattle and horses. Travelers would see a farmhouse or two and even a frontier log cabin sitting by the wayside. While some of that is still in evidence, the rural view is giving way to housing subdivisions and shopping centers. It is not until visitors reach the heart of Gallatin that they get a feel for the way things used to be. The town square, while filled with modern shops, still retains its old-time charm. It also retains a gaggle of ghosts, which is why it has been billed as "the Most Haunted Public Square in America." From frontier days, when the Bowie clan rode Gallatin's dusty streets and Andrew

Jackson plied his trade as a lawyer, through the upheaval of the Civil War and into the twentieth century, the town square and the adjacent buildings have seen many generations come and go. And more than a few spirits have refused to move on.

In the historic district around the square, for example, is an old house that was once the home of Miss Betsy Boyers' Dance School for Young Ladies, which operated from the 1920s to 1980. Today, the spirits dance on. Reportedly, Miss Betsy held only day classes because the girls were afraid to be in the old house after dark, when the ghosts were more active.

The building that takes the prize for spectral activity is a law office fronting the square that is host to no fewer than fourteen ghosts. Several of the spirits date to the Civil War, when the town was alternately occupied by the Blue and the Gray. The lawyer's office also has at least two female entities. One is garbed in a deep blue period costume, while another fancies yellow. The attorney and his staff have become accustomed to sharing the premises with its resident ghosts, although seeing the occasional discarded soda can levitating through the air can still be a bit unnerving.

Then there is the building on West Franklin Street that has served as both a county jail and a brothel. In recent decades, it has housed various restaurants, the most recent being Oliver's. Upstairs in the restaurant, people have reported hearing disembodied voices. Knocking sounds come from within the walls. The doors slam all by themselves. One of the restaurant's booths (#43) is a favorite of one of the specters. The ghost allegedly is a customer who died when he tripped and fell down the stairs.

One last site in Sumner County lies along the old frontier trail that led to Knoxville—today's Highway 25. Castalian Springs is the site of old log cabins, Indian mounds, and the home of frontier leader James Winchester, whose Cragfont is most definitely haunted.

General James Winchester was a contemporary of Andrew Jackson. Like Jackson, he commanded an army in the War of 1812. Unlike Jackson, he didn't win glory but rather earned ignominy.

When attempting to save a town from British and Indian attack, he managed to get himself surrounded and was forced to surrender. That would have been bad enough, but the helpless wounded he left behind were massacred by the Indians. He was never able to live down the shame or the blame.

Some of the paranormal incidents at Cragfont are minor: pebbles tossed in the driveway by invisible hands, a diary that insists on opening to a certain page, a chair that wishes to stay only at a certain window no matter where docents place it. Candles are seen burning in windows at night, a no-no in a historic house, due to the chance of fire; sometimes, figures are spotted peering out those same windows. Some have witnessed full apparitions; the general has been spotted standing on the roof for reasons unknown. There have also been reports of ghosts dancing in the garden. One legend claims that star-crossed lovers who took a swan dive off the "crag" of Cragfont still haunt the place. Civil War ghosts—both Blue and Gray—have also been attested to by locals.

Country-music star Conway Twitty once asked to spend the night to see if he could get in touch with the spirits. After a couple of hours alone, he fled the property. The spirits started tossing things at him. Apparently, the cantankerous general of Sumner County prefers his privacy.

Monthaven (Fite House)
1154 West Main Street
Hendersonville, TN 37075
(615) 822-0789

The former bed-and-breakfast is now the clubhouse for the surrounding apartment complex and a cultural center for the local community. Located at Exit 2 (Vietnam Veterans Parkway), it is open year-round.

Gallatin Town Square
Intersection of TN 109 and TN 25

You may not encounter a ghost during the daylight, but the square is still worth a look-see. Have lunch, browse the antique mall, and ask the local historian at the county archives as to the whereabouts of David Lang.

Cragfont (Historic Cragfront of Tennessee)
300 Cragfont Road
Castalian Springs, TN 37031
(615) 452-7070
www.cragfont.com
(open April 15 to November 1)

Take Highway 25 out of Gallatin; if you reach Bledsoe's Fort, you've gone too far. I didn't see any dancing ghosts in the garden when I was there, but ask the docent about Cragfont's haunted heritage. If the right one is on duty, you'll get an earful.

CHAPTER 19

Cumberland Witches
Buckner, Bell, and Beyond

Mention Tennessee and witches in the same breath and the first thing that comes to mind is the Bell Witch of Adams. While the old girl has long since departed the Highland Rim of Middle Tennessee, there is no shortage of folks willing to tell—and retell—the story to newcomers. Given all that has been said about "the Mysterious Spirit," her ears must be constantly burning.

In truth, the Bell Witch was not a witch in the usual sense. Rather, the story involves the bewitchment of a particular family. But as unusual as that bewitchment was, it was not unique. It had a sequel—less famous, to be sure, but eerily similar and every bit as terrifying for the family that was its target. The Bell Witch's spiritual sister was known to people on the eastern part of the Highland Rim as the Buckner Witch.

For those not familiar with Tennessee lore, it should be noted that the alleged witch responsible for the Bell family's curse was believed to be a neighbor named Kate Batts, who had a feud with John Bell, the family patriarch. But in fact, the entity bedeviling the Bells was never finally identified as any particular flesh-and-blood being. The Bells themselves referred to it only as "the Mysterious Spirit" or "Our Family Troubles." The so-called witch was more a poltergeist-like entity than a broomstick-riding, cackling-over-a-cauldron variety of witch. The Bell Witch singled out one family for its malicious pranks and focused on one member of that family in particular, for reasons still unknown. It is in these essential elements that the Buckner Witch most resembles her more famous sister.

Around the town of Monterey, visitors can still get an earful about the Buckner Witch, if they ask the right people. Off and on for many years, the witch has bothered and bewildered various members of the Buckner family and their neighbors. This has gone on since the town was still known as Standing Stone.

Sometimes, the Buckner Witch is merely felt as a presence. Other times, she is actually seen as an apparition. Eyewitnesses describe her as looking like a little old lady dressed in black. Many in Monterey claim she still follows people around the town. People passing the old Buckner place at the end of Cates Road have seen the house all aglow with eerie lights. This, too, is thought to be a manifestation of the witch.

Various explanations have been put forward as to the cause of the Mysterious Spirit of Monterey. One version has it that the Buckner Witch is guarding buried family treasure. Many years back, a member of the Buckner clan actually tore up the kitchen floor in the old homeplace in search of it. However, the strongest local tradition holds that the witch is the vengeful spirit of a woman who tried to come between Aunt Margaret and Uncle Alec Buckner in the 1870s.

The name of this aspiring home wrecker is said to have been Polly Brewington. She appeared in the Monterey area sometime after the Civil War, accompanied by her two brothers. People disagree on exactly where she came from but concur that she and her siblings settled near an old sawmill. By all accounts, she was a small, dark-complexioned woman who always wore a long black dress trimmed with white cuffs and collar. On her head was a bonnet as black as night. Polly carried a satchel or purse of the same color. Her personality matched her clothing, for she had a black heart with a mean streak a mile wide.

To make ends meet, Polly hired herself out as a domestic. The trouble began when she came to work for Alec and Margaret Buckner. After a time, Polly took a shine to Uncle Alec. Whether or not anything actually went on between the two is unknown. Family tradition says that Polly's attentions were unwanted and that Alec Buckner spurned her romantic overtures.

In any case, Polly's infatuation turned into an obsession. It is said she even had her two brothers threaten Margaret with violence in order to drive her away. But Aunt Margaret refused to be intimidated. Polly did not succeed in breaking up the Buckners' marriage. In fact, their union, if anything, became stronger.

Whether she did it to bind her husband closer to her or whether it was simply the natural course of events, Margaret became pregnant. On December 4, 1881, she gave birth to a son, William Buckner. Within a few days of the delivery, Margaret exclaimed out of the blue, "Well, the old witch is dead!" Female friends visiting her were taken aback by the outburst and asked her to explain. Margaret grew wide-eyed. With a strange expression on her face, she told them Polly Brewington was dead. The woman who had made her life miserable was gone. But Margaret had bad news, too. "Now she's come to haunt me in death," she added.

How Margaret knew all this is a mystery. She was still abed recovering from childbirth and had no way of finding out about Polly Brewington's health on her own. Nevertheless, she was right. Polly was indeed dead, from causes unknown. Soon thereafter, the Brewington boys departed the area, taking their dead sister's body with them. But if Polly Brewington's mortal remains departed Monterey, her spirit did not.

While most in Monterey felt the departure of Polly Brewington was good riddance to bad news, a few whispered dark rumors about what had really happened. Some said Aunt Margaret did more than just get pregnant to hold onto her man. They said she murdered Polly to eliminate her rival and that now the spirit of the dead woman was haunting the Buckner family. But how could that be so? Margaret was birthing and laid up in bed afterward; she couldn't have left her house to do Polly harm. Unspoken was the possibility that Polly was not the only witch at work. Nobody ever dared voice that thought to Aunt Margaret's face.

In the weeks, months, and years that followed, the image of a woman clad all in black was repeatedly seen by the people of Monterey. The mysterious spirit that haunted the city made Margaret Buckner the focus of its unwanted attention. When Aunt Margaret sought to busy herself with household chores, the Buckner Witch would interfere with her sweeping or quilting. At times, Margaret would take a broom to the underside of her bed—not to sweep the dust but to make sure the witch was not hiding there. Once, the witch appeared in Margaret's bedroom. Aunt Margaret took a swipe at the apparition with her walking stick, which passed right through it. Even in death, Polly tried to come between Margaret and Alec. The spirit was reputed to have climbed in bed with the couple. As far as Aunt Margaret was concerned, three was definitely not company.

After Uncle Alec died, Aunt Margaret moved in with one of her sons in town in the hope that the spirit was bound to her old homeplace. But it continued to bedevil her. It soon became apparent that the witch could get about quite easily. Not only did it haunt the path around the old Buckner place, it also began to follow folks other than the Buckners, although its preferred target remained Aunt Margaret.

When Aunt Margaret also died, people in Monterey thought for sure that would put an end to matters. But the Buckner Witch continued to haunt the countryside. By all accounts, the witch has never actually harmed anyone. It is, however, unnerving to wake up in the middle of the night and see a pair of strange eye staring at you in the dark, or to have a wizened old hag in black follow you as you walk. For the Buckner clan in particular, there is no doubt that witches are real.

The Buckner Witch and the Bell Witch are not the only hags to ever inhabit the Cumberland Plateau. Although no one will admit to practicing the dark arts, plenty once knew the proper spells and rituals to ward them off. And one ignores the old ways only at one's peril.

Some years back, a fellow named Charles Marlowe lived on the southern end of the Cumberland Plateau around Summerfield in Grundy County. He knew all about Cumberland witches. In fact, he was related to one. Coming under a spell placed on him by Margaret, the second wife of his uncle Rufe, Charlie fell ill, unable to walk. Rufe's wife often came by and borrowed things in groups of three—a sure sign she was a witch.

To break the spell on him, Charlie and another relative drew a picture of Margaret and burned it up with red cedar shavings. A few days later, Margaret turned red as a beet. She looked like she'd been scorched in a fire. She claimed she'd gotten sunburned. But it was the middle of winter, and people in Tennessee don't get sunburned that time of year.

Before World War I, a woman named Frost was thought to be a witch by some in the Summerfield area. John, a neighbor of hers, went deer hunting regularly and by all accounts rarely came back empty handed. One time, John was in the woods when a large deer jumped right out in front of him. It was an easy shot, yet he missed. The same thing happened the next week, and the next. The farmer began to suspect that witchcraft was at work on his gun.

A friend told John to load his gun with a silver bullet to break the spell. Sure enough, the next time the deer jumped out at him, he shot the silver bullet and hit it squarely in the leg. Curiously, even though the doe was lamed and couldn't have run far, neither the hunter nor his dogs found any trace of her.

The Frost woman stopped by pretty regularly to borrow things. When she didn't show up the next day, John's wife paid her a visit to find out why. The wife came back and told her husband Miz Frost was laid up in bed with a broken leg. That was when John knew *she* was the deer he'd hit.

These days, few on the Cumberland Plateau remember such old haint tales. If you come across a Buckner or a Bell, however, they may still have a story or two to tell about Cumberland witches.

III
In High Cotton

Uncanny Encounters in
West Tennessee and Memphis

Chapter 20

Savannah Spirits

Once upon a time, Savannah was a bustling port town on the Tennessee, alive with all manner of activity as merchants and travelers came and went and cargo was loaded onto the sternwheelers that plied the big river. Today, the steamboats are mostly gone, although sportsmen and pleasure boaters still motor by in the spring and summer when the fishing is good and the weather pleasant. One thing the graceful city by the bank of the Tennessee has retained through the years, however, is its reputation as the abode of restless spirits.

Today, the city's main claim to fame is not its trade or its ghosts but its place in history, for it was here that General Ulysses S. Grant made his headquarters in the spring of 1862. A stroll through town still conveys much of the charm and beauty that attracted Grant. Of course, the reason that Grant and company visited Savannah had something to do with a war—although one might not guess it from his surroundings here. Grant and his staff relaxed in comfort at Cherry Mansion, while most of his men pitched their tents any which way they chose several miles upstream on the opposite bank—the enemy side of the river.

Grant and his boys are long gone, but Cherry Mansion stands as majestic as ever, rising high on a hill overlooking the broad Tennessee.

If local reports are true, at least one Federal still resides within the venerable mansion.

Located at 265 Main Street, Cherry Mansion was built in 1830 by David Robinson, who gave the house and grounds as a wedding present to his daughter and son-in-law, William H. Cherry. A wealthy landowner in his own right, Will Cherry improved and enlarged the house, turning it into a showplace.

Despite the fact that Cherry was a slave owner, he proved a staunch supporter of the Union, as were many other townsfolk. When the Federals came upriver, Cherry welcomed them and offered his home as headquarters for the Union commander. It was while eating breakfast in the mansion one April morning in 1862 that Grant heard distant gunfire coming from Pittsburg Landing, several miles away. And it was from the porch of Cherry Mansion that he hurried down to the river to his waiting steamboat to go preside over the first day's debacle at Shiloh.

If that alone were all that ever transpired in Savannah, the town's claim to fame would still be assured. But the tides of war brought much sickness and death to the city, as it filled with casualties from the battle. Two Union generals—Major General C. F. Smith and Major General W. H. L. Wallace—died within Cherry Mansion's walls soon after the battle. Which one haunts the mansion has never been determined for certain.

On more than one occasion, people on Main Street have looked up at Cherry Mansion to see a man in a dark blue uniform peering at them from an upstairs window. Details of the paranormal activity inside the house remain limited, as the home has been in private hands since it was built. It is known that previous owners experienced loud noises at odd times, as well as the sound of voices coming out of thin air when no one was there. Only very recently has the historic mansion been opened to the public for tours. Perhaps as time goes by, more of the spectral activity inside Cherry Mansion may be documented.

In the 1970s, an incident just outside the house attracted notoriety. In broad daylight, a man dressed in a white suit walked up to the large historical marker that stands in front of the house. After reading the sign for a minute or so, the gentleman disappeared into thin air!

Although the specter in white does not sound like a Civil War ghost, it may well be. His clothing sounds very much like that worn by gentlemen in the summertime in the decades *after* the war. In the late nineteenth and early twentieth centuries, many veterans of the war revisited the battlefields of their youth. Could some elderly veteran who died with memories of the places of war still strong in his mind have been revisiting one of them in the afterlife?

A number of other ghosts have been sighted in downtown Savannah, but many of the reports are fragmentary or vague. Some may have been Civil War–era ghosts. One report, for example, told of a ghost "in army attire" searching for his hat in a parking lot in the early-morning hours. Another spirit was sighted around midnight near Chalk Bluff, apparently giving orders to a company of ghosts. Upstream a few miles at Pittsburg Landing, the Shiloh battlefield has gobs of ghosts, park rangers' denials notwithstanding. Nor are the shades of Shiloh limited to the national park proper, for the fighting during April and May 1862 ranged all the way from the banks of the Tennessee to Corinth, Mississippi.

The Savannah area boasts other hauntings besides those dating to the Civil War. During the 1890s, a small building called the Red Sulfur Springs Hotel stood near Pickwick Landing. On New Year's Eve in 1894, what has been described as "the most atrocious murder ever committed in the area" occurred there.

A party was going on in the hotel. Some local moonshiners by the name of Thomas provided both the liquor and the music. The Thomas boys were talented musicians but meaner than spit. A day or so before the party, for example, one of the boys' banjos needed a new head to cover the frame. The boy simply grabbed a cat, killed it, skinned it, stretched the fresh hide out before the fireplace to dry, then fitted it over his instrument. For the Thomas boys, life was cheap but banjos weren't.

During the party, a man named Alvin Martin, who wasn't from around those parts, happened to flirt with one of the local girls. He danced with her and made advances. And she seemed to encourage it. The Thomases' white lightning may have been what made Martin frisky—more frisky than suited the Thomas boys. The outsider was even seen stealing a kiss from the local girl.

The Thomas boys, Gus and Ed, took offense. The two lured Martin onto the porch with the promise of free whiskey, then shot him in the leg. Lying there helpless, Martin pleaded for his life. Instead, one of the Thomases placed a big horse pistol about an inch away from Martin's mouth and pulled the trigger twice.

As the clock struck midnight and everyone inside cheered the new year, the Thomases loaded the headless corpse into a buggy, hog-tying it so it sat upright. Then they whipped the horses. The wagon carrying the mutilated corpse ran some three miles down the road, over the state line into Mississippi. Martin's headless corpse was found the next day, still grotesquely sitting upright in the carriage, which was wedged between two trees.

Now, Alvin Martin was not the first man to lose his head over a woman, but the fact that he left this world without it may have something to do with why his ghost haunts the old Red Sulfur Springs Hotel. The current residents of the old building frequently hear footsteps. Occasionally, the doorbell rings on its own. At other times, the owners suddenly feel a deathly cold come over the place, even on hot days. Still more uncanny is the piano in the parlor that has been known to play all by itself. The tune sounds like old-time music such as might have been heard in the 1890s.

The former hotel was not the only haunted place on Red Sulfur Road. Built in the late nineteenth century and since torn down, the Blakney House was pretty spooky in its day. Witnesses heard eerie organ music emanating from the home at odd hours of the night; the last time its old pump organ was played by human hands was at a funeral for a spinster aunt of the Blakney family who lived all her life in the house and died there as well. At other times, passersby saw strange lights illuminating the shadowy silhouettes of figures moving about inside the house.

Life along the Tennessee has changed quite a bit since the old days. The TVA tamed the wild and unpredictable river—at least a bit. Dams like the one near Pickwick Landing control the river's outbursts and make life easier for locals and visitors alike, as well as providing cheap and abundant electricity. Still, if the river has changed its ways, the spirits at places like Savannah, Pickwick Landing, and Shiloh have not. Visitors may still hear their voices calling—if they've a mind to listen.

Cherry Mansion
265 West Main Street
Savannah, TN 38372
(731) 607-1208

For many years, the mansion was much talked about but closed to the public. Fortunately, it is now accessible to both Civil War buffs and fans of haunted houses. Tours are available by appointment.

CHAPTER 21

Purdy Scary

Way back when, the community of Purdy was an up-and-coming place. The county seat of McNairy County, it boasted its own college and was a political and economic hub. When the railroad came through, however, the city elders decided they didn't want any newfangled trains belching smoke, disturbing the horses, making noise at all hours, and generally disturbing their serenity. In the end, the railroad bypassed Purdy and went through nearby Selmer instead.

Unfortunately, with the railroad went prosperity. One by one, businesses relocated to be near the rail line. So did the people. Eventually, the county seat was relocated to booming Selmer. Today, Purdy isn't even a gravy stain on the state map. Such places are commonly called ghost towns. In Purdy's case, the place really does have ghosts.

About the only things left to remind folks of the old days are an empty house and a cemetery of equally antique vintage. The house—known as Dodd House or the Hurst Mansion—has been known for many years to be haunted. Of late, it is in bad shape due to the actions of thrill seekers and amateur ghost hunters.

The Dodd House holds fast to many mysteries. That it retains at least one resident spirit is certain. As to the ghost's identity, some dispute exists even among those familiar with the house's history. According to some, the ghost is that of a Confederate officer named Dodd who was cruelly tortured and murdered in the house by pro-Union marauders. Others claim it is actually the ghost of the leader of the Unionist guerillas, a man named Hurst. It was he who died there fighting Confederate troops, the story goes. And it is he, not some Rebel, who haunts the decaying mansion.

Regardless of the spirit's name, no one disputes its continuing presence. A bloodstain on the second floor is said to mark the spot where the man was murdered. Previous owners tried to erase the stain, but it always came back. Some say it returns on the anniversary of the man's death. There is also a gouge in the stairwell, a mark left by a bullet from one of the murderers' guns as they fired at their victim.

Over the years, visitors to the house have heard the screaming of the man's tortured spirit reliving his grisly death. One reporter from a local newspaper attempted to snap a photo of the exact place where the soldier was slain, but his camera refused to work. Oddly, it operated fine before and after and even in other rooms of the house—just not in that one spot.

Some visitors have not seen or heard anything creepy while tramping about the house, only to notice a woman in a white dress peering from one of the windows when they later developed their photos. Still others have reported seeing a similar woman in white in the nearby graveyard. Who the woman may be is not known for certain. The last full-time residents were two sisters, Bessie and Mary Dodd. Either one of them is a likely candidate.

The nearby Purdy Cemetery is even more of a haunted hot spot. Numerous encounters experienced by visitors and locals alike attest to the active spectral presence there.

One curious fact about the Purdy burial ground is that it contains an unusually large number of children. While no one has ever provided a reason for such a high rate of child mortality in old Purdy, it does provide an explanation for some of the spectral encounters reported there.

People commonly tell of hearing children screaming in the dark at the cemetery. One visitor who saw nothing while exploring the graveyard later had one of his pictures come out showing the face of a little girl. Others have seen similar apparitions on the tombstones.

The woman in white also frequents Purdy Cemetery. And she is far from the only adult apparition there. In one case, an old-timer was clearing some trees when a spectral horse-drawn carriage passed by, complete with a man, woman, and child all dressed up in vintage nineteenth-century clothing. The farmer's modern machinery went dead when the apparition appeared and stayed that way until it passed by.

Other visitors to the graveyard have had encounters with Civil War ghosts—which is not surprising, considering Purdy's proximity to the Shiloh battlefield. People have reported hearing a group of Rebel soldiers in the graveyard. Some even claim to have seen the ghosts of black slave gravediggers at work interring the Confederate dead. During the war, both sides often employed blacks to do the gruesome task of gathering up battlefield remains—often badly decayed—and burying them.

Even during daylight hours, it is not uncommon for visitors to Purdy Cemetery to have weird experiences. People may feel a chill in the graveyard on hot summer days. Others hear the sound of footsteps close behind, as if some invisible being were following them.

Unfortunately, Purdy's notoriety has caused both the graveyard and the nearby house to suffer damage from modern-day marauders whose main goals are drinking, partying, and vandalism. Tombstones have been deliberately broken or tipped over. Refuse has been thrown all over the place.

Some local residents deny that anything supernatural goes on in Purdy, perhaps in hopes of discouraging vandals and thrill seekers. Others don't deny Purdy's hauntings but resent the continued trespassing by both the living and the dead.

One longtime resident claims that the spirits have been angered by all the desecrations. The resident lives just down the road from the cemetery. Disturbed spirits have invaded his home. Doors open and close with a bang. Screaming ghost children keep his own youngsters awake at night. The spirits have been known to spook wildlife as well.

All these spectral goings-on led one newspaper reporter to describe Purdy—despite its rustic beauty and the generally genial temperament of the folks thereabouts—as "one of the scariest places on the planet."

CHAPTER 22

Adams Family Phantoms
The Haunts of
Victorian Village

In its glory days, Adams Avenue in Memphis was famed as a millionaires' row. During the late nineteenth century and into the early years of the twentieth, a series of ornate and elegant mansions arose along the avenue. These many-storied homes were peopled by wealthy merchants, industrialists, and the city's social elite.

Back before the Civil War, the area was actually on the outskirts of town. Following the war, ambitious entrepreneurs and other newly affluent families rewarded themselves with opulent homes in the trendy new neighborhood. As the river trade revived and families moved out of the overcrowded core of the city, more homes arose along elegant Adams Avenue. As the nineteenth century came to a close, the millionaires' row reached its peak as the city's elite met, made merry, and married.

The twentieth century brought changes. World War I, the Great

Depression, World War II—all affected the bluff city by the big river. The social elite of Memphis moved farther and farther into the countryside, and Adams Avenue went into a slow decline. Although the millionaire and socialite "Adams families" long ago moved on, their ghosts linger. To this day, they dwell in the elegant, graying homes.

The neighborhood that once was suburban is now a part of the inner city called Victorian Village. Only a select few of the magnificent mansions remain. The oldest and humblest is the Magevney House at 198 Adams. A small white clapboard cottage, it was built in the 1830s, when the area was still very much frontier wilderness. The original owner, Eugene Magevney, was a hardworking Irish immigrant whose home reflected his simple, industrious lifestyle. The ghost of old Eugene Magevney—or at least some member of his family—is thought to frequent the homestead. Strange noises, cold spots, and similar odd occurrences have been witnessed over the years. Since 2005, when access to the house was reduced for the public, reports of spectral activity have diminished, although that is due to fewer visitors and not a lessening of paranormal goings-on.

Far more actively haunted is the Lee House. The grand and stately mansion at 690 East Adams Street sometimes goes by the name of the Harsson-Goyer-Lee House, reflecting the series of families that once inhabited it—and perhaps still do.

At the time of its construction, the house looked nothing like it does now. The original home, which now forms the rear wing of the mansion, was built in 1843 by William Harsson, a lumberman from Baltimore. Often called "the little square house," it was built of brick. It was not grandiose by any means, but it served the needs of Harsson and his family, even when his daughter Laura married an up-and-coming young man named Charles Goyer and the couple moved in.

Charles Wesley Goyer had arrived from Indiana by flatboat in 1841 with little money but great expectations. In a short period, he started making a name—and, more importantly, money—for himself in Memphis. He and the beautiful Laura quickly became the proud parents of a growing family. Goyer bought the little square house from his father-in-law in 1851. By 1860, he built a large addition onto the front. As director and president of Union and Planter's Bank of Memphis, he could well afford the expense.

Charles and Laura weathered the war years but saw their happiness come to an abrupt halt in 1867. That year, both Laura and her father died of yellow fever, leaving Charles a widower with ten children to take care of. With a large family and a growing business on his hands, Charles did not remain single for long. When he married the next year, his bride was none other than Laura's sister Charlotte, making her both aunt and stepmother to his large brood. Charles died in 1881. As his children grew up, married, and moved out, they eventually decided to sell the mansion.

Captain James Lee bought the grand home from the Goyer estate in 1890. James Lee was the son of the founder of the Lee line of "floating palace" river steamers that were a familiar sight along the Mississippi in the 1800s. Lee's daughter Rosa grew up surrounded by beautiful art objects and grand architecture. Not surprisingly, she became a patron of the arts in later life. When Rosa died in 1936, she deeded both the Lee mansion and the next-door Woodruff-Fontaine Historic House to the city as the James Lee Memorial, which operated the buildings as an art center until 1958.

It is not certain when it came to light that the Lee House was haunted. In recent decades, the most visible presence has been called "the Lady in Red." Although the Lee House is generally not open to the public, its older wing—"the little square house"—was converted into an apartment for the caretaker of all the city-owned properties on the block. It is in this section that the Lady in Red has most frequently been seen. By all accounts, she is young and beautiful, brightly clad in a Victorian-era dress. She is generally identified as Laura Goyer, who is said to have returned to the house after her death to watch over her children and see they were properly cared for. Of course, she may also have come back to check up on her husband and her sister Charlotte, who seems to have wasted no time filling in for Laura.

Occasionally, psychics and paranormal investigators have been permitted to explore the house. In the 1980s, a group from the University of Memphis documented the Lee House's hauntings. More recently, local amateur groups have gone to the mansion in search of spooks. While the results have never been published in detail, such visits to the Lee House and other Victorian Village properties rarely fail to turn up ghosts.

Perhaps the weirdest happening at the Lee House was reported by a former caretaker. Having had numerous spectral encounters himself while staying alone in the Harsson section of the mansion, he invited a friend to room in the Goyers' old master bedroom as his guest. The caretaker preferred to sleep in the kitchen.

One night, the houseguest came into the kitchen and woke the caretaker. He had been half-asleep when he felt a naked female body next to him in bed, pressing against him. Gradually, it dawned on the man that whoever was next to him was not alive. With that, he jumped out of bed and departed the room. Whether or not this ghost was the Lady in Red is unknown—she didn't have any clothes on, for one thing, and it was dark. The scared houseguest didn't stay in the room long enough to ask questions.

Next door to the Lee House is the Woodruff-Fontaine Historic House. Of all the haunted homes in Victorian Village—and there are quite a few—the most familiar to the public is this grandiose French Victorian–style house with the mansard roof at 680 Adams Avenue.

The Woodruff-Fontaine Historic House is a favorite not only with tourists but also with academic parapsychologists, psychics, reporters in search of Halloween stories, and ghost-hunting groups. Visitors don't need high-tech gear to detect ghosts in here. The five senses will do just fine.

Like Charles Goyer, Amos Woodruff was a self-made millionaire. In 1843, he arrived in Memphis from New Jersey at the age of twenty-three and set up shop as a carriage maker. Where Woodruff made his fortune, however, was in a newer form of transportation. He organized the Memphis and Charleston Railroad and eventually wound up owning not only that but two banks, a hotel company, a cotton business, and a lumber company. He also served a stint as president of the city council.

Having accumulated his fortune in Memphis, Woodruff lured his wife from New Jersey with the promise that he would build her a grand mansion in the finest part of town. In 1871, he kept his promise when he built Phoebe the four-story mansion that still stands today. Estimates suggest that it cost Woodruff a hundred thousand dollars to complete the palatial home—a princely sum in those days, when the dollar was backed by gold.

Woodruff, his wife, and their four daughters were happy in their new home—so much so that when the eldest daughter, Mollie, wed, she and her new husband moved into a suite of rooms on the second floor. Today, that suite is known as "the Rose Bedroom." Unfortunately, Mollie's marital bliss was not fated to last. In quick succession, her first-born died of yellow fever and her husband contracted pneumonia and also passed away. Both died in the Rose Bedroom. Mollie later remarried and lost another baby to yellow fever. Although the Woodruffs sold their mansion to Noland Fontaine in 1883, it is believed that when Mollie died in 1917, her spirit returned to the Rose Bedroom and has continued to haunt the place to this day.

Visiting psychics have actually seen Mollie in the Rose Bedroom and given curators detailed descriptions of her dress—descriptions that match Mollie's clothing stored in the house museum's clothing collection. More often, however, visitors and staff encounter her unseen but sometimes very vocal ghost. Her old four-poster bed often shows the impression of someone's having slept in it, even though it is roped off from the public. Staff members sometimes hear muffled crying coming from Mollie's room. Visitors and volunteers alike have reported a baby's cries from the Rose Bedroom.

Mollie isn't the only spook inhabiting the Woodruff-Fontaine Historic House. A male presence has been identified on the third floor. This particular spirit is less sad than mad and exhibits a particular dislike of women. Although the spirit seems amiable enough toward males, it has been known to jostle and push female visitors with unseen hands.

More commonly, females experience an overall sense of discomfort on the third floor—a feeling that they are unwelcome there. The same misogynistic male spirit has occasionally made its presence known on the first floor as well. On one occasion, a female museum worker's necklace was torn off on the first floor by the bad-boy ghost!

Who this male entity is remains a mystery. Beginning in 1883, the home was occupied by Noland Fontaine's clan. Someone connected to either the Woodruff family or the Fontaine family could be responsible. Moreover, although General Nathan Bedford Forrest never lived here, his black walnut bed is part of the furnishings on the third floor. Perhaps his cantankerous aura emanates from the old bed. Whoever the male ghost may be, he is certainly no Southern gentleman.

Like the Woodruffs, the Fontaines had a daughter named Mollie. When she married, her father gave the couple the house directly across the street at 679 Adams Avenue as a wedding present. Once described as "a Victorian Valentine," that home is now the site of Mollie Fontaine Lounge, a trendy watering hole for mortal Memphians. Not surprisingly, Mollie's ghost is believed to be the mostly unseen hostess of the place.

Noland Fontaine's widow died in 1929, after which Rosa Lee added the Woodruff-Fontaine Historic House and the carriage house in back to her holdings. The complex thereafter became a haven for art students, the carriage house even serving the Memphis Little Theatre as "the Stable Playhouse." Although not heavily visited by tourists, the carriage house is sometimes rented out for weddings. At least a few such groups have had uncanny experiences there. Whether the ghost is a disgruntled dead art student or some deceased actor hamming it up is unknown.

The city-managed house museums of Victorian Village receive the most publicity regarding their haunted history. But they are hardly the only Adams Avenue homes that are occupied by the spirits of the past. However, since most of these are privately owned, their hauntings remain largely a family affair—an Adams family affair.

Woodruff-Fontaine Historic House
680 Adams Avenue
Memphis, TN 38105
(901) 526-1469
www.woodruff-fontaine.com

This is the most accessible of the Victorian Village haunts but by no means the only one.

Molly Fontaine Lounge
679 Adams Avenue
Memphis, TN 38105
(901) 524-1886
www.molliefontainelounge.com

The specialty here is billed as "Food and Spirits." What the ads don't mention is that the spirits include Mollie Fontaine herself. *Bon appétit!*

CHAPTER 23

The Oakslea Place Haunting

Lying nearly halfway between Nashville and Memphis, Jackson is a convenient stop for weary travelers passing through Madison County. But the city has much to offer in its own right, from an ancient and mysterious Indian religious center to the home of the legendary Casey Jones to a pleasant bed-and-breakfast that provides a scenic boo! at no extra charge.

John Read was the presiding judge for two different county courts and a highly respected local citizen. In 1860, he built Oakslea Place on a quiet branch of the Forked Deer River. Back in those days, the house was deep in the countryside and surrounded by a stately stand of oak trees on a large tract of land.

When Judge Read died in 1865, the property passed to other members of the family. It remained with his heirs until the turn of the twentieth century. At that time, a real-estate magnate bought the home and developed the surrounding property. In 1917, Dr. Jere Cook and his wife moved into Oakslea and made further improvements. They and their family continued to enjoy the mansion's amenities until 1958. From then until 2004, another prominent physician and his family reveled in Oakslea's spacious quarters and quiet dignity.

As the years passed, Jackson grew up around Oakslea. Sections of the plantation were parceled out for other houses. Today, Oakslea is situated in the middle part of Jackson on a quiet, tree-lined boulevard. One of the oldest homes in town, it has accumulated a long history. It has also accumulated a few things not of this world.

In 2004, Oakslea Place came into the possession of its present owner, Richard Testani. From the first, Testani recognized the house's uniqueness and set about restoring it with a view to turning it into a bed-and-breakfast. Meanwhile, he began to suspect he was not the only one to possess the house. After Oakslea opened to guests and others began having similar encounters, Testani realized that some of the house's dearly departed had not quite departed.

At first, the new owner experienced things that might be easily dismissed as the products of an overactive imagination—the sounds of footsteps and of voices whispering. Then he began to notice things not so easily dismissed—the strong scent of a woman's perfume and the distinct aroma of fresh flowers. Finally, the master of Oakslea started seeing full-blown apparitions. Nor was Testani the only one to witness the elegant bed-and-breakfast's spectral residents. Guests staying in the four well-appointed suites experienced an assortment of paranormal phenomena and even had ghosts materialize before them.

Despite all the spectral activity, no one at Oakslea has expressed any fear at having to share their stay with the resident spirits. In fact, by all accounts, the ghosts who haunt Oakslea have impeccable manners.

Perhaps the most interesting apparition is a rather dignified spirit named Hampton. According to eyewitness accounts, Hampton appears as an elderly African-American gentleman always dressed in formal attire such as a butler might wear. His name is known because he once materialized before a bartender working a catered party in the mansion. The bartender was busy dispensing beverages when the tuxedo-clad ap-

THE OAKSLEA PLACE HAUNTING   153

parition appeared and introduced himself by saying, "I am Hampton the butler."

Over the years, the owners of Oakslea Place employed house servants. Hampton, by all accounts, was one of the home's more devoted domestics, serving as butler there for most of his adult life. He has appeared to the present owner on a number of occasions and has occasionally materialized before visitors and staff. Apparently, his spirit still looks after Oakslea and its guests, making sure things run smoothly. Hampton's dignified demeanor in death, as in life, adds a touch of class to the ambiance.

Hampton is by no means the only spectral presence known to haunt Oakslea. Two female apparitions are present as well. It is believed that they are mother and daughter and that they are former residents. It is to these ghosts that Testani attributes the various olfactory phenomena commonly experienced at Oakslea. At unexpected times, the scent of a woman's perfume will flood a room. Similarly, guests may come into a room thinking it contains a large bouquet of flowers, only to discover that no such arrangement is there.

Testani and his guests have continued to experience the kinds of spectral encounters that the new owner first noticed—the sounds of footsteps and of barely audible voices, as if a conversation is being held in another room. Testani has even felt the touch of unseen hands. What ghosts are responsible for these phenomena and how many of them haunt Oakslea in this manner remain two of the house's several mysteries.

A common element among all the uncanny experiences that guests and staff have had at Oakslea Place in recent years is that the specters definitely seem to be the protective sort. Apparently, these particular ghosts grew so fond of their abode in life that they have chosen to also abide there in the hereafter.

CHAPTER 24

Reelfoot Encounters

Tucked away in Tennessee's northwest corner, Reelfoot Lake is a natural wonder. Created amid the death and destruction of the New Madrid Earthquakes of 1811–12, the lake was formed virtually overnight, as if by magic. The few Native Americans who survived the quakes and flood shunned the area ever after as cursed and ill-omened. The great Indian leader Tecumseh declared that the Great Spirit had "stamped his foot" to punish the tribesmen of the region for being too friendly with whites.

Indeed, when the Great Spirit stamped his foot upon the earth around Reelfoot Village, the Great River—Mishasi-pokni Huch-cha, or "He whose age is beyond counting"—ran backward, rushing to fill the footlike depression created by the quakes. Legends grew about the lake. For many, it became a place of mystery and wonder—and dread.

Some of the best-known haint tales about the lake relate to the legend of Kalopin, the lame Indian chief who had a forbidden love for a neighboring princess, Laughing Eyes. At various times, fishermen and duck hunters have reported Native American ghosts on the lake and sounds coming from beneath it. That many Native Americans died in the quakes and the subsequent flood is fact. That the Southern tribes regarded Reelfoot as the result of divine punishment is also fact. Is it so far-fetched, then, that the spirits of some of those who died in the quakes and flood should still haunt the lake?

The Indians shunned Reelfoot as cursed, but whites embraced the area as a wilderness paradise filled with game, fish, and fowl. Davy Crockett hunted here in the 1820s, although he called it Redfoot Lake. In the wake of the hunters came settlers. They, too, found the place to their liking.

Despite its scenic beauty, Reelfoot Lake has continued to have a turbulent history. During the Civil War, several battles were fought in the area. At nearby Island Number Ten, a major siege took place for control of the Mississippi. At Tiptonville, ten thousand Confederates surrendered to the Yankees. Every now and again, farmers dig up bullets and cannonballs even today.

At the turn of the twentieth century, outside developers wanted to turn the lake into their private pond and displace the local folks. The men who made a living off the lake's abundant wildlife did not take kindly to strangers destroying their way of life. Soon, Nightriders—a local group unrelated to the Ku Klux Klan but part and parcel of the post–Civil War vigilante phenomenon—began a reign of terror against the outsiders. The Nightriders ultimately lynched a land-company lawyer near the spot on the lake called Walnut Log. Although a number of men were prosecuted, no local jury was willing to convict them of actions most local folks thought justified. A sense of dread continues to hang over Walnut Log. To this day, locals can point out the tree where the lawyer was hanged.

The lake remains a sportsman's paradise. Fishing, boating, hunting, and hiking are accessible to all. Visitors find the area a scenic wonderland. But beneath the placid lake lie secrets. Places seemingly normal by day may instill terror by night. The still waters of Reelfoot do not run deep, but they cover an awful lot of mysteries nonetheless.

Take, for example, the apparition seen around Champey's Pocket on the east side of the lake. It first came to light several years ago when two coon hunters were out at the lake one chill, windy night in late November. Around one in the morning, they decided to return to their truck, parked at Champey's Pocket Landing. After hooking up the boat and loading their guns and hounds, the two drove off. The truck hadn't gotten far along the road when one of the hunters noticed something strange coming out of the weeds. The figure was dressed in what seemed to be a long gown. Her face was indistinct, as if there were a veil over it, and neither her hands nor her feet could be made out. The ghost was pale and transparent and floated above the ground. After staring transfixed for a few seconds, the two men didn't wait for her to get any closer and hightailed it out of there. They went back to Champey's Pocket on other occasions to investigate but were never able to make sense out of their experience.

On another occasion, visiting fishermen had a similar experience late at night. Just as they were loading their boat onto their trailer, they, too, spotted "the Lady in White." When one of them later inquired of some locals about their encounter, it came out that others indeed had experienced similar run-ins with the ghost over the years. Apparently, many people had kept silent about it for fear of ridicule or being accused of drunkenness. Comparing different accounts of the ghost—often separated by years—a pattern emerged. The apparition was always spotted in the vicinity of Champey's Pocket, and always at night. Those with nerve enough to hang around more than a few seconds noted that the ghost eventually floated into the lake and disappeared. One witness in the 1990s added the detail that she was dressed like a bride.

That same witness believed he had an explanation for the haunting. Several generations earlier, a certain local landowner had the reputation of being mean as a snake. As the story went, he lured his ex-girlfriend into the woods and beat her brutally. The landowner had found out she was going to marry a man from Kentucky and resolved that if he could not have her, no one else would. Leaving her for dead, he returned to his house. A few days later, however, she managed to crawl out of the woods. When he discovered her still alive, the man tied her up in fishing nets and dumped her, still breathing, into the lake. The sheriff at the time was a close friend and allegedly helped him cover up the crime.

On rare occasions, visitors to Champey's Pocket have seen a male ghost in the area as well. He is dressed in a suit, like that of a groom. Some claim to have seen him joining the ghost bride near the lake. One old-timer who knew the story claimed the couple were named Linda and Peter. Apparently, they were both murdered by the jealous ex-boyfriend and dumped in the lake. Since the landowner got away with his crime, the ghosts are the only witnesses to his vicious act.

Another female ghost also haunts the area. A resident of Proctor City and his brother-in-law were headed home along the road on the west side of the lake in 1997 when they spotted it in a lot near the old prison nearby. The ghost glowed all over. Her legs tapered to nothing. No feet were visible as she hovered above the ground. The two kinfolk resolved never to talk about the incident. But in 2003, one of them had to take his niece to the emergency room because she was having a panic attack. On the way, she told him what had caused it. She had spotted a glowing woman in a red dress floating above a field along Highway 78, going toward Proctor City. It was almost exactly where he'd seen the ghost. After the first witness subsequently related his family's encounters with the Lady in Red, other local residents came forward to tell of their experiences with the ghost. Again, it came out that the sightings went back several generations in the vicinity of the old prison.

Nor was that prison—now closed—immune from strange doings. One old-timer who now lives in Kentucky used to work the third shift there. This particular guard happened to have an intense dislike for the smell of coffee. When he began his shift, he would make a point of unplugging the large coffee urn the second shift had put on to brew. One night around three in the morning, hours after he had unplugged the urn, he was at his work station writing up reports when the lid of the urn suddenly came off for no reason and flew across the room. Nor was he the only guard to see and hear strange things while working in the prison.

The Indians had their tales of Reelfoot Lake. White settlers added to the lore. For outsiders and even some locals, however, learning the lake's secrets is a difficult task. One longtime resident confessed, "Most people won't open up about any ghosts they might share a home with." Another local informant put it this way: "To admit that you have seen something can cause ridicule from others."

So, for now, while casual visitors can enjoy its natural beauty, Reelfoot Lake will continue to keep most of its mysteries safe beneath its placid surface.

Reelfoot Lake State Park
2595 State Route 21E
Tiptonville, TN 38079
(731) 253-8003
www.state.tn.us/environment/parks/
ReelfootLake/

The lake is located close to the Mississippi. Numerous resorts and campgrounds in the area cater to sportsmen and nature enthusiasts; I'm sure they wouldn't mind hosting a few ghost hunters as well. The state park is a good place to learn about local history and culture. The park is home to the R. C. Donaldson Memorial Museum; for information, call (731) 253-9552.

Chapter 25

Ernestine and Hazel's
Spirits, Soul, and Rock-'n'-Roll

The proprietors of most bars might take offense at having their place characterized as a dive. At Ernestine and Hazel's in the heart of downtown Memphis, however, they revel in that title. In fact, they boast that their establishment is "the best dive in Memphis." No less an authority than *Esquire* magazine rated Ernestine and Hazel's "one of the coolest dives in the United States."

The food and the jukebox in this venerable dive are legendary. The menu features the "Soul Burger," which lays claim to being the best hamburger in the city. The jukebox is packed with classic soul, funk, country, and blues, with a distinct bias in favor of homegrown hits. It is said the old jukebox has a mind of its own. But that is not the only peculiar thing about Ernestine and Hazel's. The drinks served at the bar are not as renowned as the other spirits this mythic dive serves up, for Ernestine and Hazel's is one of the most haunted bars in the nation.

Now part of the revived historic arts district of downtown Memphis, the funky-looking building that houses Ernestine and Hazel's has seen a lot of wild times and gone through many changes over the years. The old whitewashed two-story brick structure on Main Street wasn't always the best dive in Memphis. Built before the end of World War I, it was once a pharmacy. Some of the old drawers where drugs were kept are still intact in the bar. According to local tradition, this is where St. Joseph Aspirin for children was originally concocted. Made in the form of chewable candy, St. Joseph Aspirin was the medicine that unwittingly taught the sixties generation to associate pill-popping with *fun*, much to the chagrin of authorities. The building also housed a dry-goods store and a soda fountain. The marble-topped counter where old-fashioned sodas were dispensed still survives in the bar as well. That is typical of the place. Things—and people—seem to accumulate and hang around for decades. Perhaps that is how the bar has earned its haunted reputation as well. The spirits of former patrons and musicians linger long after it was their time to go.

The bar owes its name to Ernestine Mitchell and Hazel Jones, its proprietors in the days when it became a music mecca. In 1944, Andrew "Sunbeam" Mitchell opened the Mitchell Hotel above Pantaze's Pharmacy. Shortly thereafter, he started his first nightclub, the Domino Lounge, also on the second floor. When Sunbeam took over the old pharmacy portion of the building, his wife, Ernestine, oversaw the food preparation, serving up soul food and chili to customers. Sunbeam later opened additional nightclubs in the black neighborhoods and started a variety of other music-related enterprises in Memphis.

After World War II, large numbers of Southern blacks returned home, their wallets full with pay from Uncle Sam. Although they had enjoyed a taste of the wider world—a world where prejudice was less in evidence—it would still be years before the civil-rights movement gained momentum. In the meantime, blacks wanting to enjoy themselves could not go into white nightclubs, so in Memphis and elsewhere in the South arose "the Chitlin' Circuit," a network of juke joints and nightclubs. Black entrepreneurs like Sunbeam Mitchell saw this need and did their best to fill it with places like the Mitchell Hotel. Their establishments were raucous, rowdy, and a little bit dangerous, but they featured great blues and R&B music, the like of which could not be heard anywhere else. In fact, white blues legend Mose Allison claimed that what some consider "the original rock-'n'-roll band"—Tuff Green and His Rocketeers—got its start at the Mitchell Hotel in the late 1940s.

Sunbeam, wife Ernestine, and Ernestine's sister Hazel not only had a jammin' juke joint, they also looked after struggling musicians. They had soft hearts when it came to music makers and often let one or another stay for weeks at the hotel for free. Many a struggling bluesman and R&B artist survived on Ernestine's chili. According to Sunbeam, Little Richard once stayed at the Mitchell for weeks when he hit a hard patch.

Upstairs, in addition to providing a place to sleep, the Mitchell Hotel offered female companionship—for a fee—to those patrons so inclined. Musicians coming to town would often stay at the Mitchell, play music, write songs, and party the night away with "the girls" before their scheduled recording sessions the next day. One time, Wilson Pickett came to town to record at Stax Record Studios, located a few blocks from the hotel. Steve Cropper, guitarist for Booker T. and the MG's—another Stax group—stopped by and learned that Pickett didn't have any new material to record the next day. Using the old upright piano still upstairs at Ernestine and Hazel's, the two jammed through the night, working on new songs. The next day, Pickett recorded two of his greatest hits, "The Midnight Hour" and "Mustang Sally," both obviously inspired by his stay upstairs.

Although blacks could not patronize white clubs in the late 1940s and the 1950s, whites could and did go to black clubs in Memphis and elsewhere. And what they heard, they liked. As Sunbeam became busy running other music venues, Ernestine and Hazel were the ones most in evidence at the Mitchell Hotel on a day-to-day basis. Eventually, everyone came to call the place "Ernestine and Hazel's." It has been known that way ever since.

Whatever they came for—good food, good times, good music, bad girls—patrons black and white alike generally went away satisfied.

Ernestine and Hazel's became popular not only with native Memphians but with out-of-town celebrities as well. In the bar are pictures of legendary bluesman Howlin' Wolf with some female "admirers" sitting on his lap. Ray Charles was a regular visitor as well. The bad boys of rock-'n'-roll, the Rolling Stones, frequented the place in its heyday. Allegedly, the girls upstairs were the inspiration for "Brown Sugar." B. B. King, Tina Turner, Otis Redding, and many others visited Ernestine and Hazel's at one time or another. The two sisters ran the hottest spot in town. It had a reputation for being so bad it was good.

In the late 1960s, however, times changed. Ironically, integration proved the death knell for Ernestine and Hazel's and the Chitlin' Circuit. Blacks were no longer restricted to their own clubs, and whites could hear once-taboo black music in nightclubs closer to home. Eventually, the venerable juke joint, honky-tonk, and house of ill repute that was Ernestine and Hazel's went the way of all flesh. The building was boarded up. Only its ghosts were left to party on.

Then, in the early 1990s, a movement began to revive Beale Street and the old downtown area of Memphis. A local developer and the building's owner recruited a successful bar owner to revive Ernestine and Hazel's on the principle that if they could attract a hip new generation to the legendary club, other businesses would follow. Russell George, Ernestine and Hazel's current owner, and bar manager Vivian Jones worked hard to get the place into shape while retaining the decadent charm of the old Ernestine and Hazel's. By all accounts, they and their crew have succeeded admirably.

Music is a big part of the attraction here. Ernestine and Hazel's boasts an ample dance floor and the best-stocked jukebox in Memphis. The jukebox has an eclectic collection of hit songs that feature the Memphis sound. Guests have witnessed an odd thing about the jukebox, however: it seems to have a mind of its own. It is supposed to play songs in random order. But since the reopening, both staff and patrons have noticed that it often plays songs eerily in tune with people's conversations or states of mind. It is as if the old machine can actually read their thoughts.

For example, a group of women came in to celebrate one of their number's recent divorce. No sooner had they sat down than the jukebox started playing Tammy Wynette's "D-I-V-O-R-C-E." Another time, the manager, Vivian, had just arrived at the bar after attending the funeral of a beloved regular, Freddie Newman. As soon as she came in the door, the jukebox began to spin Curtis Mayfield's "Freddie's Dead." Both Vivian and the owner were more than a little surprised. Other nightclubs may well be haunted, but how many have ghosts that also double as DJs?

The place seems to be inhabited by both male and female ghosts. A male phantom has been sighted carrying a candle in the bar. At other times, photos have been snapped of a male ghost on the stairs and of the face of a female ghost. Electronic voice recordings have been captured in the building after hours, especially upstairs.

Because the place is so psychically active, it is a favorite haunt of ghost hunters. On occasion, the management has allowed serious groups to stay overnight to document the hauntings. One ghost hunter who has been there several times observed, "We have never been disappointed."

The exact identities of the ghosts that haunt Ernestine and Hazel's have never been determined. Given the nightclub's bawdy history, it is likely the male ghosts all go by the name of John, while the ghosts of the working girls wish to remain anonymous. The shades of a few old bluesmen and other celebrities may also reside at Ernestine and Hazel's, still jammin' the night away.

It is not hard to guess why old ghosts haunt the legendary hotel turned juke joint, for there is one spirit that continues to dominate the place to this day. Upstairs and down, it draws both the living and the dead to it. It is the spirit of the Memphis blues.

**Ernestine and Hazel's
531 South Main
Memphis, TN 38103
(901) 523-9754**

Eat, drink, dance—just make sure the partner you're dancing with is flesh and blood!

CHAPTER 26

Haunted Bolivar
The Friendly Phantoms and Restless Revenants of Hardeman County

Traveling south along Highway 18 about half an hour out of Jackson, drivers come upon the town of Bolivar. Although not a big urban area, Bolivar is known in West Tennessee for two things: its bounty of beautiful Victorian homes and its abundance of ghosts.

Passing along the tree-lined streets, travelers might easily see Bolivar as a town that time forgot. That, however, would not be true, for when I visited Bolivar one dreamy summer day, the downtown was abuzz with activity. Restoration and renovation projects were in evidence all around the square, and people were everywhere. It was not hard to see that folks thereabouts live very much in the present even as they work to preserve the past.

Far and away Bolivar's most famous—and best-loved—ghost is that of Uncle Dave Parran. For eighty-six years, Uncle Dave was a local fixture. Born before the Civil War, he witnessed a lot of history, much of it from the front porch of his home. In his prime, Uncle Dave held court in the town square, where he could be seen any day of the week. An undertaker by trade, he also owned an iron foundry. Many of the finer homes in Bolivar sport his foundry's fine iron decorations. When he wasn't about his profession, Uncle Dave would sit outside and watch folks come and go. He often engaged friends and acquaintances—that is to say, just about everyone in town—in conversation. If need be, he brought additional chairs onto the porch so he could chew the cud with visitors.

Even after Uncle Dave retired from the funeral business, he still hung out in the square. As he got up in years, however, he spent more and more time in his rocking chair. People became used to the sight of Uncle Dave rocking on the front porch of Wren's Nest, the beautiful Victorian home where he lived. Uncle Dave also referred to Wren's Nest as "the Wedding Cake House." He would explain to the curious that he called the house that because the decorations and trim were as ornate as those on any wedding cake. However, the fact that the home was built as a wedding present by the town's wealthy industrialist, John Houston Bills, for his daughter Lucy may also have had something to do with the nickname.

When Uncle Dave passed away in 1936, he was sorely missed. People half expected to see him still there, rocking in his old chair. Then someone noticed something strange: Uncle Dave's chair was rocking all by itself! To those who dismissed it as being caused by the wind, people pointed out that the chair rocked even on calm days. Folks passing the ornate house on Bills Street got used to seeing the haunted chair in motion and accepted the fact that Uncle Dave's ghost was out people-watching.

Nor was the rocking chair the only evidence of Uncle Dave's spectral presence. Later occupants of Wren's Nest noticed strange goings-on inside the home. In the middle of the night, residents inside the Wedding Cake would hear noises as if someone were rummaging around for something. The sounds of bureau drawers opening and closing and invisible footsteps padding about the house became familiar to subsequent owners over the decades. Although living in a haunted house was initially a shock to some of them, they eventually got used to the notion that Uncle Dave was still on the premises.

Across the street from Uncle Dave Parran's house stands McNeal Place, whose haunting is a sadder affair. The mansion dates to 1862 or thereabouts. It was built by Ezekiel Polk, a relative of James K. Polk, so his wife, Ann, could be close to the grave of their daughter Priscilla in nearby Union Cemetery.

Priscilla died in 1854 while still in her teens. Ann never got over it and visited the grave every day of her life. Even when the Yankees occupied the city and their lines blocked access, Ann obtained a special pass to visit her daughter's grave. It is said that no stronger emotion exists than a mother's love for her children. So it is not surprising that after Ann herself crossed over, her ghost continued to visit Priscilla's grave. Over the years, numerous witnesses have seen Ann passing between the mansion and her daughter's resting place.

The home passed to Thomas McNeal, a son-in-law of Ezekiel and Ann Polk. Thanks to its three-foot-thick walls, its hand-painted frescoes in the hallway, its Carrera marble, its elaborate wrought-iron grillwork, and its finely manicured gardens, McNeal Place, as it came to be known, seemed less a Southern mansion than some Renaissance palace. But nothing could ever console Ann Polk, whose presence is still felt inside and outside the house. Either she or another family ghost has been caught in wedding photos taken on the front porch as a strong glow emanating from inside the house. Others claim to have seen her gazing out an upstairs window toward the graveyard.

When it comes to melancholy spirits, however, the nearby Western Mental Health Institute claims first place. It is believed to be the abode of more than a few restless spirits. A state-run facility, the institute is closed to the general public. For that reason, reports of hauntings there are hard to verify, and rumors abound. However, generations of Bolivar citizens have worked at the institute. A few have spent time there as patients.

Today, WMHI is a modern facility. But during the nineteenth and early twentieth centuries, the treatment of patients more resembled medieval torture than medical science. Lobotomies were common, as were electric shock and "water therapy." In the basement of one building, the iron shackles fixed to the walls were used to restrain uncooperative patients.

As one of the oldest mental institutions in the South, WMHI has had a long and often tragic history. Many patients in the old days were not even mentally ill by modern standards. For example, women who were promiscuous ("sex-crazed") or suffering from postpartum depression were frequently institutionalized there. Persons suffering from Alzheimer's, mental retardation, and epilepsy could be committed either by families choosing not to deal with their conditions or by teachers or other authorities who neither cared about nor understood their maladies. Such folks may not have been insane when they entered the hospital but sometimes became so due to the terrible conditions there.

As one Bolivar citizen described them, the ghosts of WMHI are not just lonely spirits but "tortured souls"—spirits unable to pass beyond the painful memories of their mortal existence. Reports of apparitions by former patients are common but have generally been ignored. However, staff members have had similar experiences while working at the hospital. Many former employees have heard voices or seen people in units not in use. At other times, ghosts have been spotted in outbuildings long since shut down.

Access to the institute is restricted even for family members, so would-be ghost hunters are advised not to trespass. The only part of the facility accessible to the public is the administration building, and even that requires permission to visit. It, too, is allegedly haunted.

By contrast, those wishing to get up close and personal with the spirit world can find no better place than Magnolia Manor. This grand old mansion built in the Georgian style has been a bed-and-breakfast since 1995. It has been recognized by Fodor's for its excellence and has been featured on network television and in *National Geographic*. For those who don't mind sharing their room with a ghost or two, Magnolia Manor is definitely the place to stay.

Built in 1849 of bricks made by slave labor, it was the home of Judge Austin Miller, a leading citizen of the county. The Miller family resided in Magnolia Manor for three generations, accumulating several lifetimes of memories within its walls.

The main house has four guest bedrooms, two of which are suites. It boasts nine fireplaces, thirteen-foot ceilings, and antique furniture that would do any museum proud. In the rear stands the slave quarters, now converted into a cozy guest cottage. In the main house, guests can choose among the 1849 Room, Annie's Room, the C. A. Miller Suite, and the Austin Miller Suite. All the lodgings have had reports of spectral activity at one time or another.

The most active seems to be the 1849 Room. Elaine Cox, the innkeeper and owner of the house, has heard footsteps there late at night when the room was empty and the house locked. The room's antique wardrobe is a favorite haunt of a playful spirit that likes to rattle the hangers inside and bang against the wooden sides. Guests in the room occasionally feel something touching their feet at night.

In Annie's Room, paranormal investigators have had motion detectors go off when the room was vacant. Moreover, the spirit is quite talkative. During several sessions, ghost hunters recorded spectral voices responding directly to questions. The voices seemed to be female.

In the C. A. Miller Suite, a ghost hunter mistook a male apparition for a fellow investigator one night. Another time, a guest in the room was awakened in the middle of the night by the sound of a person humming. Sitting up with a start, she saw a woman seated in the room's rocking chair. That same female ghost has been seen elsewhere in the house walking with a candle. She is believed to date to the home's earliest era.

The Austin Miller Suite has had its share of unusual events as well. A piece of electronic equipment placed in the room to detect unseen entities was found to have turned itself off. It had not malfunctioned. The ghost simply didn't like its movements being monitored. It seems this ghost busted the ghost busters.

Even the guest cottage is haunted. A female voice has been heard there on more than one occasion. The apparition of a young girl is thought to reside in the former slave quarters.

Combining the known history of the house with the results of the investigations of a number of paranormal researchers, Elaine Cox and her staff have been able to identify who they feel the ghosts may be. One of the female haunts is short, stout, and elderly and has been described as dressed in old-fashioned clothing. It is thought she is the ghost of Annie Miller, who lived all her eighty-four years and ultimately died in the home. Another female apparition has been described as young and pretty and also dressed in antique clothing. Thought to be a cousin of the Millers who died at age eighteen, she is frequently seen in the 1849 Room. A male presence has also been detected in the house. He, too, is presumably one of the Miller clan.

At least one Civil War phantom has been sighted roaming the grounds outside the mansion. The fact that both Grant and Sherman used the house as their headquarters may have something to do with this haunting. The house even has a feline phantom, believed to be the ghostly pet of the last Miller to live here.

Bolivar is a hidden treasure in southwest Tennessee. Beautiful homes and a bounty of ghosts make for a town full of more surprises than meet the eye.

CHAPTER 27

Ghost Lights and Other Frights

Tennessee's spook lights have been alternately scaring and fascinating folks for as long as anyone can remember. Moreover, reports of uncanny lights span the state from one end to the other.

The Cherokee Indians used to talk about a mysterious spirit they called Atsil-dihyegi, or "Fire-Carrier." Tradition was a bit vague about exactly what sort of spirit it was and what it looked like, for whenever Cherokees sighted it, they never stayed long enough for a good look.

The only things known about Atsil-dihyegi were that it was very dangerous and that it went about carrying a light. A mixed-blood Cherokee named Wafford related how his mother encountered it when she was a young girl in frontier days. She was returning home one night from a trading post in the Carolinas when Fire-Carrier suddenly appeared behind her. According to her son's account, the fiery spirit seemed to follow her along the trail. The Indian maiden didn't wait for the spook light to catch up. She whipped her pony and hightailed it straight home.

In the high country not far from the North Carolina border lies

Doe Mountain. While not so famous as other mountain luminaries, the Doe Mountain Fireball has a long history. Reported to be about three feet across, it seems to remain earthbound as it rolls up and down the slopes. Even more unusual, it has been seen in daylight. That it is no ordinary fire is indicated by eyewitness accounts of its rolling over dry leaves and tinder without setting them afire. Its nature and origin are mysteries.

Spook lights aren't limited to the countryside. In 1810, a mysterious fireball appeared on Gay Street in downtown Knoxville, causing an uproar among local folks. Unlike the later White Mule, it did no damage. Nevertheless, the citizenry was glad it never made a reappearance.

In Middle Tennessee, travelers don't even have to leave the interstate to encounter a spooky illumination. The Cumberland Mountain Ghost Lights occur all around the mountain but scare motorists along I-40 at one particular spot. Allegedly the result of a grisly murder, the lights play at night right where the freeway crosses the Obed River.

Down in the Cumberland Valley, little Leipers Fork has hosted occasional visits by a ghost light. What sets the light off is unknown. Perhaps it signifies a protest against all the transplants from elsewhere.

Mostly, ghost lights prefer to haunt rural areas, either on lonely country roads or along railroad tracks. Up around Adams, lights continue to appear in the vicinity of the old Bell farm. Although the legendary Bell Witch has long since headed for greener pastures, all manner of weirdness continues to manifest itself in the area. Whether the fact that an old frontier trail crosses the property or that the area is dotted with Indian mounds has anything to do with the ghost light is a matter for speculation.

The most famous spook light in Tennessee is the one that hangs out along the railroad line running through Chapel Hill. Sightings of this light have clustered along the CSX railroad crossing in town. Reputedly, it is the ghost of a headless brakeman who slipped on the tracks one night and is still looking to recover his missing cranium. The spook light has been seen by many curiosity seekers over the years. But of late, the local constabulary has taken to arresting trespassers who wander onto private property in search of it.

Across the Tennessee River in West Tennessee, McKenzie lies about midway between Paris and Milan. McKenzie has an old cemetery, also called Chapel Hill, that boasts a spook light. At night, eerie lights are seen cavorting about the graveyard. The cemetery is near not only an old church but also ancient Indian mounds. Likely, the place is doubly haunted. Even more ominous than the lights are reports of shadowy figures lurking about the area.

Farther south, down along the Alabama border, is Flintville. Although small, the town is rich in paranormal activity. The Flintville Light is similar in many ways to the Chapel Hill railroad light, but its origin is better documented.

The story goes that a local man was walking along the tracks one night when he was hit by a speeding train. Bits and pieces of him were spread along the track for some distance. Ever since then, the light has appeared along that same stretch. The Flintville Light approaches as if it were the headlamp of an oncoming train. When observers approach the light, however, it withdraws and then disappears. At an elementary school in Flintville adjacent to the old roadbed, the light has been reported to look like an old man carrying a lantern. Most witnesses who have seen it, however, describe it simply as a disembodied, eerie white glow lacking shape or form.

In truth, it's been many years since trains went through Flintville. The bed where the tracks once ran is still there. In some places, sections of rusted track may still remain where no one has bothered to take them up. But if the trains are gone, nobody told the spook light.

Flintville has seen many strange sights besides the ghost light. In 1905, for example, the Hicks clan had a reunion. When the group portrait came back from the photographer, Grandpa Hicks was in the photo. What was the problem with that? Well, only that old Marion Hicks had died eleven months and twenty days before the photo was taken.

Phantom photos and phantom lights—for a small town on the Alabama border, an awful lot of things seem to happen in Flintville. For example, there's that eight-foot-tall hairy-looking gent who has been hanging around of late. But that's another story.

CHAPTER 28

Elvis Lives!

Marc Cohen may or may not have seen the ghost of Elvis Aaron Presley when he visited Graceland in 1985, an experience he wrote about in his hit song "Walking in Memphis." But since Elvis's death, many folks who have come to pay homage to "the King of Rock-'n'-Roll" most certainly have.

Some, in fact, claim their encounters with the postmortem Elvis were really meetings with him in the flesh—that he never really died, that the autopsy lied, that the King is still in hiding. In recent years, a few writers have even speculated that perhaps Elvis has returned from the grave, Christlike. Many devout Elvis fans have problems with the theory of the King as "King of Kings," however. A less blasphemous suggestion is that perhaps he should rather be regarded as St. Elvis, that all the postmortem encounters are akin to beatific visions of a beloved patron saint.

The fact that Elvis was born and raised a fundamentalist Protestant, not Catholic, makes this interpretation of his apparition a mite difficult. But aside from the inconvenience that most Protestant denominations do not go in for the veneration of saints, the idea may have some merit, as outlandish as it seems. Saints, it is said, bridge the

gap between the here and the hereafter. Although their flesh may (but not always) molder into dust, their spirits continue to abide, appearing to the faithful to guide and inspire them. Their continued presence is why Catholic saints are generally referred to in the present tense. They are dead but not gone.

So, yes, Virginia, there is a Santa Claus. And yes, Elvis lives on in spirit. Hundreds, if not thousands, of eyewitness have testified to the continuing presence of St. Elvis.

The basic fact is that Elvis died in his mansion of a heart attack on July 20, 1977—from, it is said, straining too hard on the toilet. Since then, his postmortem career has been nearly as active as his life. Unfortunately, in recent years, since the demise of that great journalistic institution *Weekly World News*, it has become far harder to track details of the King's busy afterlife.

Certainly, the epicenter of all the paranormal activity is Graceland. It is said that a man's home is his castle. In his domain, the King held court, surrounded by faithful retainers. He received visits not only from supplicants but also from foreign dignitaries—such as the Beatles. Since Elvis's passing, however, Graceland has become less castle and more secular shrine. Today, it is a place of pilgrimage where the faithful may view sacred relics associated with the object of their veneration. It is the second-most-visited home in the country, right behind the White House. Given the intense emotions swirling about the place, is it any wonder that Graceland is a center of psychic activity?

In the decades since Graceland opened to the public, numerous visitors have seen the image of Elvis. He has been witnessed peering from both a second-floor window and a first-floor window. He has been spotted sitting inside a screen door at the back of the mansion. Elvis has also been seen riding in mysterious black limousines and other cars, entering and leaving Graceland in the dark of night. One Memphis cabdriver swears he drove Elvis to Graceland on a stormy night, much in the manner of the "phantom hitchhiker" legend.

Of course, on any given day, a visit to Graceland does not automatically entail a spectral encounter with Elvis. The majority of his dedicated fans have come and gone and seen his mementos and nothing else. However, it is interesting that a number of those who have witnessed Elvis's ghost at Graceland were not devoted fans of the King but just ordinary visitors. One informant, a woman named Ana, recalled visiting the mansion as a child with her parents years ago. While staring at the King's bejeweled jumpsuit behind glass, she thought she caught sight of something out of the corner of her eye. Looking back at the exhibit case, she then noticed a reflection in the glass of Elvis's face. Outside, behind the mansion, still with her parents, she saw a black horse gallop across the pasture to the horse barn. Shortly afterward, the audio tour informed her that Elvis's favorite horse, Jack, was a black thoroughbred. It turned out that no horses were on the property that particular day. Had she seen the equine specter of Jack? Finally, as she and her family arrived at the meditation garden and Elvis's grave, the little girl again saw the King's reflection in the glass casing.

Later, when the photos from the trip were developed, it turned out that Ana's mother had snapped one of her daughter sitting at a picnic table with the blurry image of a man walking behind her, even though no one had been visible there at the time. Was it coincidence? Confusion? Or was Elvis reaching out to a new generation from beyond the grave?

The report of the specter of Elvis's favorite horse raises the interesting prospect that more than one ghost haunts Graceland—a possibility that tabloids and psychic researchers have mostly ignored. A number of witnesses have sighted Elvis's mother at Graceland as well. Gladys Presley has been seen near the mansion's kitchen window—the same window whose pane she broke when she fell on the day she died. Elvis's mother has also been reported wandering the hallway upstairs outside Elvis's bedroom, quietly singing an old gospel song. It is as if she is still looking over her son, even in death.

Just as Graceland is home to more than just Elvis's ghost, the King's shade has been known to visit a number of other places associated with his life.

A short distance from Graceland is the Pepper House. Gary Pepper was one of Elvis's most devoted fans and a close friend. He was president of one of the King's first fan clubs, The Tankers, EPFC. Gary Pepper suffered from cerebral palsy. As time went on, he was more and more debilitated by the disease. On his own initiative, Elvis hired a twenty-four-hour caretaker for Pepper and even paid the mortgage on his house. He frequently popped in on Pepper at odd hours of the day and night and was always welcome. In fact, the Pepper House was something of a refuge for the often-harried superstar. Elvis often went there to sing or play music for his own and Gary's pleasure. Over the years, Elvis bestowed on his favorite fan a number of souvenirs from his career, including his gold lamé jumpsuit and his 1957 Chevy. Clearly, the Pepper House was a place the King associated with happy memories.

A range of paranormal activities has been reported inside the Pepper House. Elvis still pops in for visits from time to time. The house has been featured on at least one television documentary on the paranormal. On one occasion, two cynical local deejays attempted to broadcast from inside the house, virtually daring Elvis's ghost to visit them. From the start, the crew was plagued with a variety of technical problems. Apparently, Elvis had been listening to the two sarcastic deejays mouth off and was not amused.

Across the street from Graceland stands the 128-room Elvis-themed Heartbreak Hotel. This modern hostelry with all the amenities is decorated in a manner aimed to please die-hard fans of the King. Its richly appointed gift shop is filled with everything Elvis. Although the hotel is named after the song that made him famous, Elvis never actually stayed here—in life, at least. Allegedly, however, the King has popped in at least once postmortem—to get married!

A sixth-grade class from the Midwest was visiting on a field trip. Its students got an inkling something strange was up when, as they approached the main entrance, they noticed the glass doors were all steamed up. The students then spied Elvis in the lobby making out with the ghost of Marilyn Monroe. But once the clerk turned up the lights, Elvis and Marilyn disappeared right before their eyes!

Other witnesses present at the time claimed the ghostly couple had been sighted in the hotel's "Chapel of Love" a short time earlier. They were supposedly the principals in a phantom nuptial ceremony. Instead of wedding bells, however, the eyewitnesses claimed they heard "Diamonds Are a Girl's Best Friend," Marilyn's signature song.

Many are highly skeptical of this latter report, including the Presley estate. Still, when it come to Elvis Presley sightings, anything is possible.

Since Elvis was such a dynamic individual, it is not surprising that ghostly encounters with the King have not been limited to Graceland or even Memphis. Elvis's ghost has been reported as far afield as blue Hawaii, Palm Springs, and, of course, (viva!) Las Vegas. Although it is not generally appreciated by the general public—or even by some of his most avid fans—Elvis spent quite a bit of time in Nashville during his career. Many of his greatest hits were recorded there. And his legendary manager, Colonel Tom Parker, lived in the sedate suburb of Madison.

Elvis even played the Grand Ole Opry early in his career—but only once. In those days, the Opry was straight-laced and traditional in the extreme. For example, saxophones were not even allowed as backup instruments on stage. How Elvis and his original group managed to get booked is unknown. Certainly, his swiveling hips and Negro blues–inspired singing style would never have been allowed had management known. In any case, Elvis went on and did his rockabilly best. Not only did he fail to win any applause, the audience actually booed him off-stage. As Elvis departed, humiliated, a local producer took him aside and gave him some free advice: "Son, get out of the business. You'll never make it in music."

Elvis did not follow that advice. Neither did he ever perform live in Nashville again. Nevertheless, over the years, he made many friends in Music City—producers like Chet Atkins, songwriters like Mae Axton, and a whole host of session musicians, studio engineers, and others. They were all devoted to the King not because of his fame but out of respect for him as a performer and singer. That Elvis's ghost should pay occasional visits to Music City is not at all surprising.

In 1988, for example, a local gas station attendant was working the graveyard shift when a man came into the store to pay for fuel. He was the spitting image of Elvis. The attendant was even more stunned when the customer opened his mouth. By his speech and mannerisms, the tall stranger was identical to the King in ways no mere impersonator could mimic. After the customer disappeared into the night, the gas jockey was convinced he'd encountered Elvis.

Then there was the time Elvis was sighted in broad daylight in downtown Nashville. He was strolling up Lower Broad among the cluster of honky-tonks and tourist shops catering to the country-music faithful. Wearing his signature white jumpsuit, he could not be mistaken; in the full light of day and under close scrutiny, no impersonator could possibly pass for the King. Passersby stopped and stared. One fan even approached for an autograph. Shortly thereafter, the jump-suited stranger disappeared as mysteriously as he had come.

Were these genuine sightings or just extremely good imposters? An objective answer is impossible. All that can be said is that those who witnessed Elvis were convinced he was real.

More in line with standard paranormal experiences is the reported haunting of the old RCA Studio on Music Row, where Elvis recorded his breakthrough hit, "Heartbreak Hotel," in 1956.

The song has an eerie, haunting quality to it, and the story of its origin is stranger still. "Heartbreak Hotel" was written the year before, in 1955, by Mae Axton and country musician Tommy Durden. It is one of those great songs that came into existence in a flash of inspiration, rather than being hammered out, as is the norm. The lyrics to "Heartbreak Hotel" were inspired by a young man's suicide note. One of the lines in the note said, "I walk a lonely street." Something about the words clicked with Mae Axton and her writing partner. They composed the entire song, lyrics and all, within half an hour.

Mae Axton was a Jacksonville, Florida, teacher who caught the country-music bug. It wouldn't let her go. Early on, she was the publicist for Hank Snow, whose manager happened to be Colonel Tom Parker. At that time, Elvis had another man managing him. Mae approached that manager with the song, pressing him to have Elvis record it. Mae was certain that if Elvis sang "Heartbreak Hotel," it would go straight to number one on the charts.

On January 10 and 11, 1956, Elvis and his band went into the RCA Studio at 1525 McGavock Street, within sight of the city's famous skyline. It was their first recording session for their new label. In those days, Nashville was not yet Music City. Only a handful of recording studios were located in town. "Heartbreak Hotel" would change all of that.

Although Chet Atkins was in charge of the session, he let Elvis and the band have free rein. They picked what songs to record. "Heartbreak Hotel" was one of them. The song was released later that month. By the end of 1956, it had become the top-selling single of the year, earning Elvis his first gold record. Mae Axton's intuition was right.

The runaway success of "Heartbreak Hotel" not only made Elvis's career but also put Nashville on the recording-industry map. Within a few years, the quiet, tree-lined residential neighborhood that stretched from the old studio at 1525 McGavock all the way to Belmont Mansion was transformed into Music Row, as record labels, producers, sound engineers, songwriters, singers, and musicians all flocked to Nashville to be part of the booming recording business there. While many hands made Music City what it is today, it all began with the simple two-story RCA Studio on McGavock Street.

RCA moved to new quarters—the famed "Studio B." The old studio went through various changes in the ensuing decades, including serving as the offices and studios of country television pioneer Jim Owens. In the years following Elvis's death, the old building acquired a reputation for being haunted. People working there had odd things happen to them on a number of occasions. It seemed these events occurred whenever Elvis's name came up in conversation. A ladder would fall over for no reason, or lights might suddenly explode or blink out. Strange noises would come through the sound equipment, yet recording engineers could find no cause. Although no paunchy, gold-lamé-clad ghost ever appeared before the stagehands and editing crews at the

McGavock studio, the assumption was that Elvis's ghost was responsible for the unusual happenings.

In January 2008, the famous studio at 1525 McGavock was bulldozed to make way for a parking lot—a not uncommon occurrence for historic sites in Nashville. So, in this case, Elvis has not so much left the building as the building has left Elvis!

Graceland
3734 Elvis Presley Boulevard
Memphis, TN 38116
(800) 238-2000
www.elvis.com

"Thank you very much."

Appendix

Haunted Hotels of Tennessee

The following is by no means a complete list of all the Tennessee hotels, inns, and bed-and-breakfasts that have been reported as haunted. As a sampler of what the state offers, however, it may serve as a quick guide for those who wish to explore the state's paranormal heritage up close.

Edgewater Hotel (The Edgewater at the Aquarium)
402 River Road
Gatlinburg, TN 37738
(800) 423-9582
www.edgewater-hotel.com

Falcon Manor B&B at Falcon Rest
2645 Faulkner Springs Road
McMinnville, TN 37110
(931) 668-4444
www.falconmanor.com or www.falconrest.com

Watches stop ticking in one of the guest rooms here. Phantom footsteps are heard in the hallway. The resident spirit has even been known to pose for wedding photographs.

Franklin-Pearson House
108 East Cumberland Street
P.O. Box 593
Cowan, TN 37318
(931) 962-3223
www.franklinpearson.com

The permanent residents of this nine-room bed-and-breakfast in an old railroad hotel are ghosts. The house is located close to "mystery mountain"—Monteagle.

Garden Plaza Hotel (formerly the Holiday Inn Sunspree Resort)
520 Historic Nature Trail
Gatlinburg, TN 37738
(800) 435-9201 or (865) 436-9201

Hawley House
114 East Woodrow Avenue
Jonesborough, TN 37659
(800) 753-8869 or (423) 753-8870

This 1793 inn is located in the oldest town in Tennessee. Not only the inn but the whole town is host to ghosts.

Heartbreak Hotel
3677 Elvis Presley Boulevard
Memphis, TN 38116
(877) 777-0606 or (901) 332-1000
www.elvis.com/epheartbreakhotel/

This fashionable boutique hotel dedicated to the life of the King features Elvis-themed rooms and suites. If you're lucky, he and Marilyn may drop in for their wedding anniversary.

Hermitage Hotel
231 Sixth Avenue North
Nashville, TN 37219
(888) 888-9414 or (615) 244-3121
www.thehermitagehotel.com

The oldest hotel in Nashville, the Hermitage has played host to everyone from presidents to the legendary Minnesota Fats. Currently, it is home to several ghosts believed to be former tenants.

The Inn at Hunt-Phelan
533 Beale Street
Memphis, TN 38103
(901) 525-8225
http://www.huntphelan.com

During the Civil War, the Hunt-Phelan Mansion served first as a Confederate headquarters, then later as Ulysses S. Grant's abode. The male spirit haunting the place is thought to be that of a devoted servant of one of the families that lived here.

Little Greenbrier Lodge
3685 Lyon Springs Road
Sevierville, TN 37862
(800) 277-8100 or (865) 429-2500

Magnolia Manor (1849)
418 North Main Street
Bolivar, TN 38008
(731) 658-6700
www.magnoliamanorbolivartn.com

The specters in this bed-and-breakfast have been documented by ghost-hunting groups. Ghost tours are offered in October.

Newbury House
5517 Rugby Highway
Rugby, TN 37733
(423) 628-2441
www.historicrugby.org

This is a great little place to stay in one of the most haunted towns in America.

Oakslea Place Bed-and-Breakfast
1210 North Highland Avenue
Jackson, TN 38301
(731) 554-1760

This cozy bed-and-breakfast is located in one of the oldest homes in Jackson. Guests' comfort is assured with Hampton the butler on duty.

Prospect Hill Bed-and-Breakfast Inn
801 West Main Street
Mountain City, TN 37683
(800) 339-5084 or (423) 727-0139
www.prospect-hill.com

This six-bedroom bed-and-breakfast lies in the heart of the haunted Smokies.

Sheraton Read House
827 Broad Street
Chattanooga, TN 37402
(800) 325-3535 or (423) 266-4121
www.sheratonreadhouse.com

The present hotel replaced one that stood on the same spot during the Civil War. Apparently, one of the former hotel's residents decided to stay put. Room 311 is haunted by a Yankee soldier who murdered a prostitute in the same-numbered room of the old hotel. Reportedly, he is not a happy trooper.

Rocky Top Village Inn
311 Historic Nature Trail
Gatlinburg, TN 37738
(800) 553-7738 or (865) 436-7826
www.rockytopvillageinn.com

The Thomas House
520 East Main Street
Red Boiling Springs, TN 37150
(615) 699-3006
www.thomashousehotel.com

Located in an old mineral spa and resort town, this hotel features fine food, fun, and phantoms. Investigations have documented numerous paranormal phenomena.

Historic Tower House Inn (J.P. Adams House)
300 West Fort Street
Manchester, TN 37355
(931) 723-7888

Union Station Hotel
1001 Broadway
Nashville, TN 37203
(615) 726-1001
www.unionstationhotelnashville.com

This former train station was converted into a small but elegant hotel. Several ghosts roam its halls, including that of Major Lewis, the man who oversaw the building's construction in 1898.

Woodlawn
110 Keith Lane
Athens, TN 37303
(800) 745-8213 or (423) 745-8211

The identity of this bed-and-breakfast's resident ghost is unknown, but he is thought to be a Civil War soldier.